Maya® Studio Projects

PHOTOREALISTIC CHARACTERS

Autodesk®
Official Training Guide

Maya® Studio Projects

PHOTOREALISTIC CHARACTERS

Autodesk®
Official Training Guide

TODD PALAMAR

WILEY
Wiley Publishing, Inc.

Acquisitions Editor: Mariann Barsolo
Development Editor: David Clark
Technical Editor: Campbell Strong
Production Editor: Dassi Zeidel
Copy Editor: Tiffany Taylor
Editorial Manager: Pete Gaughan
Production Manager: Tim Tate
Vice President and Executive Group Publisher: Richard Swadley
Vice President and Publisher: Nfil Edde
Media Associate Project Manager: Jenny Swisher
Media Associate Producer: Shawn Patrick
Media Quality Assurance: Doug Kuhn
Book Designer: Caryl Gorska
Compositor: Maureen Forys, Happenstance Type-O-Rama
Proofreader: Publication Services, Inc.
Indexer: Jack Lewis
Project Coordinator, Cover: Katie Crocker
Cover Designer: Ryan Sneed
Cover Image: Todd Palamar

Dear Reader,

Thank you for choosing *Maya Studio Projects: Photorealistic Characters*. This book is part of a family of premium-quality Sybex books, all of which are written by outstanding authors who combine practical experience with a gift for teaching.

Sybex was founded in 1976. More than 30 years later, we're still committed to producing consistently exceptional books. With each of our titles, we're working hard to set a new standard for the industry. From the paper we print on, to the authors we work with, our goal is to bring you the best books available.

I hope you see all that reflected in these pages. I'd be very interested to hear your comments and get your feedback on how we're doing. Feel free to let me know what you think about this or any other Sybex book by sending me an email at nedde@wiley.com. If you think you've found a technical error in this book, please visit http://sybex.custhelp.com. Customer feedback is critical to our efforts at Sybex.

Best regards,

Neil Edde
Vice President and Publisher
Sybex, an Imprint of Wiley

Acknowledgments

The versatility and flexibility of Autodesk Maya never ceases to amaze me. This book started as a question: could you simulate muscle contraction using a human performance to drive the motion of the muscle? That quickly led to another question: could the muscles be used to simulate lip syncing and facial expressions, and would the results be believable? The questions didn't stop after that. After a little testing, the answers became clear: simulating muscles using data captured from a human performance would work. Not only does it work, but it can simplify or make unnecessary many of the laborious procedures used by the industry today. Of course, the process has issues of its own, but the idea was worth pursuing. I built a prototype, and the book began. ■ Without the love, friendship, and participation of my wife, Brindle, this book would never have been written. Her devotion and belief in me are amazing. I am grateful for every day I get to spend with her. In addition, this endeavor would not have been possible without the trust, patience, and understanding that embody the entire Wiley Publishing team. Your support is greatly appreciated. Furthermore, a big thanks to Vcom3D, Inc., for allowing me the use of their facility and cameras. I also thank my daughter, Makenna, for deciphering my meanderings and taking them down as dictation. Lastly, I want to thank my biggest fan: my son Reece. His motivation, input, and assistance were priceless throughout the process of writing this book.

About the Author

Todd Palamar is a 21-year veteran in the computer animation industry. After transitioning early in his career from traditional special effects to computer-generated imagery, Todd did effects work for several direct-to-video movies. He later went on to work on numerous video games, including Sega of Japan's coin-operated title *Behind Enemy Lines,* as well as *Dukes of Hazzard* and *Trophy Buck 2* for the Sony PlayStation console. For six years, Todd taught at Full Sail University. During this time, he received numerous accolades as an outstanding educator. Additionally, Todd was a trainer at the DAVE School, bringing postgraduate students up to speed in Maya. Todd has written five books, including *Maya Cloth for Characters* and *Maya Studio Projects Dynamics.* His breadth of experience has allowed him to work in location-based entertainment, military simulation, television commercials, and corporate spots. Todd is currently Technical Art Director at Vcom3D, creating real-time characters capable of sign language and lip syncing.

CONTENTS AT A GLANCE

Contents

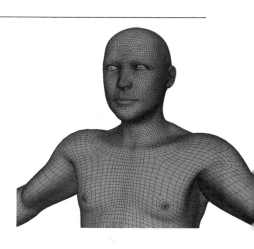

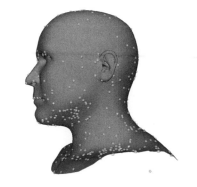

Introduction

The term photorealistic is thrown around a lot and is often undefined. Although it seems obvious—*photorealistic* means something looks like a photo—the word requires a greater explanation. There are many facets to photorealism. This is true because as a CG artist, you have control over everything. Achieving 100 percent realism takes teams of people to pull off. Their combined talent is paramount, but so are their perceptions.

Different things make each one of us believe something looks real. For some, if a character moves properly, then they believe it can exist. For others, it's the lighting that has to be perfect. Most people can't say for sure what it is they don't believe—they just know something doesn't look right. Therefore, when we talk about photorealism, each step in the process needs to have its own level of expectation. CG animated family movies are a great example. The characters are intentionally stylized, but the lighting is done in a real-world fashion, giving the movie a realistic look. In this book, our goal is to look at the individual elements and establish a photorealistic foundation.

Who Should Read This Book

If you're interested in building computer-generated characters that move and act realistically and also look real, you should read this book. Individuals working or interested in film, television, or games can benefit from the procedures and techniques outlined. Furthermore, those in the scientific or medical simulation industry can benefit from the anatomy sections.

The book is designed for the intermediate Maya user. It's assumed that you have a thorough working knowledge of Maya's interface and understand each module. You should have expertise in one or more of the following: modeling, animating, texturing, and rendering.

What You'll Learn

In this book, you learn how to build individual elements and assemble them into a photorealistic character. At its heart, the book teaches you how to capture an actor's performance and apply it to dynamically driven muscles and skin. We give you the steps to build your own personal motion-capture studio and describe methods for transferring the results onto a character's body and face. In addition, you're taught how to add hair, fur, and clothing to a character. When finished, you'll be able to create your own virtual character of any design.

Hardware and Software Requirements

Building photorealistic characters requires every facet of Maya. This book also requires Adobe Photoshop and Autodesk's MatchMover. At a minimum, you should have a 2.8 GHz CPU and 2 GB of RAM. For more specific information, check out Autodesk's system requirements page:

    http://usa.autodesk.com/maya/system-requirements/

It's also recommended that you run only Maya-certified graphics cards. Although most graphic cards can run Maya, they don't support every feature; icons may be missing, and software may crash. You can find a list of certified graphics cards through the following link:

    http://usa.autodesk.com/adsk/servlet/index?siteID=123112&id=
    14959955&linkID=9242259

Finally, to access all of Maya's tools, you need to use Maya 2011 or later. Versions prior to 2011 don't have all the features required to complete the projects in this book.

How to Use This Book

This book progressively builds a character, with each chapter adding a new element. But the chapters aren't interdependent, with the exception of Chapter 8—you can work through chapters out of order. The material covered in each chapter is as follows:

Chapter 1, "Character Skeletons," introduces you to the main character of the book. You'll review his geometry and build him a basic joint skeleton. The geometry is then weighted to the skeleton.

Chapter 2, "Face Rigging," describes each muscle used in human expression and speech. You'll model muscles and convert them to nCloth. You'll then rig them using dynamic simulation tools and connect them to each other via constraints.

Chapter 3, "Hair," takes a look at different hair styles and the techniques used to make them. You'll create hair for the character by growing, cutting, styling, and coloring it.

Chapter 4, "Fur," focuses on using fur to build facial hair. The importance of good fur UVs is discussed as well as using multiple UV sets. You'll learn how to paint fur attribute maps in Maya and Photoshop. By the end of the chapter, you'll have added a beard, eyebrows, and eyelashes to the character.

Chapter 5, "Blood and Sweat," utilizes the power of nParticles to create blood and sweat. Characters don't always need these things, but using them can increase realism. Learning how to use these tools also opens the door to other effects, such as tears and drool.

Chapter 6, "Clothing," teaches you how to take regular geometry and convert it to nCloth. You'll learn how to fit garments properly to your character. When the clothing is the proper size, you'll adjust attributes to make it react like denim, cotton, or any other type of material. In the end, your character will be running around in a new shirt, jacket, and pants.

Chapter 7, "Performance Capture," introduces you to a low-cost solution for creating your own motion capture. You'll learn how to construct a motion-capture suit, place markers on the body, and set up a space in which to record a performance. After the performance is captured, you can use the footage to create three-dimensional data. The data is then applied to your character.

Chapter 8, "Composition," brings all the elements together. You'll attach the character's face to simulated muscles driven by motion capture. Subsurface scattering shaders and textures are added to the geometry. You'll also produce an image-based lighting setup and render the scene.

When you start a project, it's best to copy the files from the DVD to your local hard drive. In Maya, set the project directory to the root of the copied files. Doing this ensures that all the scenes and other referenced files will be mapped properly.

The DVD included with this book contains incrementally saved Maya scene files, most of the figures that appear in the book, and movies showing the results from several projects. All of the Maya scene files are called out in the text of the book; use these to confirm your settings or test new ideas. The electronic versions of the figures are useful to scrutinize detail that doesn't show up in print. Some can also be used for reference, to match colors and shapes.

Contacting the Author

I welcome any and all feedback you might have about this book and the simulations within it. You can contact me at tap@speffects.com. To see my latest endeavors please visit www.speffects.com.

Sybex strives to keep you supplied with the latest tools and information you need for your work. Please check their website at www.sybex.com/go/mspphotoreal, where we'll post additional content and updates that supplement this book should the need arise.

Maya® Studio Projects

PHOTOREALISTIC CHARACTERS

Autodesk®
Official Training Guide

CHAPTER 1

Character Skeletons

Getting a character to move properly begins and ends with a good skeleton. It takes proper positioning and the right number of joints. The skeleton provides functionality and at the same time limits the ways geometry can deform. In this first chapter, you'll construct a skeleton and weight it to a modeled character. You'll then apply stock motion capture to test the character's deformations and the skeleton's validity.

In this chapter you will learn to:

- **Evaluate your characters geometry**
- **Paint weights**
- **Mirror and copy weights**
- **Apply motion capture**
- **Use the FBX file format**

Character Pipeline

The details of a character pipeline vary based on the character and change from company to company, and artist to artist, but for the most part, the overall process doesn't change. In this book, the pipeline is as follows:

PHOTO REAL PIPELINE

1. Establish the geometry.
2. Build a skeleton with basic functionality.
3. Add traditional skin weighting.
4. Create the facial anatomy.
5. Set up skin simulation.
6. Add facial hair using Fur.
7. Create and style hair.
8. Dress the character.
9. Implement secondary character effects.
10. Capturing a performance.
11. Add lighting and rendering.

Traditional skin weighting or binding only goes so far. The character in this book is fully clothed; therefore, his body doesn't need intense skin deformations. But the character needs to act. He needs to be able to speak and be convincingly expressive. To achieve this level of realism, it's crucial to match the real world as much as possible. Driving the character's face is an anatomically correct muscle system. The muscles squash and stretch and push and pull on the skin like real muscles.

Replicating human anatomy is half the battle. The muscles may move perfectly by themselves, but it's a different story when you need all of them to work together to form a smile or a frown. In comes *performance capture*. The term was coined by James Cameron while working on *Avatar*. Performance capture is the recording of every movement made by an actor. Well, maybe not every movement, but enough motion to identify speech, expressions, and of course full-body activities.

Skin Evaluation

Prior to adding joints, you should always evaluate your character's geometry or *skin*. It should have proper edge flow and enough faces for detailed deformations. Computer speed is constantly on the rise. Thanks to more RAM and accelerated GPUs, software has been able to increase production complexity. In the past, numerous techniques were used to push as much of the character's geometry as possible off until render time. This is still practiced today; but you can add more geometry to the character's actual bind. The increase makes it possible to have deforming wrinkles and folds with accurate collision. This increase also demands a more intricate setup.

In this book, the character you'll create is clothed. Most of his skin is covered; only his hands and face are exposed. As a result, his body can have basic deformations, while his face is complex. Figure 1.1 shows the geometry of the character named Jack who is the focus of this book.

Figure 1.1

Jack's geometry

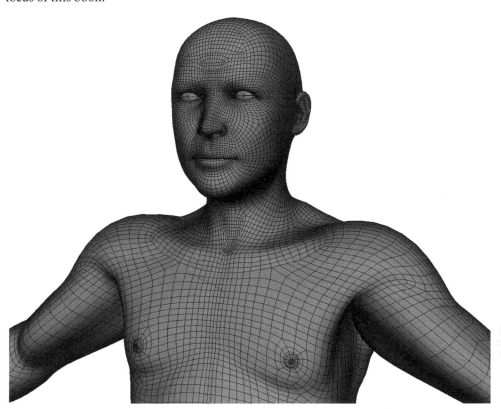

The geometry's density is consistent across the entire surface. Using predominantly quadrangle polygons funnels the edge flow from the body and arms up into the head. The head, which is significantly smaller than the overall body, benefits from compacting the incoming geometries into less space. Therefore, you have a good balance of geometry to support simulated clothing over the body and detailed deformations on the exposed face.

You use a muscle-based rig to drive the face. Blend shapes or morph targets are often used to animate facial expressions. However, they generate unnatural motion between each target and cause the development artist to generate hundreds to thousands of shapes to counteract the effects of the process. Muscle rigs make sense. Real muscles move in a linear fashion, and replicating this motion in computer graphics (CG) is simple. The combined motions of groups of muscles create a facial expression. Tweaking this expression is a matter of moving a muscle a little up or a little down.

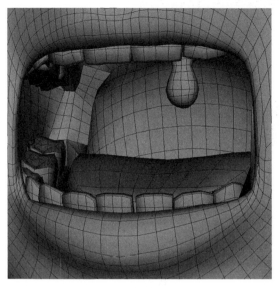

Figure 1.2
The interior of Jack's mouth

The geometry of the head is attached to the muscles. The muscles drive the geometric skin using nCloth for both the muscles and face geometry. This creates very complex deformations. It also makes it necessary to isolate the head from the rest of the body. You use basic weighting to control everything but the face. Detaching the head from the body allows the head to be nCloth. Ultimately, the head is a hybrid of nCloth and traditional weighting. The seam where the head and body connect is hidden by the character's clothes, but it's nevertheless held together by the basic weighting.

It's also important to mention the mouth. Having a character realistically express emotion and speak places a significant emphasis on the teeth, tongue, and rest of the mouth. Modeling these parts isn't as critical as modeling the exterior skin, but it's essential that they exist. Figure 1.2 shows the interior of Jack's mouth.

Base Skeleton

Building the skeleton is more of a technical achievement than an artistic one. The skeleton's functionality in the overall pipeline is primary. You must name the joints and orient them properly. You need to establish layers to toggle a joint's visibility as well as its selection status. These things are important; above all, however, is joint placement.

In the final setup, the character has two skeletons: a base skeleton and a motion-capture skeleton. The *base skeleton* is nothing more than a joint hierarchy that has been properly oriented. Its construction is simple but its joint placement is meticulously arranged.

Joints in the human body aren't always centered within the skin's volume. For instance, the bones along the spine are pushed to the back of the torso, with the ribcage protruding from the front. On a CG character, it's best to position the spine joints centered within the body; doing so makes the deformations function more naturally. The reason is that the human body is filled with bones, organs, and fluid, all of which play a factor in motion. A CG character is an empty volume, and its anatomy is implied. Figure 1.3 shows the CG character's spine placement.

Most often, what works best when placing joints is old-fashioned trial and error. You can bind the joints to the skin and test their rotation. Choosing Skin → Edit Smooth Skin → Move Skinned Joints Tool lets you make rapid changes to a joint's location. The tool works great for determining the position of the hip and knee (see Figure 1.4).

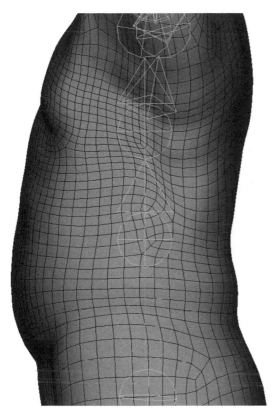

Figure 1.3

Jack's spine is positioned almost centered in his body and is vertically aligned.

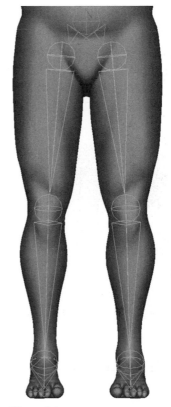

Figure 1.4

After testing several positions, the locations of the hip and knee are determined.

The arm joints are positioned in a similar fashion to the leg. However, their joints are located based on the shape of the character's skin. You want to pay close attention to the angle of the fingers to ensure proper rotation. Figure 1.5 shows the hand and the joint placement.

Performance Capture

Performance capturing is an important element in the photoreal character pipeline. Part of this process is creating a capture skeleton. You want the skeleton to match your character's skeleton as closely as possible. The more it deviates, the harder it is to transfer its motion. There will inevitably be some difference, but it's possible to calibrate to different skeletons.

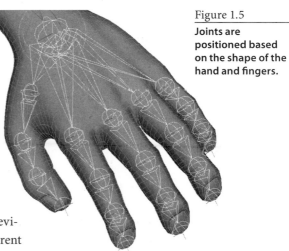

Figure 1.5

Joints are positioned based on the shape of the hand and fingers.

To maintain the freedom to design and build any character, you need a system for calibrating the two rigs. The better your calibration process, the greater your freedom. The capture skeleton is based on the actor whose performance you're capturing. For this book, the capture skeletons are generated using Autodesk's MatchMover program (see Figure 1.6).

Figure 1.6

The interface for Autodesk MatchMover

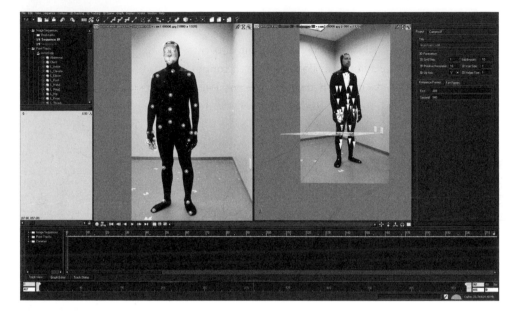

Many other tracking applications are available that you can use in place of MatchMover. Autodesk's MatchMover program offers the benefit of compatibility. Because it's an Autodesk product, files can be exchanged between Maya and MatchMover easily.

After you import multiple angles of video or film footage of the same action into MatchMover, you track points that are identifiable in all the camera views. The points in the footage are typically markers that were manually placed for the sole purpose of tracking. MatchMover turns these markers into points in 3D space (see Figure 1.7).

The track points are then used to derive an animated skeleton by literally connecting the dots (Figure 1.8).

The track points are exported to Maya. In Maya, multiple skeletons are created and connected to each other. Scale plays an enormous role, no pun intended, in setting up both rigs. (Scale is addressed in detail in Chapter 7, "Performance Capture.")

The motion-capture skeleton and data aren't the critical part of the pipeline. The skeleton can change, and the data can change. It's what you do with the data that is decisive. With that said, you can't use any old data. For instance, there is a lot of downloadable

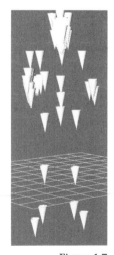

Figure 1.7

Markers from the imported footage turn into track points in 3D space.

motion-capture data. Getting such data to work on your character is possible, as shown in the last two projects in this chapter, but it often fails for numerous reasons.

First, downloaded motion-capture data may fail due to unknown factors. You don't know how the data came to be. The actor's physique doesn't need to match your character, but knowing what the person looked like is helpful. Having a video of the actual performance is invaluable. Seeing the motion on joints in Maya isn't good enough: The data may be missing keys, or the actor's physique may be the opposite of your character. As mentioned earlier, it's possible to use differently proportioned skeletons, but not knowing why the data moves the way it does is a huge impediment. The rotation of a joint isn't a good representation of the joint's position. This is especially true for incomplete data sets like hands. Capturing finger motion is difficult, so the hand is sometimes a single joint or made up of a hand and a thumb joint. Regardless, the twisting motion of the wrist and upper arm is difficult and sometimes impossible to decipher without having a video reference of the actor. Remember, the skeleton must be calibrated first before the motion can be applied properly. If you can't align your character to the motion-capture skeleton, you've already lost the battle.

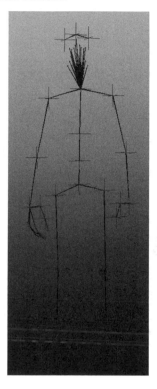

Figure 1.8

The track points are linked together to form a skeleton.

Another issue with motion-capture data is frame rate. Most capture sessions are done at 60 fps or higher to help in the tracking process. This is especially true for quick actions. A higher frame rate helps the software accurately track the data. It also helps when markers become obscured. Having more frames allows you to interpolate through the missing track points more smoothly.

The third problem with downloaded motion capture is the number of joints and marker placements. Motion capture is done for different reasons. The downloaded session may have been to get arm data only, so the lower half of the body was neglected. Again, having video of the capture session can reveal where the markers were placed. But videos may not reveal all them. Not having their exact locations makes it difficult and sometimes impossible to determine the differential between the motion-capture joint center and your CG character joint center.

All these reasons reinforce the need for your own personal motion-capture studio. Having your own setup gives you complete control over the data.

Weighting

Quaternion weighting helps skin deformations tremendously. You no longer need additional bones to help support the volume of skinned parts; you only need to add joints where your character needs them, making the process far more intuitive.

This also helps with the weighting process. Instead of the skin caving in at a bent joint, the volume is maintained, causing the skin to penetrate the opposing side. You can counteract the penetration by painting weight from the opposing side. You can even mix the quaternion weighting with classic linear weighting to have the skin lose some volume in the area, creating the illusion of collision. Both options create a more lifelike fold in the deformation. In the first project, Jack is weighted to his skeleton using quaternion weighting techniques.

Project: Painting Weights

You've evaluated the geometry and built the skeleton. Everything is in place for skin weighting. All of Jack's weights are done with quaternion weighting. The geometry to be weighted is one complete mesh. Ultimately, the mesh is divided into two pieces; but it's easier to weight a single mesh and then copy the weights to the final broken-up mesh. The following tutorial takes you through the entire process.

1. Open the jackWeights_v01.ma scene from the chapter1\scenes folder on the DVD. The scene contains the character's geometry as a single mesh and his skeleton. The geometry and skeleton have been assigned to respective layers.

2. Open the Outliner, and Ctrl+select the root_JNT node and the jack node. Choose Skin → Bind Skin → Smooth Bind tool options.

3. In the default settings, change Skinning Method to Dual Quaternion. Use Figure 1.9 to confirm your settings. Click Bind Skin to accept the options.

The default bind does a decent job of weighting the character. It's far from perfect, of course, but it provides you with a clear path. Most of the needed corrections center on the torso. Figure 1.10 shows the torso's deformations.

4. Select clavicleLft_JNT, and rotate it to –15.0 in the Z. Select shoulderLft_JNT, and rotate it to 45.0 in the Z.

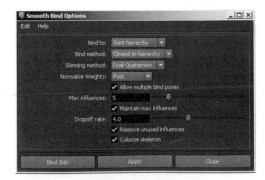

Figure 1.9

Change the Smooth Bind options.

CLAVICLE ROTATION

In the final rig, the clavicle will rotate only a little in the Z axis. To achieve a proper shoulder shrug, most of its motion will come from the joint's local X translation. Rotations are being used here simply for convenience. All the rotate values are at 0.0, making it easy to return the joint to its original position. Otherwise, you'd keyframe the joint's translation to retain its original value.

5. The spine and left shoulder joints are the first to tackle. Getting these deformations along the spine correct makes it easier to add the appendages. Select the skin, and choose Skin → Edit Smooth Skin → Paint Skin Weights Tool.

6. Knowing the target area to fix lets you customize the Paint Weights tool. Ctrl+select the following joints:

   - root_JNT
   - spine1_JNT
   - spine2_JNT
   - clavicleLft_JNT
   - shoulderLft_JNT
   - elbowLft_JNT
   - radiusLft_JNT
   - collar_JNT

   Choose the tack icon in the upper-right corner of the Influences list. The selected joints are now isolated.

7. Open the Gradient section, and select Use Color Map. The weight maps go from black and white to color. Select clavicleLft_JNT. Toggle the check box for Use Color Map a few times, and notice the difference in the display. The information is identical for both, but your eyes can't perceive the subtleties in the grayscale shading. Figure 1.11 shows the difference between the default weight maps and the colored ones.

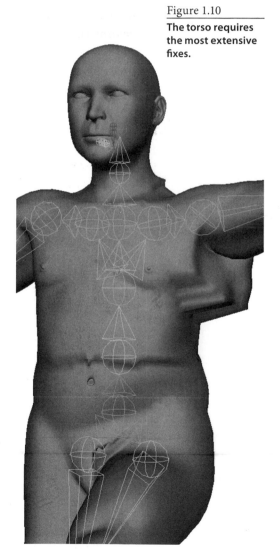

Figure 1.10

The torso requires the most extensive fixes.

GRADIENT WEIGHT MAPS

There are two ways to display a joint's influence: grayscale shading and color ramps (also known as a *heat map*). The grayscale shading is straightforward: black is zero, and white is one. Heat maps increase the amount of visible contrast by displaying weight values as colored intensities. They facilitate the ability to paint without knowing the actual value of the weight. In other words, you can paint with greater accuracy. You can also see variants in the weighting that wouldn't normally be noticeable in traditional grayscale maps, such as values in the hundredths.

8. The first objective in the weighting process is to remove all the unnecessary weights. You could begin by choosing Skin → Edit Smooth Skin → Prune Small Weights, but this can also remove some necessary weighting. Instead, using the heat map, you can easily paint out what you don't need.

    Select radiusLft_JNT from the Influences list. The radius shouldn't have any effect on the skin past the elbow. Using a Replace value of 0, paint out all the blue weights up to the elbow.

9. Select elbowLft_JNT from the Influences list, and remove all of its blue values up to the elbow as you did for radiusLft_JNT in step 8.

10. Do clavicleLft_JNT next. Remove all the weights except a large area around the upper shoulder. Use your own body as reference. Place your hand over your heart, and then raise your shoulder. Feel the skin move? Slide your hand down and around the bottom of your ribcage. Keep raising your shoulder to feel how far the effects of the clavicle go. Figure 1.12 shows the remaining weight values.

Don't worry about getting the weights perfect or taking away too much. The weights are far from being finished, and it's much easier to come back with the Smooth Paint operation to fine-tune the results.

11. Spine2_JNT is a little out of hand. Its influence spreads across most of the body. Instead of trying to paint this out, it's easier to flood the weight to 0 and paint it from scratch. Change Paint Operation to Replace, set Value to 0.0, and click Flood. All of its weights are removed.

12. Change Value to 1.0, and change Brush Profile to the Solid brush. Paint from the bottom of the breast to just under the collar bone. Go from the center of the chest to the center of the back. Use the edge flow of the geometry as a guide. There is no need to paint the right side because you'll eventually mirror the weights. Use Figure 1.13 as a reference.

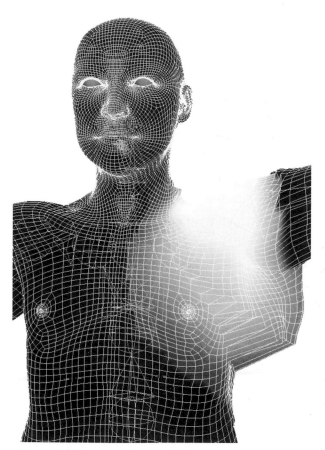

Figure 1.12
The weights for clavicleLft_JNT

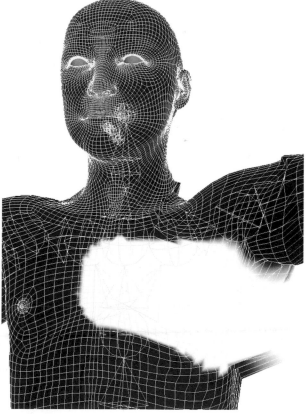

Figure 1.13
The weights for spine2_JNT

13. Switch the Paint operation to Smooth, and click the Flood button six times.

14. Choose shoulderLft_JNT. Change the Paint operation to Replace, and use a Value of 0.0. Paint out all the weights up to the shoulder. Use Figure 1.14 as a guide. Remember to do the back of the character as well.

15. You should start to see some progress. At this point, you can use the Smooth operation to refine the weighting. Keeping shoulderLft_JNT selected, smooth the weights around the shoulder area. You should end up with weighting similar to Figure 1.15.

16. Go through all the other joints, and continue to smooth the weights around the shoulder. The shoulder will look pretty good when you're finished. This is a good time to save your scene.

To check your work so far, you can compare it to `jackWeights_v02.ma` on the DVD.

17. With the shoulder basically finished, let's move down the arm. Select elbowLft_JNT, and rotate it –30.0 units in the Y.

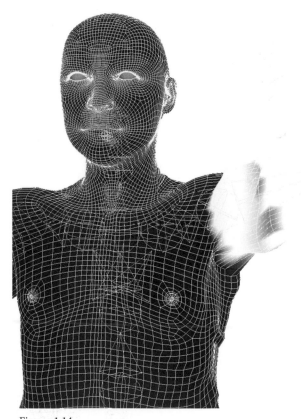

Figure 1.14
The weights for shoulderLft_JNT

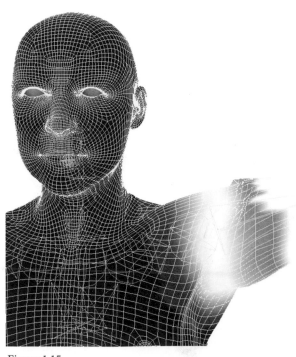

Figure 1.15
Smooth the weights for shoulderLft_JNT.

18. Select the character's geometry, and open the Paint Weights tool options. Select the following joints from the Influences list, and pin the selection:

    - clavicleLft_JNT
    - shoulderLft_JNT
    - elbowLft_JNT
    - radiusLft_JNT
    - wristLft_JNT

19. Click shoulderLft_JNT. Replace any weighting with 0.0 below the elbow.

20. Switch to elbowLft_JNT, and replace all the weights above the elbow with 0.0. Repeat for radiusLft_JNT.

21. Switch to wristLft_JNT, and replace all the weights with 0.0 down to the wrist joint itself.

22. Select the Smooth Paint operation. Toggle back and forth between the elbow and shoulder joints, smoothing the weights until they're blended nicely. When you're satisfied, clean up the smaller weights by painting them with a 0.0 value. The weights of the two joints should only bleed over the elbow area by a couple of edge loops. Figure 1.16 shows the finished results.

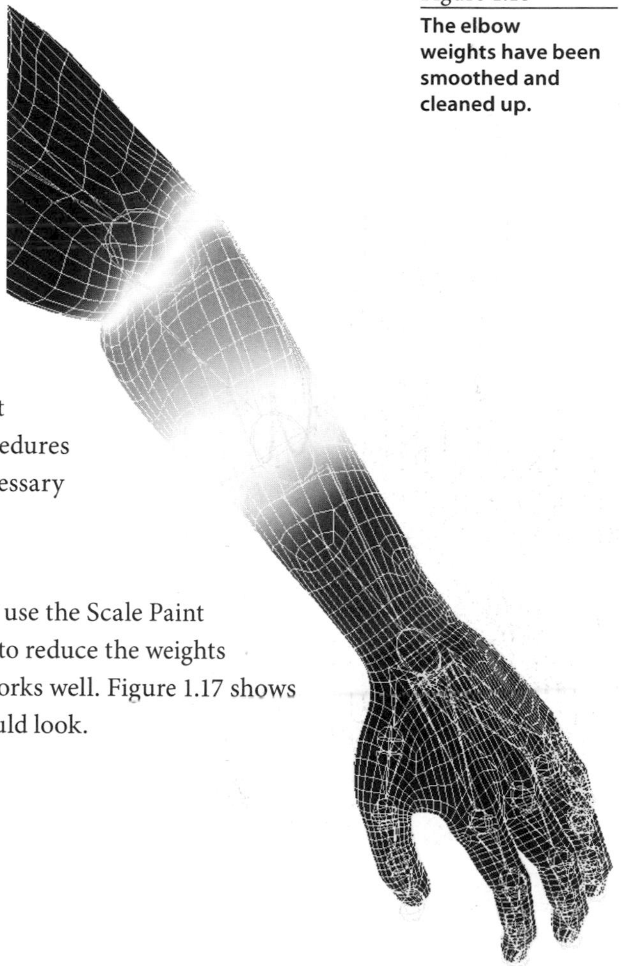

23. The radius and wrist joints work together; the radius rotates in the X while the wrist handles the Y and Z axes. The radius weights are good, except where they influence the wrist. Follow the same procedures you used for the previous joints to remove the unnecessary weighting.

24. Rotate wristLft_JNT to 40.0 units in the Z.

25. After you smooth the weights around the wrist joint, use the Scale Paint operation on both wristLft_JNT and radiusLft_JNT to reduce the weights and create a tight crease in the skin. A Value of 0.9 works well. Figure 1.17 shows how the wrist and the wristLft_JNT weight map should look.

Figure 1.16

The elbow weights have been smoothed and cleaned up.

Figure 1.17

Scale the weights to get a crease around the bent wrist.

To check your work so far, you can compare it to jackWeights_v03.ma on the DVD.

26. Do the hip, leg, and neck using the same procedure you've followed for the other joints in this project. You can try them on your own or continue to the next project.

Mirror and Copying Weights

Symmetrical characters are great because you only have to build half of them. You can mirror just about every aspect. Skin weighting is no exception; mirroring significantly reduces the amount of redundant work.

Perhaps an even greater tool than mirroring is the Copy Skin Weights tool. It allows you to copy weights from one skin to another, regardless of the skeleton. It works on entire meshes as well as components. Copy Skin Weights is very flexible and a time saver.

Project: Mirror and Copy Weights

Half of the character is weighted. In the next project, you'll mirror the weights and then clean them up. In the latter half of the project, you'll copy the single mesh weights over to the divided mesh with the head separated from the body. Follow these steps:

1. Open the jackWeights_v04.ma scene from the chapter1\scenes folder on the DVD. The scene picks up where the previous project left off. Half of the character is weighted.

2. Select Jack's geometry. Choose Skin → Edit Smooth Skin → Mirror Skin Weights. Use Figure 1.18 to set the mirror options. Click Mirror to apply the settings.

3. The Mirror Skin Weights tool is highly effective, but you can still have a few stray vertices. Rotate shoulderRght_JNT to 50.0 units in the *Z*. A single vertex from the torso is attached to the upper arm (see Figure 1.19).

   Stray vertices like these are easy fixes. Select the problem vertex, and choose Skin → Edit Smooth Skin → Weight Hammer. In an instant, the vertex is averaged with the surrounding vertices and deforms naturally.

4. A closer inspection reveals a second vertex just above the armpit. Select it, and use Weight Hammer to fix it. Rotate the rest of the joints to make sure they all look good.

5. The weights are finished; you can now transfer them to the separated head and body geometries. Choose File → Import, and open the jackParts.ma scene file from the chapter1\scenes folder on the DVD.

   The head and body nodes are now in the scene. The two new pieces are assigned to the layer named PARTS.

6. Turn off the visibility for the JACK_MESH layer.

7. Shift+select root_JNT, head, and body. Choose Skin → Bind Skin → Smooth Bind. In the tool options, set Skinning Method to Dual Quaternion. Click Bind Skin.

8. Turn on the visibility for the JACK_MESH layer.

9. Shift+select jack and body.

10. Using the default settings, choose Skin → Edit Smooth Skin → Copy Skin Weights.

11. Shift+select jack and head. Choose Skin → Edit Smooth Skin → Copy Skin Weights.

   The weights successfully copy over to the two separate pieces as if they were weighted together. You can now delete the jack node.

   To check your work so far, you can compare it to jackWeights_v06.ma on the DVD.

Figure 1.18
Mirror Skin Weight options

Figure 1.19
One vertex under the arm didn't mirror properly.

Motion Capture

Even the best animated characters still fall short of captured motion. You just can't beat the real thing. There are reasons why, but current hand-keyed animation isn't as convincing. Movie producers like to say it's because animators make characters do things that aren't natural. Animators say they needed more time or better direction. The truth is, the problem lies in the intricacies of the human body and the inadequacies of the current tools. To put it another way, it's bad timing.

When people and animals move, each bone is influenced by the one before it. This of course is *inverse kinematics* (IK). However, when one bone moves, the others counteract. Imagine typing on a keyboard. Your palms are resting on the desk, and it seems as though your fingers are doing all the work with your wrist keeping things stabilized. In order for your wrist to keep your fingers on the key board, your elbow shifts periodically. To support that elbow motion, your shoulder compensates. It doesn't stop there: every time you peck at a different key, different muscles are called into action. You can feel a similar effect by trying to stand still. All of your muscles fire to maintain your position. A single muscle applying force to a bone causes a chain reaction of hundreds of micromovements. Some go unnoticed, but when they're missing, we instantly recognize that something is wrong.

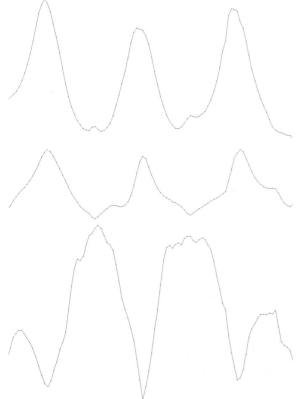

Figure 1.20

Three axes from motion-captured data

It's extremely difficult to calculate all those small motions and apply them in an animation. However, that's not the hard part. The real trick is finding the timing and patterns that exist among those motions. Look at Figure 1.20: it shows an excerpt of a motion-captured actor doing jumping jacks.

The top curve is the *Y* axis of the wrist. The middle curve is the *X* axis from the radius, and the bottom is the *X* axis of the humerus bone. Jumping jacks produce strong deviations in all the curves, but pay attention to how each curve has a relationship to the other. Even though they share the same peaks and values, how they get there isn't the same. Jitters and hiccups along the way indicate one bone supporting the other. You can see how the motion becomes seemingly more erratic as you go from the larger parent bone on top to the smaller child bone on the bottom.

Someday, computer-generated rigs will have this motion built into them, allowing animators to choose key positions and synthetic anatomy to fill in the rest. We're not far from having this technology. Maya has a precursor with full body IK (FBIK) rigs and human IK (HIK) systems. Until these are capable of delivering a convincing human performance, we still need to rely on motion capture for the ultimate in photorealism.

As we mentioned at the beginning of the chapter, it's important to know where your motion-capture data comes from. You can use material downloaded from the Internet, but it often requires a lot of work and in the end produces less than adequate results. To use motion capture to its fullest potential, you must have complete control over every aspect, from the actor to the data that the motion capture outputs. With that said, more and more websites offer motion-capture data. Using this data can save you a tremendous amount of work, and the data is relatively cheap if not free.

Project: Motion Test

The Jack character is weighted, but you don't know how he'll perform. To test his abilities, you can apply downloaded motion-capture data to his skeleton. The data used in this project is from Carnegie Mellon University's Graphics Lab. They have a larger motion-capture database that you can access at http://mocap.cs.cmu.edu/. In addition, they have numerous other resources like converters and documentation. Follow these steps:

1. Open the mocap_v01.ma scene from the chapter1\scenes folder on the DVD. The scene contains the character's geometry weighted to his skeleton. The geometry and skeleton have been assigned to respective layers.

   A second skeleton is in the scene: it's significantly larger than Jack's skeleton and has captured motion of an exercise routine. It's assigned to a layer called MOTION_CAPTURE.

2. Open the Outliner, and select the root node. Group this to an empty group node by pressing Ctrl+G. Rename the group1 node **mocap_GRP**.

3. Select mocap_GRP, and scale it uniformly to the approximate size of Jack; 0.03605 is good (see Figure 1.21).

   Make a note of the scale you end up using; it can be used for all the motion capture done with the same actor. Later in the chapter, you'll apply different motion from the same actor.

4. Turn off the visibility on the body layer.

5. The group node is mainly needed for scale. You can also use it to offset the skeleton. You want to match the root joint of the motion-capture skeleton to Jack's skeleton. Before you can do this, you need to make sure you're at the default skeletal pose for both skeletons. In the Outliner, select the root node on the motion-capture skeleton. The timeline should fill up with red keyframes. Change the start time to –100. Go to frame –100, and then click the Step Forward One Key button on the timeline controls. Doing so reveals that the first keyframe is at –13. Change the timeline to match the beginning and end.

Figure 1.21

Scale the
motion-capture
group to match the
size of Jack.

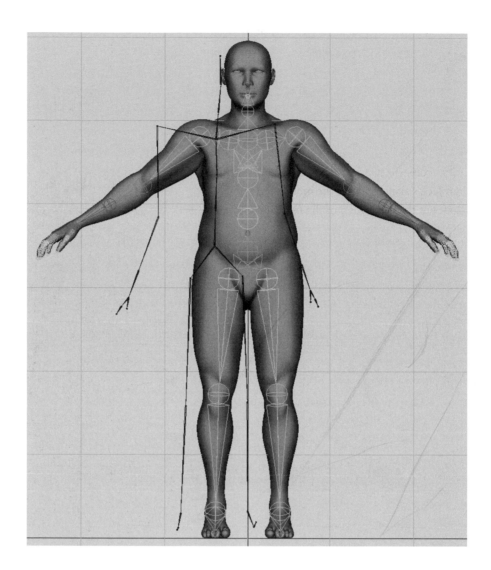

GROUP SCALE

At this point, you may want to reevaluate the character's scale. It should still be close enough. It's difficult to state whether you should scale the character in its default pose or its first frame of animation. If the first frame is a crouching or lying-down position, then you have to go with the default skeletal pose.

You don't want to go immediately to the default skeletal pose, because it isn't a true representation of the actor—it's rigid and unnatural. If you have control over the motion-capture session, it's ideal to have the actor pose in the same position as your CG character to obtain a suitable default skeletal pose.

6. Select mocap_GRP, and go to frame –13. Turn on Snap To Point. Press D, and snap the group's center to the root node of the motion-capture skeleton. With Snap To Point still on, snap mocap_GRP to Jack's root_JNT. The two skeletons are now collocated.

7. To get the skeletons to stay collocated, you need to add a point constraint. Shift+select root and root_JNT, and choose Constrain → Point. Reset the settings, and choose Add.

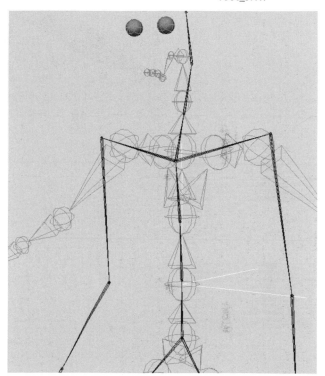

Figure 1.22

Add an IK handle to root_JNT.

Orient constraints would be the logical choice to align Jack's skeleton with the motion-capture skeleton, but the likelihood of the motion-capture skeleton being oriented with your skeleton is slim to none. The logical step is to apply the orient constraint and maintain its offset. You now have the tedious task of trying to align the joints manually.

A better solution is to use single chain (SC) IK handles. You can snap the IK handle to the end of the bone you need to align with. Adding a point constraint forces the handle to follow along. An added benefit of the SC handle is that you can also constrain its orientation, allowing you to replicate a bone's twisting motion.

8. The best place to start is at the root. Turn on Reference for the MOTION_CAPTURE layer.

9. Choose Skeleton → IK Handle Tool. Click Reset Tool at the top of the toolbar to return the settings to their defaults. Current Solver is set to ikSCsolver.

10. In Perspective, choose root_JNT and then spine1_JNT. Figure 1.22 shows the results.

11. Turn off Reference for the MOTION_CAPTURE layer, and turn on Reference for the SKELETON layer.

12. Shift+select upperback and ikHandle1. Choose Constrain → Point. Reset the tool to use the defaults, and click Add.

13. Select lowerback and ikHandle1, and choose Constrain → Orient. Make sure Maintain Offset is selected, and use the settings from Figure 1.23.

Figure 1.23

Orient constraint options

Click Play to see the constraints working. Figure 1.24 shows that the two skeleton roots are nicely aligned.

Figure 1.24

The captured character squats down with Jack's root node connected and perfectly aligned.

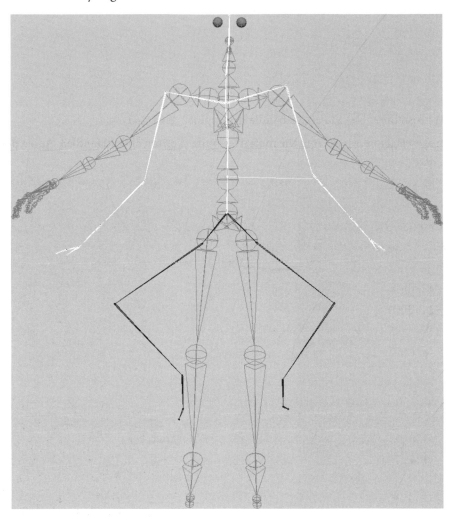

To check your work so far, you can compare it to `mocap_v02.ma` on the DVD.

Let's take a moment to review what you've just done. You point-constrained Jack's root node to the motion-capture root node. You only point-constrained the root node; none of the other joints are directly constrained. Then, you created an SC IK handle from Jack's root to his first spine joint. You point-constrained the SC handle to the motion capture's second spine joint, upperback. Doing this locked the Y and Z rotation of Jack's root joint to the pitch and yaw of the motion-capture skeleton. Next, you applied an orient constraint to the SC handle, effectively locking the X rotation to the twist of the motion-capture skeleton. The formula is to point-constrain the SC handle to the top of the bone and orient the handle to the root of the bone. Figure 1.25 illustrates.

14. Return to frame –13. You can now begin adding handles and constraints to the rest of the joints. For quick reference, Figure 1.26 shows the point and orient constraint options.

15. Add an SC handle from spine1_JNT to spine2_jnt.

16. Shift+select thorax from the motion-capture skeleton and ikHandle2. Add a point constraint.

17. Shift+select upperback from the motion-capture skeleton and ikHandle2. Add an orient constraint.

18. To finish the spine, add an SC handle from spine2_JNT and collar_JNT.

19. Shift+select lowerneck from the motion-capture skeleton and ikHandle3. Add a point constraint.

20. Shift+select thorax from the motion-capture skeleton and ikHandle3. Add an orient constraint.

21. For the left leg, follow the same procedure all the way down the skeletal chain. Here is a list of the constraint mappings:

SC IK Handle	Point Constraint	Orient Constraint
ikHandle 4	ltibia	lfemur
ikHandle 5	lfoot	ltibia
ikHandle 6	ltoes	lfoot
ikHandle 7	ltoes_end	ltoes

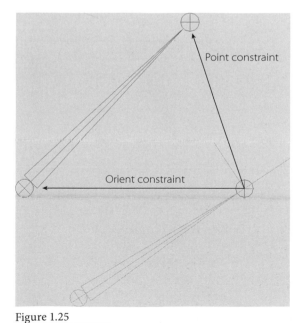

Figure 1.25

Two constraints are used to align a single bone.

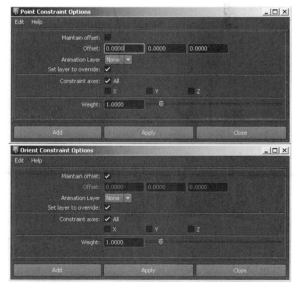

Figure 1.26

Point and orient constraint options

22. Now is a good time to check and save your work. Jack's skeleton should look like Figure 1.27 at frame 280.

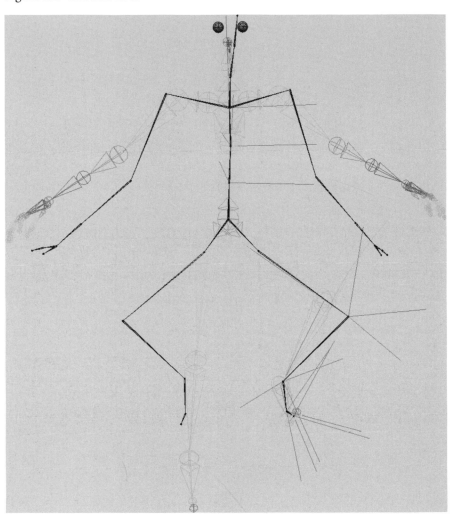

To check your work so far, you can compare it to mocap_v03.ma on the DVD.

23. The left arm is next. Use the following table to map it. For the hand, add an SC IK handle from wristLft_JNT to middle1Lft_JNT. The thumb on the motion-capture skeleton is too awkward to include; you can skip that joint.

SC IK Handle	Point Constraint	Orient Constraint
ikHandle 8	lhumerus	lclavicle
ikHandle 9	lradius	lhumerus
ikHandle 10	lwrist	lradius
ikHandle 11	lhand	lwrist

To check the alignment of the two skeletons, go to frame 424 and compare it with Figure 1.28.

Figure 1.28

Check the alignment at frame 424.

To check your work so far, you can compare it to `mocap_v04.ma` on the DVD.

24. The head and neck are next.

SC IK Handle	Point Constraint	Orient Constraint
ikHandle 12	upperneck	lowerneck
ikHandle 13	head	upperneck

25. More than half of the character is constrained. Unfortunately, IK handles and constraints can't be mirrored. You must manually assign all the bones from the right leg and arm. You can continue or skip ahead to the following saved scene file.

To check your work so far, you can compare it to mocap_v05.ma on the DVD.

26. Hide all the joints and handles. Play the animation to check the quality of the motion. Figure 1.29 shows Jack in an extreme pose at frame 550.

Maintaining Performance

Other than the obvious geometry collisions, the data transferred pretty well. The only major motion-related issue is in the shoulders: they look too high. Your first thought might be to adjust the animation or offset the IK handle. Both those solutions can cause major headaches. Adjusting the IK handle only throws the timing off for the rest of the arm. Adding keyframes over the top via a layer or secondary rig has the potential to do the same thing. More impor-tant, doing so changes the performance.

Your goal is to use the data as is. It's the performance you want. Altering it, even a little, destroys the actor's intentions and, worse, the timing of the captured motion. Maintaining its integrity is paramount. In the next project, you'll address the shoulder issue without altering the performance.

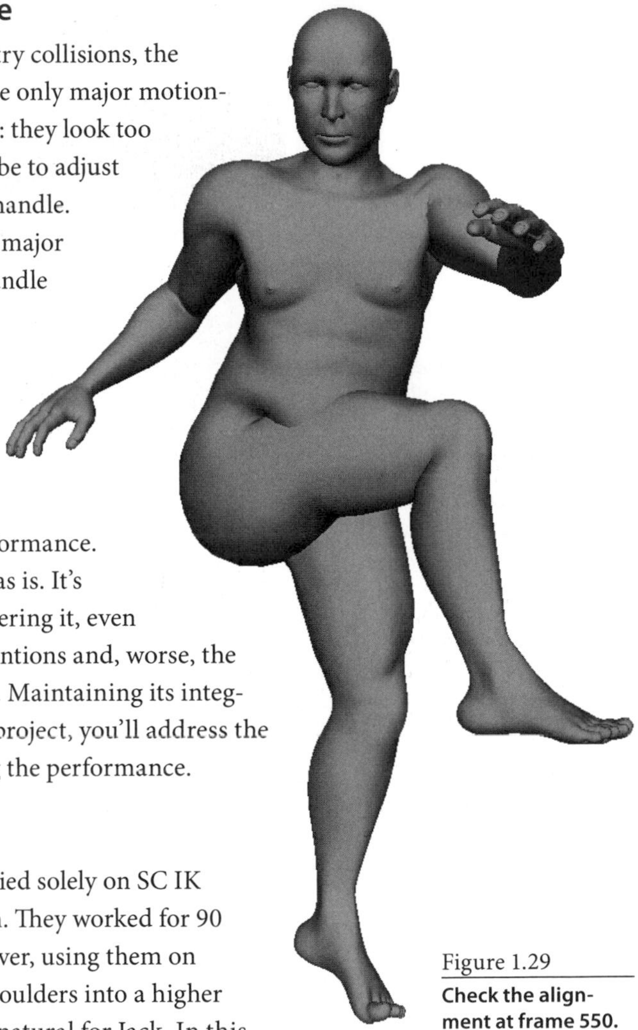

Project: Shoulder Fix

In the previous project, you relied solely on SC IK handles to drive Jack's skeleton. They worked for 90 percent of the character. However, using them on the shoulders has forced the shoulders into a higher constrained position that isn't natural for Jack. In this project, you'll remove the handle and use only an orient constraint:

Figure 1.29

Check the alignment at frame 550.

1. Open the mocap_v05.ma scene from the chapter1\scenes folder on the DVD. It's the same scene that "Project: Motion Test" ended with.

2. Go to frame 1, and look at the shoulders (see Figure 1.30).

3. Select ikHandle8, and delete it.

4. Select clavicleLft_JNT. Change all of its Rotation values to 0.0.

Figure 1.30
The shoulders at frame 1

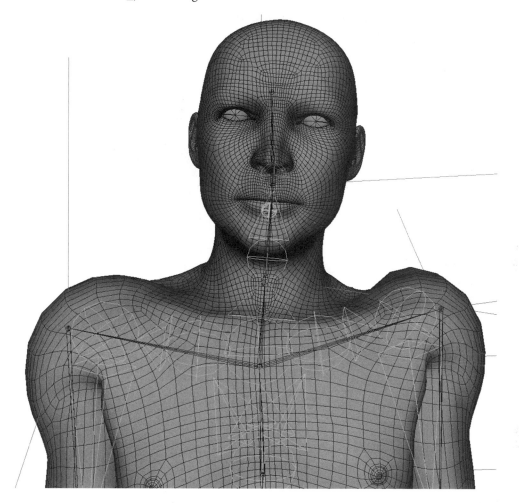

UPDATING CONSTRAINTS

When you move the clavicle, the arm moves away from the motion-capture skeleton it's constrained to. The constraints aren't broken; they simply don't update. To force the constraints to update, move to a different frame and then move back to frame 1; the arm will now be in the proper position.

5. Even without a rotation on the clavicle, it's too high based on the position of the arm. Rotate it to 7.0 units in the Z. You can see the results in Figure 1.31.

Figure 1.31

The shoulder has been rotated in the Z by 7.0 units.

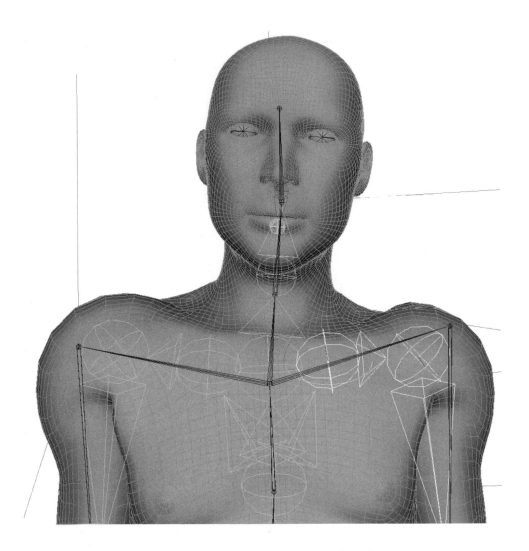

6. Shift+select lclavicle and clavicleLft_JNT. Choose Constrain → Orient. Add the constraint with the settings from Figure 1.32.

Figure 1.32

Orient constraint options

7. After evaluating the shoulder again with its new orient constraint, it becomes evident that there are weighting issues compounding the problem. You can see in Figure 1.33 that clavicleLft_JNT is too strong of an influence.

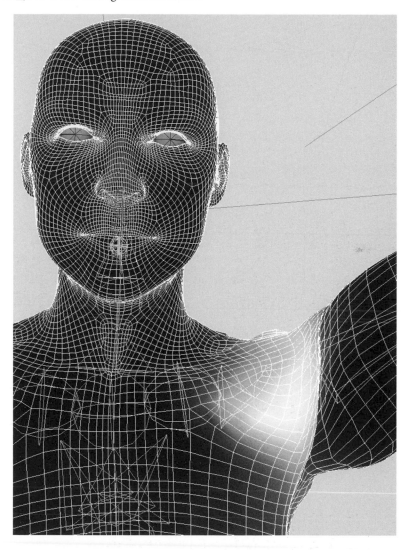

Figure 1.33

ClavicleLft_JNT weights

8. You don't want to paint the weights on this model. Doing so would break the smooth blending between the head and body. Instead, return to the single-mesh weighted character to perform the fix. Before proceeding, save your scene file.

   To check your work so far, you can compare it to shoulderFix_v01.ma on the DVD.

9. You can work on painting the weights on the single-mesh character or import the already-fixed scene file, weightFix_v01.ma, from the chapter1\scenes folder on the DVD.

10. The correctly weighted mesh is loaded into the scene. The two versions of Jack overlap each other. Turn off the layer visibility of the imported Jack nodes.

11. You can't copy the weights over to the animated Jack successfully until he is back into his bind pose. Go to frame -13.0 on the timeline, and choose Modify → Evaluate Nodes → Ignore All.

12. Now that everything is shut down, select all of the animated Jack's joints. A quick way to accomplish this is to choose Edit → Select All by Type → Joints. You can then deselect the extra joints in the Hypergraph or Outliner.

13. With all of Jack's joints selected, set their Rotation to 0.0 in the Channel Box. Jack returns to his default pose without all of his IK handles (see Figure 1.34).

Figure 1.34

Jack is now back in his default bind pose.

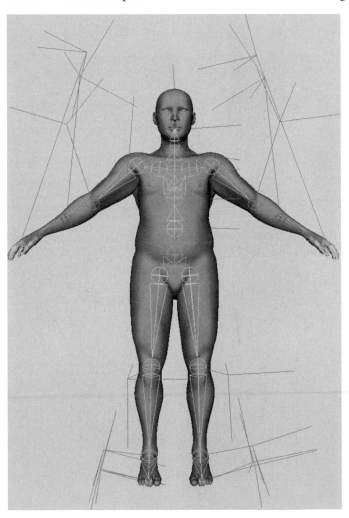

14. You can turn on the layer's visibility for the correctly weighted Jack, although doing so isn't necessary. Shift+select weightFix_v01_body1 and body1.

15. Using the default settings, choose Skin → Edit Smooth Skin → Copy Skin Weights.

16. Shift+select weightFix_v01_head1 and head1. Choose Skin → Edit Smooth Skin → Copy Skin Weights.

17. Turn all the nodes back on by choosing Modify → Evaluate Nodes → Evaluate All. Jack snaps back into place with new shoulder weights (see Figure 1.35).

    To check your work so far, you can compare it to shoulderFix_v02.ma on the DVD.

Figure 1.35

Jack looks better with his new weighting.

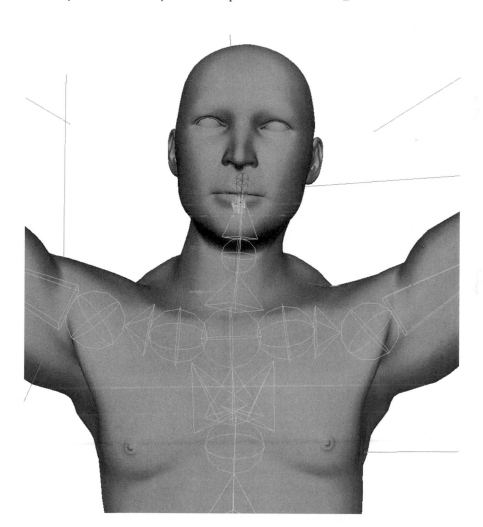

FBX

The FBX file format has a long history of exchanging hands. It's ironic, because it's labeled as a universal data-exchange format. The name is from its original owner, Filmbox. After numerous ups and downs, Filmbox eventually became MotionBuilder, now owned by Autodesk. Its current version is now supported by Maya, 3D Studio Max, Softimage, LightWave, and others, including a QuickTime format.

Project: FBX Import

In this project, you'll use the FBX file format to export and import a motion onto Jack. Here are the steps:

1. Open the boxing_v01.ma scene from the chapter1\scenes folder on the DVD. The scene file contains a skeleton with boxing motion. The timeline has been set to the beginning and end of the motion. The skeleton was derived from the same actor who provided the motion for the exercise routine in "Project: Motion Test." You can see the skeleton taking a punch in Figure 1.36.

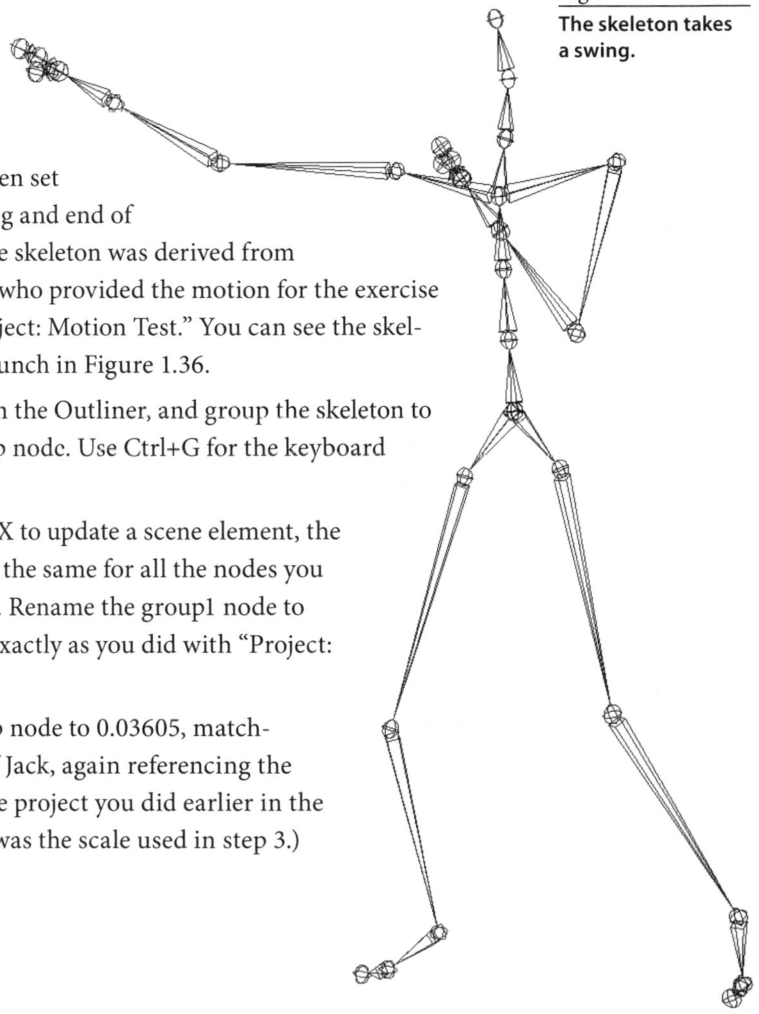

Figure 1.36

The skeleton takes a swing.

2. Select root from the Outliner, and group the skeleton to an empty group node. Use Ctrl+G for the keyboard shortcut.

3. In order for FBX to update a scene element, the names must be the same for all the nodes you want to update. Rename the group1 node to **mocap_GRP**, exactly as you did with "Project: Motion Test."

4. Scale the group node to 0.03605, matching the scale of Jack, again referencing the motion-capture project you did earlier in the chapter. (This was the scale used in step 3.)

5. Select mocap_GRP, and snap its pivot point to the root joint. You can hold D and V on the keyboard to do both actions simultaneously. This is a good time to save your scene.

    To check your work so far, you can compare it to boxing_v02.ma on the DVD.

Figure 1.37

Set the Export All options to export FBX.

6. Choose File → Export All. Change File Type to FBX Export, and click Edit Preset (see Figure 1.37).

7. When you click Edit Preset, the Edit Export Preset window pops up. The FBX file format has numerous settings you can adjust. You only need to concern yourself with the options related to animation. We'll go through each section, ignoring the ones that are irrelevant to this export.

8. Open the Animation section: it has seven subsections. Make sure Animation is selected. Under Extra Options, make sure Use Scene Name is unchecked. You don't want to alter the name of anything in the scene; doing so would prevent the identical nodes from being updated (see Figure 1.38).

Figure 1.38

The Extra Options section of the FBX options

9. Select Bake Animation. The Start and End times should be filled in already. If they aren't, check the scene and enter the appropriate numbers (see Figure 1.39).

    Resample All is optional. Selecting it redoes all the keyframes. Ultimately, you aren't using any of the keyframes on this skeleton; you're only copying its motion, so the keyframe positions don't matter. But if you like or possibly foresee the need to look at the animation curves, this option is very useful. The original boxing motion was captured at 120 fps and reduced in Maya to playback at 30 fps. This forces the keys into fractional frame numbers. Resampling the animation through the FBX export puts a keyframe only on integer frame numbers.

Figure 1.39

The Bake Animation section of the FBX options

10. You can deselect Deformed Models in the Deformed Models section. The parameter doesn't apply because there isn't any geometry in the scene (see Figure 1.40).

Figure 1.40

The Deformed Models section of the FBX options

11. The rest of the Animation options should be turned off. Curve Filters and Constant Key Reducer are useful for cleaning up animation curves, but at this point you aren't interested in cleaning the curves.

Geometry Cache Files and Constraints, the next two sections, have no bearing on the scene because none of these objects exist in the scene. Figure 1.41 shows all the settings.

Figure 1.41

The remaining Animation options

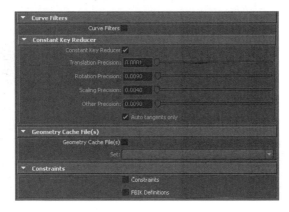

12. The only other parameters that need mentioning are under Advanced Options: the Units and Axis Conversion sections, shown in Figure 1.42.

Figure 1.42

The Units and Axis Conversion sections of the FBX options

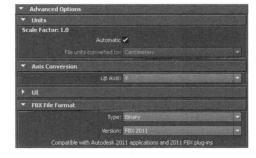

None of these need altering, but they're important if you're exporting to a different software package or want to convert the units through the export. You can also set the file format to ASCII, giving you the ability to edit the output by hand.

13. Click Save Preset, and call it **mocap**. You can call the preset anytime you need to export another motion.

14. Click Close to exit the Edit Export Preset window. The Export All Options window is still open. Click Export All to save the file. It's a good idea to create a directory named FBX in your project directory to keep things organized.

 15. Open the shoulderFix_v02.ma scene from the chapter1\scenes folder on the DVD.

16. Choose File → Import, and change File Type to FBX. Also deselect Use Namespaces, and use the settings shown in Figure 1.43.

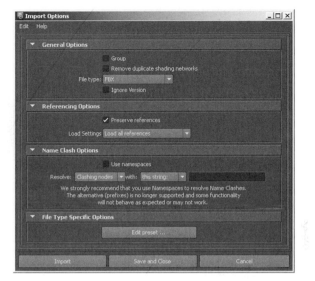

Figure 1.43

The Import Options window

17. Click Import to go to the Import browser window. Select the boxing.fbx scene from the chapter1\FBX folder on the DVD. As soon as you select the file, the FBX options appear at right in the window.

18. Under Include, change File Contents to Update Scene Elements. Make sure Animation is selected, and use the settings from Figure 1.44.

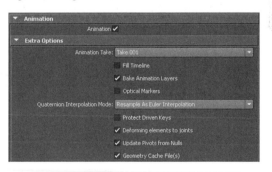

Figure 1.44

The Animation Import Options section

19. Click Import in the browser.

20. The motion loads, and the Jack character is updated. He now moves with the boxing motion capture. Figure 1.45 shows him in action at frame 87.

To check your work so far, you can compare it to boxing_v03.ma on the DVD.

For free and instant access motion capture, the results are pretty good. If you were to make extensive use of a motion-capture library, you could start with one of the skeletons provided by the library and build your character around it.

Summary

Libraries are limiting. At some point, you'll need an animation they don't have or some type of transition between captures. MotionBuilder by Autodesk is ideal for handling this type of work, but it adds more to your pipeline. In an ideal world, you'd have your own motion-capture studio! Keep reading, and you'll get there.

Figure 1.45

Jack taking a swing

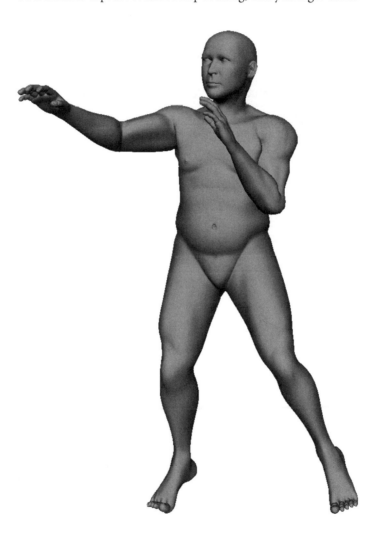

CHAPTER 2

Face Rigging

The face is the most distinguishable part of the human body. It's used to identify the people we know or don't know; but, more important, it's the principal tool used in personal communications. The computer-generated actor must be able to show emotion or give a speech.

It's easy to recognize when a face looks wrong, but how do you do it right? In this chapter, you'll replicate the muscles of the human face in order to create a functional and anatomically correct facial rig for Jack.

In this chapter you will learn to:

- Learn the muscles of the human face

- Add motion to muscles

Facial Anatomy

The human face comprises numerous muscles. The exact number is arguable, because facial muscles merge together, can be multipronged, and may perform various actions. In the end, the amount is irrelevant—what matters is replicating the correct motion.

A muscle is made up of three parts. The first is its *anchor point*, or *origin*; this is a fixed position to which the muscle retracts. The next is the muscle *belly*: the part of the muscle that does the actual contracting or tightening. The last part is the insertion, which connects to other tissues. When the muscle is acted upon, the insertion draws toward its origin, pulling the tissues connected to it. Figure 2.1 illustrates a common muscle.

Of all the muscles in the face, you'll create only 37 in this chapter. The focus is on the muscles that directly contribute to facial movement. The muscles represented aren't the only muscles the human face uses, but they're the only ones needed for this character. For instance, the jaw is moved by several different muscles. None of these need to be represented because they don't directly influence a facial muscle or skin. The jaw can be moved with a joint to simplify the setup. Figure 2.2 shows the muscles used for Jack's face.

Figure 2.1

The parts of a muscle

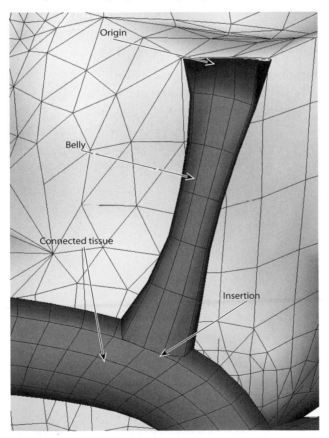

A ton of information is available about how muscles move and which muscles do what and why. This is important for you to learn, and you should do some research to truly understand the face. The purpose of this book isn't to teach you how to animate the face, but how to build it. Furthermore, captured motion is used to drive the face, not manually keyed frames.

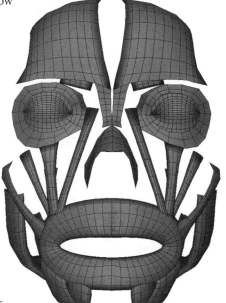

Figure 2.2

Jack's facial muscles

Many terms have been used to describe the shapes that the face makes. From expressions to phonemes, these words and/or groups have little value. When you begin itemizing individual shapes, characters become limited—their performance is controlled by a predetermined set of values. This method for creating characters is an efficient way to get the job done and essential for branded characters, but it's a contradiction for creating realistic performance-driven characters.

The reason is that all humans perform differently. And they don't just perform differently from human to human—they behave differently from situation to situation. This means different muscles are used to express what appears to be the same emotion. For instance, if you fake a smile, you're only using your zygomaticus major muscle to pull your lips apart. A real smile employs the zygomaticus major as well as the orbicularis oculi. Another scenario would be an actor exhibiting fear. Is the actor afraid of what they're seeing? If so, the actor's eyes should widen, their pupils dilate, and maybe their mouth open slightly or their lip quiver. Or are they afraid of a thought? This may cause the actor's brow to furrow and nose to flare. Each situation is different, from the muscle being used to how much it's being used.

Our goal is performance, not the individual pronunciation of words or formed expressions. To achieve a realistic performance, you must consider speech and expression as entire body motions and not singular elements. We can't stress this enough. As soon as you categorize and break down a performance into isolated reusable motions, you lose the performance.

Muscle Movement

The most important aspect of each muscle is its movement. The size and shape is almost insignificant compared to its motion. But muscle movement isn't always clear; even with an abundance of literature and online resources, finding suitable references can be difficult.

This section identifies the muscles you need to build and provides additional information to aid in their development. It's also worth noting that this isn't an exhaustive list. We could have added other muscles that contribute to skin movement, but they have been excluded for practical purposes.

ORBICULARIS ORIS

Function: The king of speech, this sphincter muscle encircles the lips. Almost every muscle that contributes to facial motion is attached to this muscle. It causes the lips to purse, kiss, tighten, and suck in.

Origin: Under the nose on the skull or maxilla

Insertion: Skin surrounding the lips

Latin name: *Musculus orbicularis oris*

Maya node name: orbicularis_Oris_MUSC

Muscle type: Sphincter

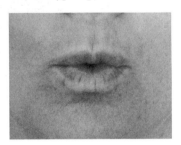

Figure 2.3

The orbicularis oris in action

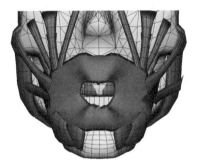

Figure 2.4

The results of clenching the orbicular oris

NASALIS

Function: Compresses the bridge of the nose, flares the wing of the nose, and depresses the nose tip

Origin: Maxilla

Insertion: Nasal bone

Latin name: *Nasalis*

Maya node name: nasalis

Muscle type: Sphincter

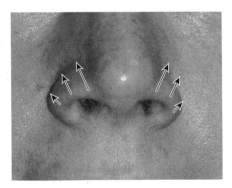

Figure 2.5

The nasalis in action

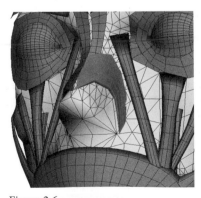

Figure 2.6

The result of flexing the nasalis muscle

LEVATOR NASI

Function: Lifts the upper lip and wing of the nose

Origin: Maxilla

Insertion: Nostril and upper lip

Latin name: *Musculus levator labii superioris alaeque nasi*

Maya node name: levatorNasi_MUSC

Muscle type: Linear

Figure 2.7

The levator nasi in action

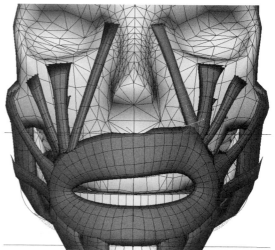

Figure 2.8

The result of flexing the levator nasi

LEVATOR SUPERIORIS

Function: Sometimes referred to as the Elvis muscle, it lifts the upper lip, forming a snarl.

Origin: Lower edge of the eye socket

Insertion: Skin and muscle of the upper lip

Latin name: *Levator labii superioris*

Maya node name: levatorSuperioris

Muscle type: Linear

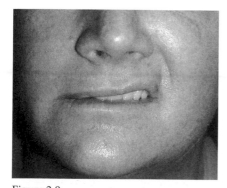

Figure 2.9

The levator superioris in action

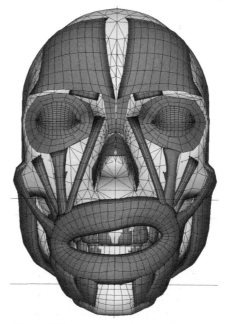

Figure 2.10

The result of flexing the levator superioris

ZYGOMATICUS MINOR

Function: Lifts the upper lip

Origin: Zygomatic bone

Insertion: Skin of the upper lip

Latin name: *Zygomaticus minor*

Maya node name: zygomaticusMinor

Muscle type: Linear

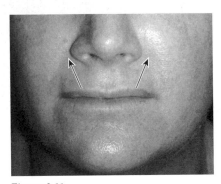

Figure 2.11

The zygomaticus minor in action

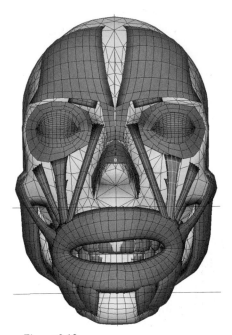

Figure 2.12

The results of flexing the zygomaticus minor

LEVATOR ANGULI ORIS

Function: Lifts the corners of the mouth

Origin: Maxilla

Insertion: Skin and muscle of the upper lip

Latin name: *Levator anguli oris*

Maya node name: levatorAnguliOris

Muscle type: Linear

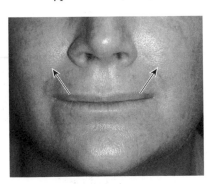

Figure 2.13

The levator anguli oris in action

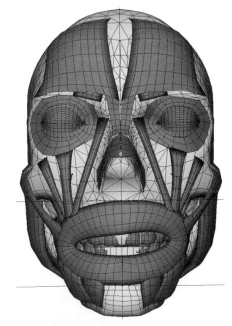

Figure 2.14

The results of flexing the levator anguli oris

ZYGOMATICUS MAJOR

Function: Pulls the corners of the mouth up and laterally

Origin: Zygomatic bone

Insertion: Skin and muscle of the upper lip

Latin name: *Zygomaticus major*

Maya node name: zygomaticusMajor

Muscle type: Linear

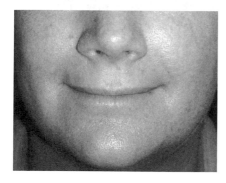

Figure 2.15
The zygomaticus major in action

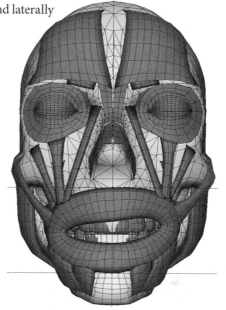

Figure 2.16
The results of flexing the zygomaticus major

BUCCINATOR

Function: Compresses the cheek against the teeth. Used in blowing and chewing.

Origin: Mandible, behind the teeth

Insertion: Back of the orbicularis oris

Latin name: *Buccinator*

Maya node name: buccinator

Muscle type: Linear

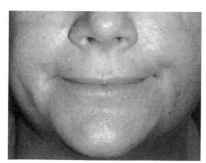

Figure 2.17
The buccinator in action

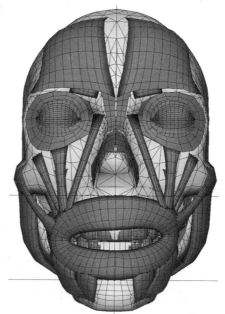

Figure 2.18
The results of flexing the buccinator

RISORIUS

Function: Pulls back the corners of the mouth

Origin: Parotid fascia

Insertion: Orbicularis oris

Latin name: *Risorius*

Maya node name: risorius

Muscle type: Linear

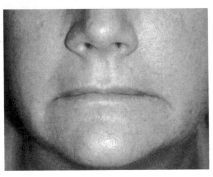

Figure 2.19

The risorius in action

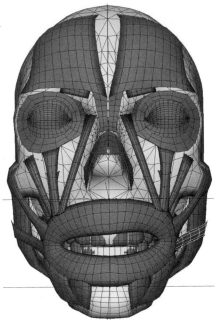

Figure 2.20

The results of flexing the risorius

TRIANGULARIS

Function: Pulls down the corners of the mouth

Origin: Front side of the mandible

Insertion: Orbicularis oris

Latin name: *Depressor anguli oris*

Maya node name: triangularis

Muscle type: Linear

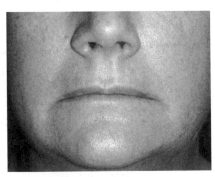

Figure 2.21

The triangularis in action

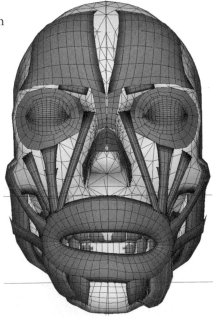

Figure 2.22

The results of flexing the triangularis

DEPRESSOR LABII

Function: Pulls down the lower lip

Origin: Oblique line of the mandible

Insertion: Orbicularis oris

Latin name: *Depressor labii inferioris*

Maya node name: depressorLabii

Muscle type: Linear

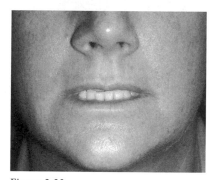

Figure 2.23

The depressor labii in action

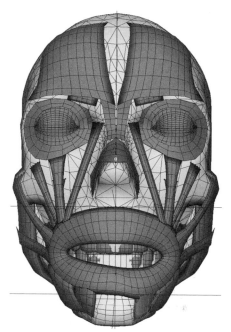

Figure 2.24

The results of flexing the depressor labii

MENTALIS

Function: Lifts the skin associated with the chin, causing the bottom lip to protrude

Origin: Bottom of the mandible

Insertion: Chin skin

Latin name: *Musculus mentalis*

Maya node name: mentalis

Muscle type: Linear

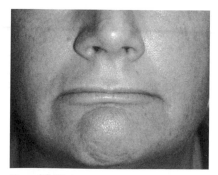

Figure 2.25

The mentalis in action

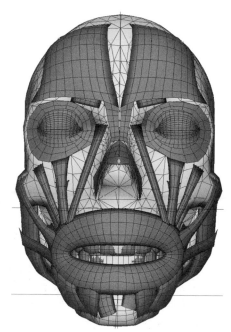

Figure 2.26

The results of flexing the mentalis

PROCERUS

Function: Draws down the eyebrow

Origin: Nasal bone

Insertion: Skin between the forehead and eyebrows

Latin name: *Procerus*

Maya node name: procerus

Muscle type: Linear

Figure 2.27

The procerus in action

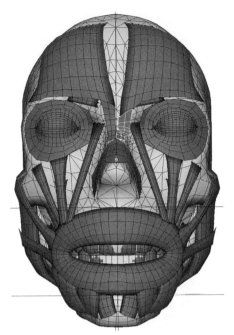

Figure 2.28

The results of flexing the procerus

CORRUGATOR SUPERCILII

Function: Wrinkles the forehead

Origin: Superciliary arch

Insertion: Forehead skin, near the eyebrow

Latin name: *Corrugator supercilii*

Maya node name: corrugator

Muscle type: Linear

Figure 2.29

The corrugator in action

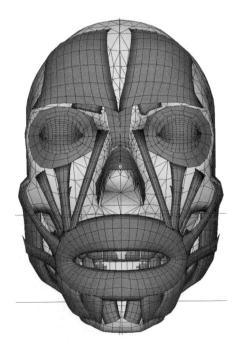

Figure 2.30

The results of flexing the corrugator

ORBICULARIS OCULI

Function: Squints and closes the eye

Origin: Frontal bone

Insertion: Lateral palpebral raphe

Latin name: *Orbicularis oculi*

Maya node name: orbicularisOculi

Muscle type: Sphincter

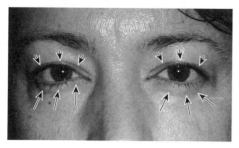

Figure 2.31

The orbicularis oculi in action

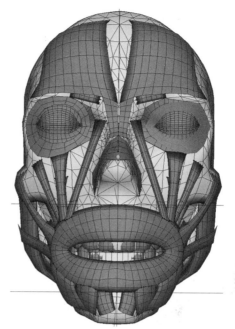

Figure 2.32

The results of flexing the orbicularis oculi

FRONTALIS

Function: Wrinkles the brow

Origin: Galea aponeurotica (top of the head)

Insertion: Skin above the eyebrows

Latin name: *Venter frontalis musculi occipitofrontalis*

Maya node name: frontalis

Muscle type: Linear

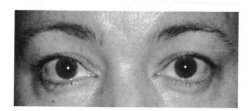

Figure 2.33

The frontalis in action

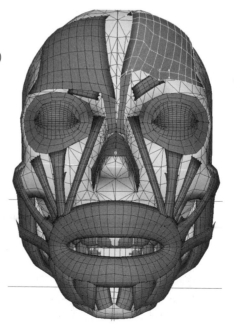

Figure 2.34

The results of flexing the frontalis

Modeling Muscles

There are three types of muscles in the head: linear, sphincter, and sheet. Of the three, only the first two are represented in this chapter. It's important that each muscle is built without penetrating another or itself. You should keep the geometry simple and low resolution. You can use any modeling method to derive the geometry as long as the end product is polygons.

Project: Sphincter Muscle (Orbicularis Oris)

The orbicularis oris muscle is the king of the sphincter muscles. Most of your time will be devoted to getting this muscle to look and act properly. This project takes you through the steps of modeling this important sphincter muscle:

1. Open the sphincterModel_v01.ma scene from the chapter2\scenes folder on the DVD. The scene contains a weighted version of Jack hidden on a layer. Jack's skull is visible and shown in Figure 2.35.

2. Turn on Visibility for the BODY layer. Select the loop of edges that border the lips. Use Figure 2.36 as reference.

3. Choose Modify → Convert → Polygon Edges To Curve.

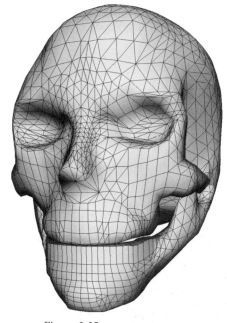

Figure 2.35

Jack's skull

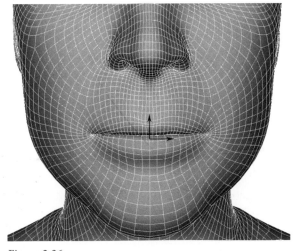

Figure 2.36

Select a loop of edges around the mouth.

4. The new curve represents the inner edge of the muscle. Duplicate the curve, and center its pivot. Scale the curve to the following (see Figure 2.37):

    > Scale X: 1.340
    >
    > Scale Y: 1.844
    >
    > Scale Z: 1.580

5. The second curve represents the outer edge of the muscle. Select both curves. Choose Surfaces → Loft, and use the default tool options (see Figure 2.38).

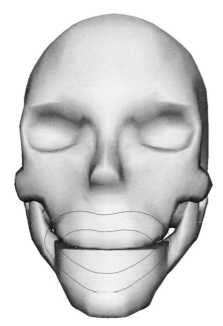

Figure 2.37

**Scale the curve
larger than the first.**

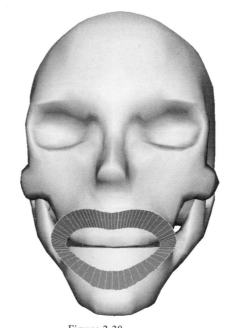

Figure 2.38

**The result of lofting
the two curves**

6. Choose Convert → Modify → Nurbs To Polygons, and use the options shown in Figure 2.39.

7. Delete the history, the lofted surface, and the curves.

8. Extrude the polygon surface to 0.01 in the Local Translate Z (see Figure 2.40).

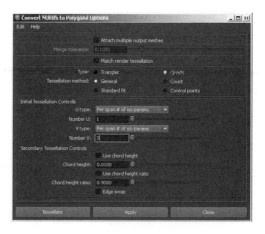

Figure 2.39

**The Convert NURBS
to Polygons Options**

9. Choose Edit Mesh → Insert Edge Loop Tool. Place an edge loop to divide the surface's thickness. Use Figure 2.41 for reference.

10. Delete the geometry's history, and center its pivot.

11. Select the edge loop you added in step 9. Scale the loop uniformly, using Figure 2.42 as a guide.

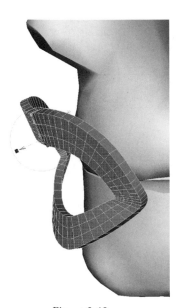

Figure 2.40

Extrude the polygons

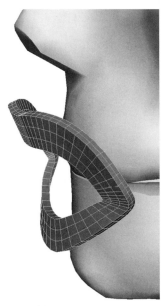

Figure 2.41

Insert an edge loop.

Figure 2.42

Scale the center line uniformly.

12. Rename the geometry **orbicularisOris**.

To check your work so far, you can compare it to `sphincterModel_v02.ma` on the DVD.

The muscle needs to be as close to the skull as possible. There are two ways make this happen: You can use the Soft Select feature of the Move tool, or you can simulate the muscle into position. Simulating the muscle has the advantage of placing the geometry at the exact desired distance from the skull.

13. Select the skull. Choose nMesh → Create Passive Collider.

14. Select the mandible. Choose nMesh → Create Passive Collider.

15. Select the orbicularisOris. Choose nMesh → Create nCloth.

16. Open nClothShape1's Attribute Editor, and switch to the nucleus1 tab.

17. Change Gravity to the Z. Figure 2.43 shows the settings.

Figure 2.43

Gravity settings

18. Switch back to the nClothShape node, and use Figure 2.44 to change the Pressure settings.

19. Click Play to watch the simulation. Stop the timeline around frame 60 or when the muscle looks good (see Figure 2.45).

20. Once the muscle has relaxed against the skull and mandible, you can choose Edit → Delete By Type → History. The nCloth attributes are removed, and the surface is normal geometry again.

To check your work so far, you can compare it to sphincterModel_v03.ma on the DVD.

Project: Linear Muscle (Zygomaticus Major)

The zygomaticus major is a key muscle in forming words and expressions. It's the epitome of a linear muscle. This project focuses on creating it and is also the foundation for creating all the other linear muscles. Follow these steps:

1. Open the zygomaticusModel_v01.ma scene from the chapter2\scenes folder on the DVD. The scene contains a weighted version of Jack hidden on a layer. Jack's skull and orbicularis oris muscle are visible and shown in Figure 2.46.

2. Choose Create → Polygon Primitives → Cylinder. Use Figure 2.47 for the settings.

Figure 2.44

nCloth pressure settings

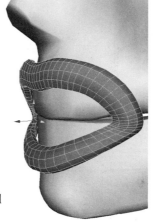

Figure 2.45

The orbicularis oris muscle after simulation

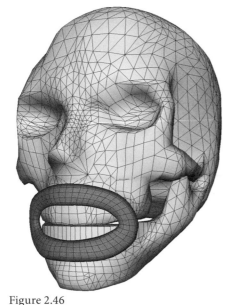

Figure 2.46

The elements of the scene file

Figure 2.47

Cylinder creation tool options

3. Rename the pCylinder1 **zygomaticusMajor_MUSC**.

4. Scale the cylinder using the following settings:

   Scale X: 0.012

   Scale Y: 0.030

   Scale Z: 0.005

5. Translate the cylinder next to the skull. Orient it to its approximate position, using Figure 2.48 as a guide.

6. Merge the vertices at the top of the muscle to close it off. In essence, you're creating a flat tendon to connect the muscle to the skull. Figure 2.49 shows the modified geometry.

7. Snap the vertices along the zygomatic process on the skull. The vertices don't have to be exact. You can snap to a curve, snap to a point, or snap to a Live surface (see Figure 2.50).

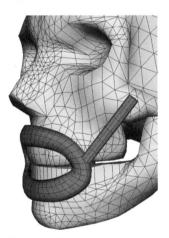 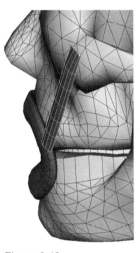 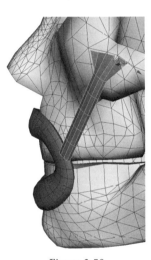

Figure 2.48
_____
Position the cylinder close to the skull.

Figure 2.49
_____
Close the end of the muscle by merging vertices.

Figure 2.50
_____
Snap the muscle vertices to the skull.

8. For the insertion, snapping to a Live surface works best. Select the orbicularis oris muscle, and make it Live.

9. Snap the end points of the zygomaticus muscle around the corner of the orbicularis oris. Use Figure 2.51 for reference.

10. Delete the muscle's history, and freeze its transformations.

 To check your work so far, you can compare it to `zygomaticusModel_v02.ma` on the DVD.

11. You can now relax the muscle into position. As with the orbicularis oris, relaxing the muscle is a good idea. Even though the zygomaticus won't collide with much, relaxation stretches the geometry into a natural state, prepping it for simulation.

     Select the orbicularis oris and the skull. Choose nMesh → Create Passive Collider. Both objects are made into rigid bodies; this is only temporary, to facilitate relaxing the zygomaticus.

12. Select the zygomaticus muscle. Choose nMesh → Create nCloth.

13. Select the row of vertices at the muscle's origin. Shift+select the skull, and choose nConstraint → Point To Surface (see Figure 2.52).

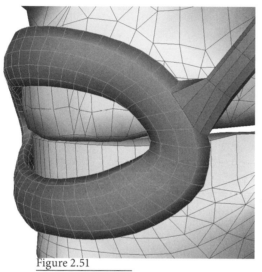

Figure 2.51
Snap the vertices of the zygomaticus muscle to the orbicularis.

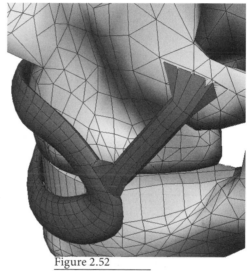

Figure 2.52
Constrain the origin to the skull.

Figure 2.53
Constrain the insertion point to the orbicularis oris.

14. Select all the vertices around the insertion point. Shift+select the orbicularis oris, and choose nConstraint → Point to Surface (see Figure 2.53).

15. Open zygomaticusMajor_MUSC's Attribute Editor, and select the nucleus1 tab. Use Figure 2.54 to set the Gravity parameters.

Figure 2.54
Gravity settings

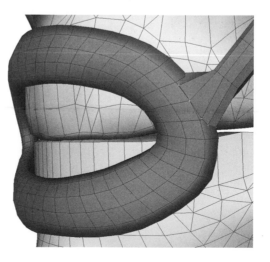

16. Play the simulation to about frame 48 or until the muscle relaxes (see Figure 2.55).

Figure 2.55

Relax the muscle.

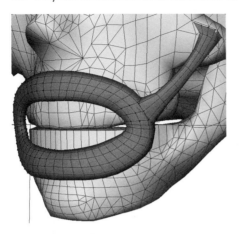

17. With the muscle selected, choose Edit → Delete By Type → History. The nCloth attributes are removed, and the surface is normal geometry again.

18. The nCloth properties are detached, but the nodes still exist. Open the Hypergraph to get a clear view of what is happening (see Figure 2.56). Delete the nRigid, nCloth, and dynamicConstraint nodes.

Figure 2.56

The nodes in the Hypergraph

19. After the deletions in step 18, the once-intermediate zygomaticusMajor_MUSCShape node is made visible. Delete it as well.

20. Rename outputCloth2 to **zygomaticusMajor_MUSCShape**. The geometry is now clean.

The muscle is finished. To check your work so far, you can compare it to `zygomaticusModel_v03.ma` on the DVD.

Muscle Motion

When you create a facial rig, you're moving nodes in a linear fashion. They might be bones that are translating or rotating. They could influence objects under the skin or the Maya muscle deformer and its utilities. Regardless, the motion is linear. As implied, linear muscles move linearly. However, when you consider a muscle under the skin, a substantial number of secondary influences are affecting its motion. It's surrounded by bone, ligament, other muscles, fluids, and more. Therefore, when it's stated that a muscle is *linear*, that means the muscle has a linear force. A linear impulse is required to make the muscle retract or flex. After the force has been applied, the muscle is at the mercy of its surroundings, and the strongest elements prevail. The result is a unique and realistic motion to the muscle. This method allows the muscle to shift along its linear path and to have jitter or shake when held tightly in a flexed position.

Mouth Muscles

Most of the muscles needed for Jack's face are located around the mouth. The majority of them are also connected through the orbicularis oris. This makes their motion difficult to solve. When a muscle like the zygomaticus major flexes, the orbicularis oris must relax, allowing it to be pulled or stretched.

The mouth muscles must behave automatically. When you're trying to animate a character, nothing is worse than constantly having to animate attributes. This is even more critical when you're dealing with performance capture. It's vital to have the performance imported onto the facial rig and work as expected. Of course, some fine-tuning will be required, but you shouldn't have to rework the relationships between each muscle every time.

The rest of this chapter focuses on getting each individual muscle to behave properly. Combining muscle motion is addressed in Chapter 8, "Composition," in conjunction with building a facial interface. Getting each muscle to move properly on its own is an important part of the process. This may seem evident; but the attributes you assign now are likely to change when other muscles are introduced. This part of the process tests the geometry, collisions, and individual motion of each muscle. When they're established, you can begin to plan and anticipate how they will affect other muscles.

Figure 2.57
The elements of the scene file

Project: Zygomaticus Major

The zygomaticus major is a great muscle to start with. It provides a lot of movement to the orbicularis oris and has a recognizable motion. In this project, you set up the zygomaticus major muscle using nCloth to simulate it. The orbicularis oris muscle is used but is locked into position temporarily. Follow these steps:

1. Open the `zygomaticusMotion_v01.ma` scene from the `chapter2\scenes` folder on the DVD. The scene contains a weighted version of Jack hidden on a layer. Jack's skull, orbicularis oris, and zygomaticus muscle are visible and shown in Figure 2.57.

2. Select the skull and mandible. Choose nMesh → Create Passive Collider.

3. In the Channel Box, set Thickness and Friction to 0.0 for the two nRigids. This allows the muscles to slide easily across the surface.

FRICTION

Although it might seem like an added bonus to have friction on the bones, it only causes problems. Having friction can cause the muscles to get caught and hang on parts of the bone. In the real world, muscles and tendons are designed to glide with little resistance. In addition, they're surrounded by fluids, easing any resistance even more.

---

4. Select the orbicularis oris, and choose nMesh → Create nCloth.

5. Choose the vertices on the right half of the orbicularis oris. Select nConstraint → Transform (see Figure 2.58).

   The transform constraint essentially locks the muscle in place. Constraining the right half allows the left half to be influenced by the zygomaticus major muscle. You do this only temporarily to keep the muscle from being pulled off the skull.

6. Select the zygomaticus major muscle, and choose nMesh → Create nCloth.

7. Select the row of vertices at the muscle's origin, exactly as you did in step 13 of the previous project. Shift+select the skull. Choose nConstraint → Point to Surface.

8. Select both muscles, and switch to component mode. Use the Lasso tool to select all the vertices around the insertion point. Choose nConstraint → Component to Component. Use Figure 2.59 as reference.

9. With the muscles connected, you can begin testing the simulation. Open the nucleus1 node, and set Gravity to 0.0. Playing the simulation should do nothing at this point.

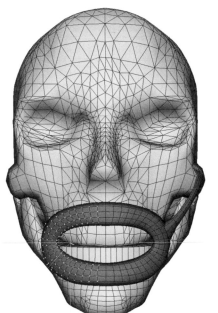

Figure 2.58

Add a transform constraint to half of the orbicularis oris.

 To check your work so far, you can compare it to `zygomaticusMotion_v02.ma` on the DVD.

10. To activate the muscle, you need to apply a force along the length of the muscle. A Volume Curve field is effective for doing this. Select a single edge at the insertion point on the zygomaticus.

    You want an edge that best follows the direction of the muscle or one that points at the origin. It's okay if it isn't perfect; you can adjust it later. Choose Modify → Convert → Polygon Edges To Curve, and use the default settings (see Figure 2.60). Leave the history intact.

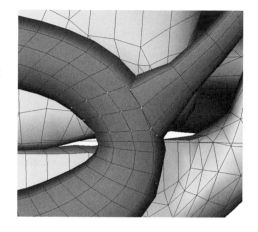

Figure 2.59

Select the vertices of the insertion point.

11. To center the curve's pivot, choose Modify → Center Pivot.

12. Assign a Volume Curve Axis field. With the curve selected, choose Fields→ Volume Curve.

13. Open the volume curve's Attribute Editor. In the Volume Control Attributes section, change Section Radius to 0.02(see Figure 2.61).

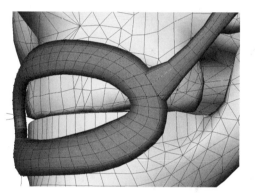

Figure 2.60

Select and convert an edge to a curve on the zygomaticus major muscle.

14. In the Volume Speed Attributes section, change Along Axis to –1.0. With the cylinder oriented so its axis runs through the length of the muscle, you use negative values for the muscles above the lips and positive values for those below the lips.

15. Set Magnitude to 20. The Magnitude value provides the force that moves the muscle.

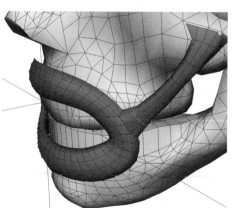

Figure 2.61

The Volume Curve field

16. Create a preset for the field, and name it **negativeImpulse**. The preset works really well because the curve holds all the translation and rotation values and not the field. Therefore, you can apply the preset without having to adjust any values.

Figure 2.62

The curve's translate and rotation values

17. Select polyCurve1, and rename it **zygomaticusMajor_CURVE**. Rotate the curve to align its direction toward the muscle's origin. You can use the values from Figure 2.62.

VOLUME CURVE

Using only a small section of curve doesn't take full advantage of the Volume Curve field. The alternate is to use a uniform field or volume axis. Both of these could work, but only to a limited degree. In addition, placing them is cumbersome. The Volume Curve immediately places the field where it needs to be. Furthermore, by retaining the curve-creation history, the volume axis field moves with the muscle. For more complex muscle shapes, you have the option of using a longer curve. Remember, the field provides an impulse to move the muscle and isn't meant to drive the muscle over a long distance.

To check your work so far, you can compare it to `zygomaticusMotion_v03.ma` on the DVD.

18. The field needs to be connected to the muscle. Don't assign the field directly to the geometry—you must assign it to the nCloth node in order for it to work properly. Select the field and nCloth2, and choose Fields → Affect Selected Object(s).

19. Play the simulation to test the muscle. Figure 2.63 shows the results at frame 20.

Figure 2.63

The zygomaticus major muscle flexes.

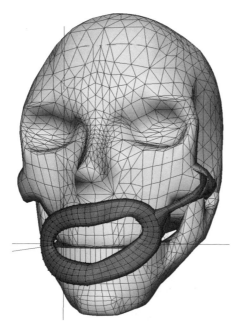

20. The results are far from perfect. You need to modify both muscles' attributes to give them proper stretch and compression abilities. Begin with the orbicularis oris: select the muscle, and open its Attribute Editor.

21. Select the nCloth1 tab. In the Collisions section, deselect Self Collide, and set Collision Flag to Vertex. Temporarily turning off Self Collide speeds up calculations. In the end, you need to use Self Collision in order to maintain stability in the muscle.

22. Open the Dynamic Properties section. Use Figure 2.64 for the settings.

Figure 2.64

Dynamic Properties settings

Stretch Resistance and Compression Resistance are the two key attributes to modify. The orbicularis oris needs to be able to stretch when other muscles pull on it. It also must resist stretching to prevent it from losing its shape. If the Stretch Resistance value is too low, the edges must stretch until they're taut before any adjacent edges are pulled. This gives the muscle a gooey type motion.

Compression Resistance plays more of a part when the muscle is pushed rather than pulled on. You'll see the full effects of this attribute on the zygomaticus major muscle described later in the project.

23. Change Deform Resistance to 1.0. Doing so helps the muscle retain its shape.

24. Change Lift and Drag to 0.0. Muscles are too dense to have these properties.

25. Play the simulation to see the new settings in action. Figure 2.65 shows the results at frame 20.

Figure 2.65

The orbicularis oris responds better.

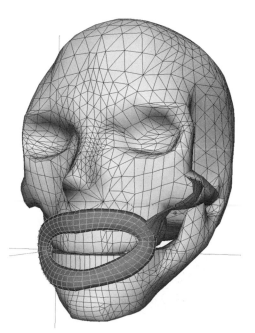

26. Select the zygomaticus major muscle, and open its Attribute Editor. Go to the nClothShape2 tab, and turn off Self Collide.

27. Use Figure 2.66 to change the Dynamic Properties section.

Figure 2.66

Dynamic Properties settings for the zygomaticus major muscle

A linear muscle relies on compression. If Compression Resistance is too high, the muscle pushes back on the force from the field and becomes stiff. Linear muscles need as little resistance to compression as possible.

Bend Resistance keeps the muscle from angling or bowing. Setting this value too high can cause the muscle to become unstable. You can tell quickly when this value is set incorrectly.

28. The remaining attributes in the Dynamic Properties section are shown in Figure 2.67. You increase Stretch Damp to help keep the muscle stable.

Figure 2.67

Remaining Dynamic Properties settings for the zygomaticus major muscle

29. When the muscles are simulated, a few vertices around the zygomaticus major's insertion point pull away from the orbicularis oris (see Figure 2.68).

Figure 2.68

Vertices are pulling away from the insertion point.

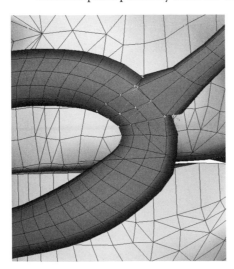

You only need to modify the constraint to fix this problem. Select dynamic-Constraint2. In the Channel Box, change the connection method to Within Max Distance.

To check your work so far, you can compare it to `zygomaticusMotion_v04.ma` on the DVD.

AUTOMATING THE PROCESS

Setting up the muscles for simulation is a repetitive process. Only a handful of attributes need to be customized per muscle. Based on this process, you can create a shelf of commonly used tools. The following is a list of the tools in the order they're used:

Choose Modify → Convert → Polygon Edges to Curve

Modify → Center Pivot

Fields → Volume Curve

Choose Fields → Affect Selected Object(s)

The muscle moves in response to the Volume Curve field. If the muscle isn't moving in the desired direction, rotate the curve to change its motion. The curve is the only node you need to adjust; the field automatically updates along with it.

The zygomaticus major doesn't move perfectly yet. It won't until you connect all the other muscles as well.

Muscle Organization

Many nodes are used in the creation of each muscle. It's important to keep them organized to prevent errors, but a clean environment also expedites the process. Renaming nodes and maintaining a good naming convention is critical to the production pipeline. Using prefixes and suffixes allows you to share a common name for all the nodes associated to a single muscle. For instance, you name the triangularis muscle named based on whether it's on the right or the left:

L_triangularis

The prefix distinguishes its position on the face in relation to the character's right or left. You can also use a prefix to describe bottom or top, and so on.

Use a suffix is used to state the type of node. The full word or abbreviation is sufficient:

L_triangularis_FIELD

L_triangularis_INSERT

The word *INSERT* is used as an abbreviation to describe the muscle's insertion point. You can use underscores and capital letters to separate the prefixes and suffixes from other letters and words. This makes it easy to call groups of similar nodes in a script or text-driven selection tool.

Quickly and reliably finding what you're looking increases the speed of any workflow. You can group muscles with all their connections under a single node without any adverse effects on performance. Creating hierarchies for each muscle puts the nodes in predictable locations and makes efficient use of Hypergraph and Outliner space. You can group all the nodes for a single muscle by its location—that is, left or right—and then group both locations under one node. Figure 2.69 shows the group in the Hypergraph.

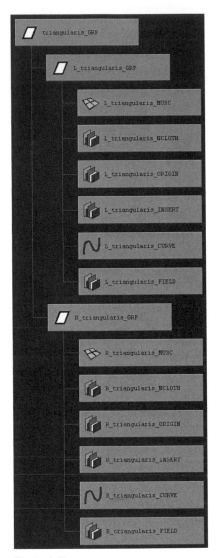

Figure 2.69

The hierarchy of a muscle group in the Hypergraph

Project: Triangularis

The triangularis muscle could be considered the zygomaticus major's opposite. You set up this muscle in a similar fashion with a few minor changes. This short project focuses on the large width of the muscle and the attributes needed to make it work. The triangularis muscle has been added to the scene and converted to nCloth. Its origin and insertion points were established in the same way as the zygomaticus muscle from the previous project. Follow these steps:

1. Open the `triangularisMotion_v01.ma` scene from the `chapter2\scenes` folder on the DVD. The scene contains a weighted version of Jack hidden on a layer. Jack's skull, orbicularis oris, zygomaticus major, and triangularis muscles are visible and shown in Figure 2.70.

2. Select an edge along the length of the triangularis. Convert the edge selection to a curve and center its pivot (see Figure 2.71).

3. Make a Volume Curve field from the selected curve.

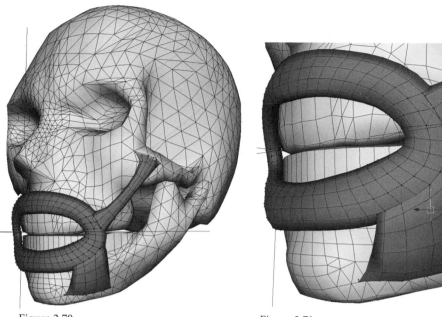

Figure 2.70
The elements in the scene

Figure 2.71
Convert an edge to a curve.

4. Open the field's Attribute Editor, and assign it the negativeImpulse preset you created in the previous project.

5. The triangularis is located below the mouth, and therefore it needs to have a positive impulse. Change the Along Axis value to 1.0.

6. You can now save this as a new preset named **positiveImpulse**.

7. The triangularis is a large muscle. To accommodate its width, it requires a Magnitude value of 40.

8. Select the field and nCloth2, and choose Fields → Affect Selected Object(s).

9. The zygomaticus major's attributes are common to most of the linear muscles. Select the zygomaticus major muscle, and open its Attribute Editor. Click the nCloth Shape tab, and make a preset from its settings. Save it as **linearMuscle**.

10. Select the triangularis muscle, and open its nCloth Shape tab in the Attribute Editor.

11. Assign the triangularis the linearMuscle preset.

12. Select polyToCurve1. Move the curve into the center of the muscle.

13. Play the simulation to see the muscle in action. Figure 2.72 shows the results at frame 20.

Figure 2.72
The effects of the triangularis

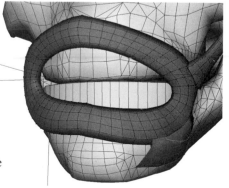

To check your work so far, you can compare it to `triangularisMotion_v02.ma` on the DVD.

Figure 2.73

The linear mouth muscles

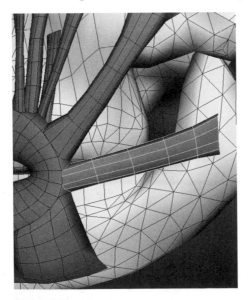

You can set up the rest of the mouth muscles in a similar fashion. They include the levator nasi, levator superioris, zygomaticus minor, levator anguli oris, buccinator, and depressor labii. They all share the same linearMuscle preset for the nCloth attributes. Each field uses the positive or negative preset depending on its position in relation to the mouth. Delete the transform constraint applied to the orbicularis oris at the beginning of "Project: Zygomaticus Major." The completed muscles are shown in Figure 2.73.

The risorius and mentalis muscles are also mouth muscles. The mentalis is really in the chin, but it contributes greatly to the shape of the lips and so is included as a mouth muscle. These muscles' origins and insertion points differ from the other muscles. The risorius's origin connects directly to the character's skin, pulling the corners of the lip back toward the ear. The mentalis, on the other hand, has its insertion connected to directly to the character's skin, pulling up toward the lips. The risorius is shown in Figure 2.74 and the mentalis in Figure 2.75.

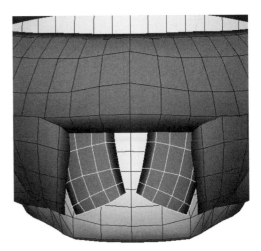

Figure 2.74

The risorius muscle

Figure 2.75

The mentalis muscle

Project: Orbicularis Oris

The motion of the orbicularis oris is the most difficult to reproduce. This is partly true due to the resistance of the other muscles connected to it. This project focuses on establishing new parameters for each muscle to allow the orbicularis oris to move freely. These settings are only used when the orbicularis oris needs to clench. In addition, the buccinator and masseter muscles have been added and the jaw animated to test the full range of the orbicularis oris's motion. Follow these steps:

1. Open the orbicMotion_v01.ma scene from the chapter2\scenes folder on the DVD. The scene contains a weighted version of Jack hidden on a layer. All of Jack's mouth muscles have been attached to each other and are shown in Figure 2.76.

2. In the Select By Name entry field, type ***NCLOTH*** to select all of the nCloth nodes.

3. In the Channel Box, set the following options.

Damp	10.0
Self Collide	On
Stretch Resistance	0.0
Compression Resistance	1.0
Bend Resistance	10.0
Mass	5.0
Stretch Damp	10.0
Self Collide Width Scale	3

4. Select the orbicularis oris, and change the following options:

Damp	2.0
Self Collide	On
Stretch Resistance	1.0
Compression Resistance	1.0
Bend Resistance	1.0
Mass	1.0
Stretch Damp	2.0
Self Collide Width Scale	3

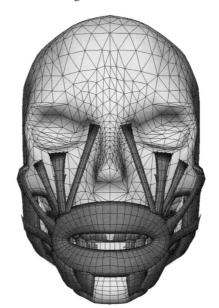

Figure 2.76

Jack's mouth muscles

   Lowering the values allows the muscle to compress inward. This is necessary to have the muscle purse the lips.

5. Select the three edges on the left side of the muscle that divide it in half. Use Figure 2.77 for reference.

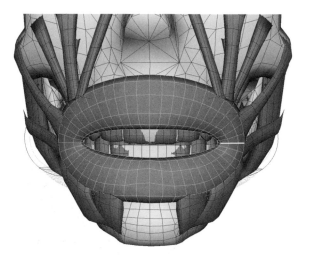

6. Convert your selection to a Volume Curve field. Rename each node to match the established naming convention.

7. Change the settings on the field as shown in Figure 2.78.

Figure 2.78

Volume Curve field settings

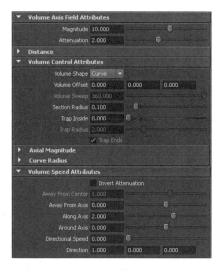

8. Repeat the procedure for the opposite side of the orbicularis oris muscle. Figure 2.79 shows the finished setup.

9. Assign each field to the orbicularis_Oris_NCLOTH node.

   To check your work so far, you can compare it to orbicMotion_v02.ma on the DVD.

10. Select three vertices in the center at the top of the muscle. Choose nConstraint → Transform (see Figure 2.80).

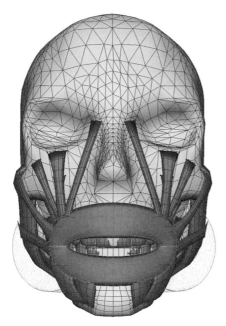

Figure 2.79

Add a Volume Curve field to each corner of the muscle.

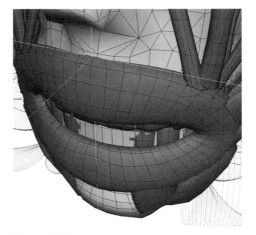

Figure 2.80

Add a transform constraint to the top three vertices.

11. Select three vertices in the center at the bottom of the muscle. Choose nConstraint → Transform (see Figure 2.81).

12. Parent the top transform constraint to the skull and the lower constraint to the mandible. With the muscle secured to the skull and mandible, you can test the fields. Click Play to see the results of the field using a Magnitude value of 20 (see Figure 2.82).

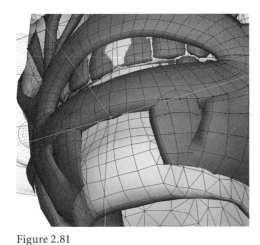

Figure 2.81

Add a transform constraint to the bottom three vertices.

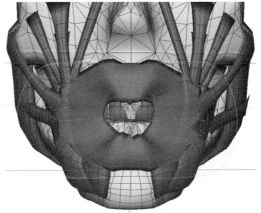

Figure 2.82

The fields push the corners of the muscle together.

13. Select the center, inside edge loop, and convert your selection to a Volume Curve field. Use Figure 2.83 for reference.

14. Change the Volume Curve field's settings to match Figure 2.84.

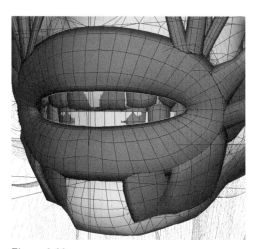

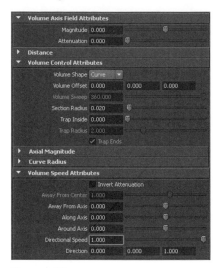

Figure 2.83

Create a Volume Curve field around the interior of the muscle.

Figure 2.84

Volume Curve field settings

The Volume Curve field pushes the lips forward as well as pulls them in. You can turn off the field by using a value of 0 for its Magnitude. Setting the Directional Speed attribute sets up the field to push the muscle in the positive Z direction whenever its Magnitude value is greater than 1. Figure 2.85 shows the field in action with Magnitude set to 5.

To check your work so far, you can compare it to orbicMotion_v03.ma on the DVD.

15. Select upperPalate_JNT from the root_JNT hierarchy.

16. Unmute the Translate Y and Rotate Z attributes in the Channel Box.

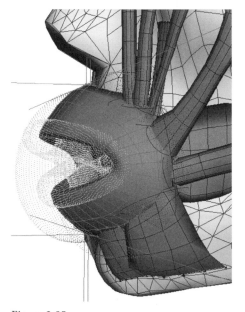

Figure 2.85

The field pushes the muscle outward.

17. Play the simulation. The mouth opens, and the muscle responds (see Figure 2.86).

    The orbicularis oris isn't moving appropriately. The corners of the muscle should pull inward when the mouth opens.

18. Select orbicularis_Oris_NCLOTH.

19. Change Stretch and Bend Resistance to 300.

20. Play the simulation: the muscle now responds correctly. Compare Figure 2.87 to Figure 2.86 to see the difference.

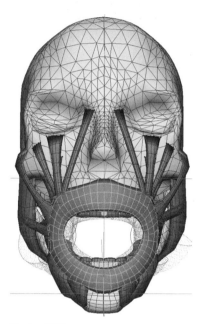
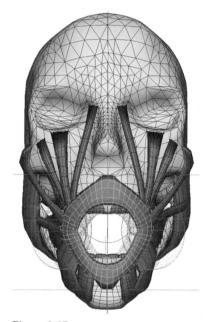

Figure 2.86
The muscle with a dropped jaw

Figure 2.87
The muscle responds correctly.

To check your work so far, you can compare it to orbicMotion_v04.ma on the DVD.

Eye and Brow Muscles

The muscles of the upper face function in a similar manner to those of the lower face. Most are linear muscles and don't require any special settings. The one exception is the orbicularis oculi muscle, which controls the eyelids. Like most of the sphincter-type muscles, it has multiple capabilities. It can also be argued that the orbicularis oculi muscle is made up of several muscles. In this book, the muscle is separated into two: the tarsus and the orbicularis oculi. The tarsus portion of the muscle is designated as the controller for opening and closing the eyes.

Project: Tarsus

The tarsus muscle is flexed in order to keep the eyelid open. When it relaxes, the eyelids close. The next project takes you through the steps to add this functionality:

1. Open the `tarsusMotion_v01.ma` scene from the `chapter2\scenes` folder on the DVD. The scene contains a weighted version of Jack hidden on a layer. The left tarsus muscle and eyeballs are visible in the scene and shown in Figure 2.88.

2. Select the superior tarsus muscle node, and choose nMesh → Create nCloth.

3. The border edges of the geometry have already been fitted to the skull. You need to pin down the muscle to prevent it from shifting and to apply a force to push against the interior muscle vertices. This is also the muscle's origin. Select the border vertices, using Figure 2.89 as a guide.

4. Shift+select the skull, and choose nConstraint → Point To Surface.

5. Select the row of edges going down the middle of the muscle. Convert it to a Volume Curve field, and apply the negativeImpulse preset to the field (see Figure 2.90). If you haven't built a shelf with these commands yet, refer to the "Automating the Process" tip at the end of "Project: Zygomaticus Major" earlier in the chapter.

Figure 2.88

The elements of the scene file

Figure 2.89

Select the vertices making up the muscle's origin.

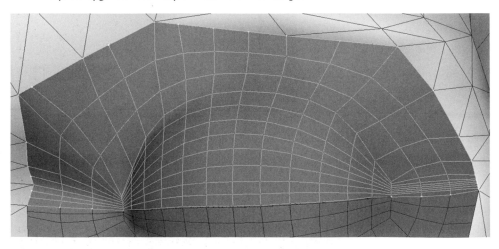

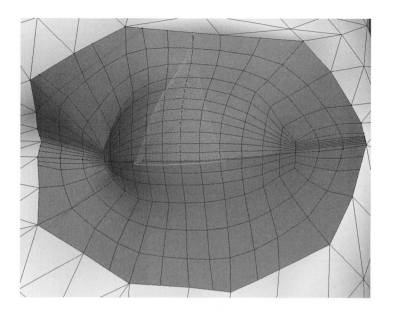

Figure 2.90

Create a Volume Curve field in the middle of the muscle.

6. By shaping the field's curve around the eyeball, you can get the muscle to retract into the skull. Use Figure 2.91 to shape the vertices. Translating the first four vertices in the Z is sufficient.

Figure 2.91

Shape the curve to match the contour of the eyeball.

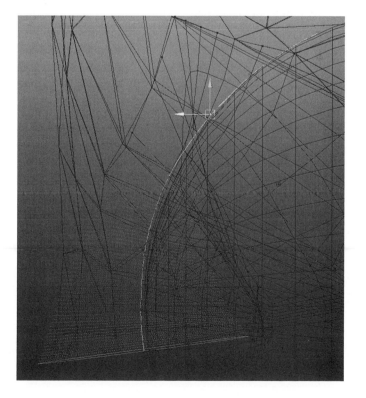

7. Attach the Volume Curve field to nCloth1.

8. Set Magnitude on the field to 8.

9. Open nCloth1's Attribute Editor. Select the nucleus1 tab, and change Gravity to 0.0.

10. Play the simulation to test the muscle. Around frame 50, the muscle pulls back, revealing the eyeball. Although effective, the overall result is less than desirable (see Figure 2.92).

Figure 2.92

The results of the field pulling on the tarsus muscle

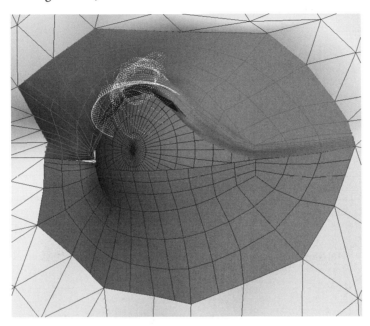

To check your work so far, you can compare it to tarsusMotion_v02.ma on the DVD.

11. Although you assigned the negativeImpulse preset to the field, you need to modify several of the attributes. Open the field's Attribute Editor, and change Section Radius to 0.04 under Volume Control Attributes.

12. Use Figure 2.93 to change the Axial Magnitude graph.

Figure 2.93

Axial Magnitude graph

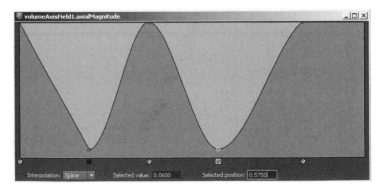

13. Open the Curve Radius section. Delete the first key to set the graph to a linear value of 1.0.

14. Open nCloth1's Attribute Editor. Use Figure 2.94 to change the Collisions settings.

Figure 2.94
Collisions settings

Self Collision is important to the functionality of the tarsus muscle. Without it, the muscle won't bunch or wrinkle as an eyelid should. The simulation is still erratic, but you can see in Figure 2.95 that wrinkles are definitely forming.

15. The muscle needs to be tight and allow for compression. Use Figure 2.96 to set the Dynamic Properties.

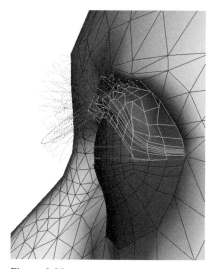

Figure 2.95
The added effect of Self Collision

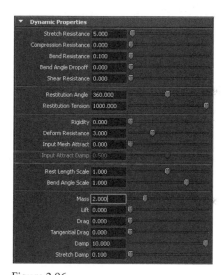

Figure 2.96
Dynamic Properties settings

The muscle shouldn't lose its shape. It needs to bend and compress freely and still be able to return to its original shape. A high Damp value keeps the muscle from having jitter.

To check your work so far, you can compare it to tarsusMotion_v03.ma on the DVD.

16. To finish the superior tarsus, you need to animate the magnitude of the Volume Curve field. Add the keyframes from Figure 2.97.

Figure 2.97
Keyframes and values

	Time	Value	InTan Type	OutTan Type
0	1	0	Clamped	Clamped
1	15	60	Clamped	Clamped
2	30	4	Clamped	Clamped

The eye needs to lift open and then stay open. It takes a substantial amount of force to raise the eyelid but only a little to keep it open.

17. When the field pulls the tarsus up, it also causes the curve to deform, which in turn causes the field's force to shift. Unlike the other muscles that you created earlier in the chapter, the curve needs to be detached from the surface. The curve can then maintain its shape despite what the surface is doing and in turn keep the field from altering the direction of its force. Select the curve and delete its history to break the connection it has to the tarsus geometry. The muscle now stays on track (see Figure 2.98).

Figure 2.98

The curve and field are now stationary.

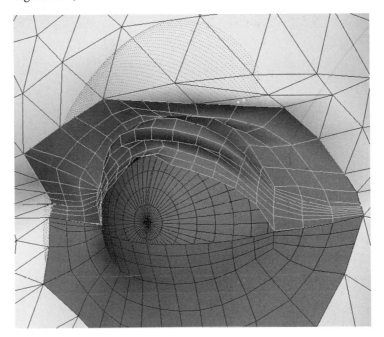

18. To get the force of the curve to push back on the muscle, forcing it to push against the eye, translate the curve –0.014 units in the Z.

19. Oddly enough, you want the muscle to stick to the eyeball when it opens. This helps keep the muscle edges from sliding. Open the Attribute Editor for nCloth1, and change Friction to 1.0 and Stickiness to 2.0. The eyeball already has a Stickiness setting of 1.0.

    That completes the superior tarsus muscle. Figure 2.99 shows it retracted at frame 60. The geometry has also been given a display smoothness of 3 just for viewing purposes.

20. Select the inferior tarsus muscle, and choose nMesh → Create nCloth.

21. Select the border vertices, using Figure 2.100 as a guide. Shift+select the skull, and choose nConstraint → Point To Surface

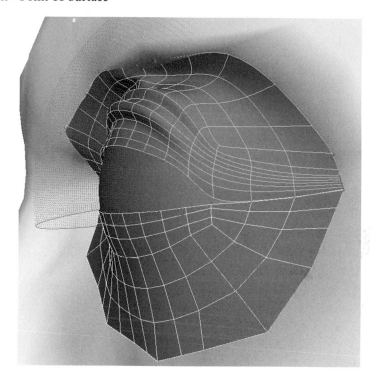

Figure 2.99

The retracted superior tarsus

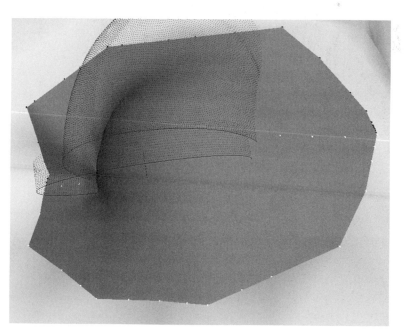

Figure 2.100

Constrain the border vertices of the muscle.

22. Create a preset from the superior tarsus nCloth attributes, and apply it to the inferior tarsus nCloth2 node.

23. Select two edges from the middle of the muscle, and convert them to a Volume Curve field. Change Section Radius to 0.04 and Along Axis to –1.0 on the field (see Figure 2.101).

Figure 2.101

Create a Volume Curve field.

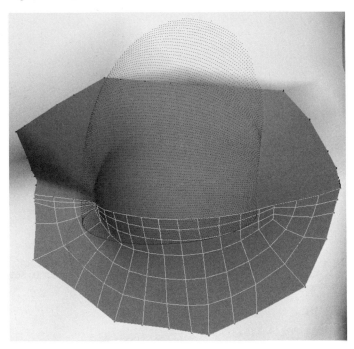

24. Apply the field to nCloth2.

25. The field needs to be animated similarly to the superior tarsus field. Use Figure 2.102 for the keys and values.

Figure 2.102

Keyframes and values

Keys			
Time	Value	InTan Type	OutTan Type
0 3	0	Flat	Flat
1 4	5	Clamped	Clamped
2 30	1	Flat	Flat

26. To finish the muscle combination, add a Component To Component constraint to the bordering edges of the two muscles. Figure 2.103 shows the finished setup.

To check your work so far, you can compare it to `tarsusMotion_v04.ma` on the DVD.

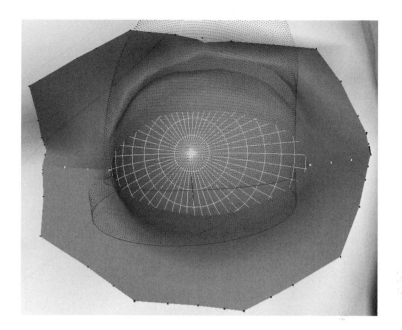

Figure 2.103
The tarsus muscles in action

Orbicularis Oculi

The orbicularis oculi is the second sphincter muscle in the face. It's much easier to set up compared to the orbicularis oris. The geometry is circular and has no thickness. It's contoured to fit around the eye socket. Add a Point To Surface constraint across its center, and constrain its vertices to the skull. The constraint keeps the middle row of edges locked and keeps the muscle in place (see Figure 2.104).

A radial field provides the muscle's force. Position it where the upper and lower eyelids come together and pushed slightly back into the eye. Using a negative magnitude, the geometry is pulled inward (see Figure 2.105).

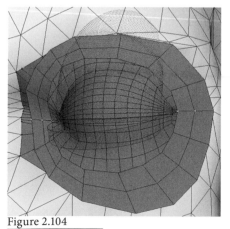

Figure 2.104
Add a Point To Surface constraint to the orbicularis oculi.

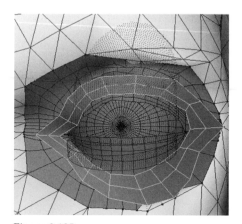

Figure 2.105
Use a radial field to draw the muscle inward.

Frontalis

The frontalis is a large, thick muscle that makes up the forehead. Although it's considered a single muscle, it moves in multiple sections. Add two separate forces to it; Figure 2.106 shows the position of the two fields.

You may need to add as many as four fields to the frontalis if your character is very expressive. Some people have great control over their frontalis muscles, giving them the ability to undulate their eyebrows. Such control should be considered when designing your character.

Corrugator

The corrugator muscle sits beneath the frontalis and on top of the orbicularis oculi. This muscle pulls the eyebrow down and inward, toward the bridge of the nose. This action is synonymous with frowning or deep thought. Figure 2.107 shows its placement and Volume Curve field.

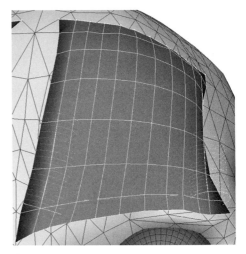

Figure 2.106
Add two fields at opposite ends of the frontalis.

The Nose

The last of the muscles of the face are in the nose. The nasalis is a sphincter muscle, despite its shape. Like the other sphincter muscles in this chapter, it too could be broken into multiple muscles. Instead, apply two fields to achieve the proper motion. Figure 2.108 shows their placement.

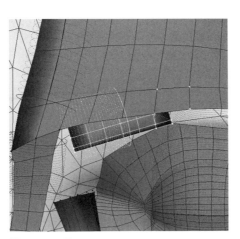

Figure 2.107
The corrugator muscle

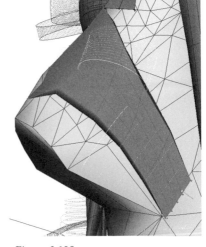

Figure 2.108
Add two fields to the nasalis muscle.

Summary

All of the facial muscles are complete. The amount of detail added to the muscle is irrelevant. It's important to have enough geometry for the muscle to deform adequately, but it does not need extra geometry to define its shape. The key is to focus on the muscle motion, as that is the only thing translated to the characters skin.

You can see the finished version of the muscles by opening the `finalMuscles_v01.ma` scene from the `chapter2\scenes` folder on the DVD. It's important to note that the magnitude and nCloth attributes in the scene aren't final—they're used for testing purposes. The final values are established in Chapter 8 to accommodate the skin.

CHAPTER 3

Hair

Geometry and texture go a long way toward make a character look real. But man or beast, those two elements alone won't suffice when completing a photorealistic character. It's the secondary details that complete the look. The next three chapters delve into the creation and management of bodily functions.

This chapter focuses on hair. Not all hair—only hair of a longer length. The longer the hair, the more control you need. Maya Hair uses dynamic curves with an adjustable point density. Attached to the curve is a Paint Effects brush with an abundance of attributes to define the rendered look of the hair.

In this chapter you will learn to:

- Undestand the basics of human and digital hair

- Grow hair

- Cut hair

- Style hair

- Color hair

Hair 101

Creating CG hair takes some real-world knowledge. Don't worry, you don't have to go cut someone's hair in order to build it in 3D, but it would help. Understanding the way hair responds based on different haircuts lets you to anticipate the hair's motion and interpret the technique. It gives you the necessary knowledge to identify the methods used in the style and allows you to derive a plan for re-creating it. Getting hair cut to the right length is the first step. Without the right haircut, there is little hope of replicating the look and motion.

To get started, let's take a look at different techniques and the terms you should be familiar with:

Layering Used to change the thickness of a hair style. It can make the hair look thinner or thicker depending on the cut. Each layer is cut shorter than the previous one to create a graduated effect (see Figure 3.1).

Bangs Also referred to as *fringe*. Bangs are hairs styled to hang over the forehead. They're done in a multitude of ways and can range from a single wisp of hair to the entire front section. An example of bangs is shown in Figure 3.2.

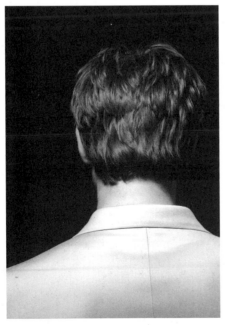

Figure 3.1
An example of layered hair

Figure 3.2
Bangs are the hairs on the front of the head that hang over the forehead.

Feathering A texturing technique to add a light, soft, wispy look to a hairstyle. Feathering is similar to layering, except the overlapping layers are made to blend more (see Figure 3.3).

Bowl Cut What you don't want. It's important to mention this style, because typically CG characters get a bowl cut. It's actually derived from placing a bowl on someone's head and then cutting off the excess hair. The style was popular during the Great Depression and remains so in the CG world because it requires no experience and can be created by anyone with a bowl and scissors.

Thinning Usually done with special scissors called *thinning shears* (see Figure 3.4). This technique reduces the weight of hair. The scissors are slotted, allowing only a portion of the hair to be cut. Doing this lightens the load of the hair, giving it more volume.

We've all had our hair cut at some point in our lives, but do you really know what's going on up there? The first step in the process is to wet the hair. Wet hair is easier to cut. Next, the hair is sectioned. It's easier to work on a small area than the entire head; working in sections allows you to move the other hair out of the way. The hair is then cut to the desired length. After one section is cut, the next one is cut using the previous section as a guide. When the hair has been shaped appropriately, it's textured. Texturing employs all of the hair-styling techniques. For instance, hair can be pulled to a 90-degree elevation and the ends cut at a 45-degree angle to achieve a layering effect like that shown in Figure 3.5.

Figure 3.3

The ends of the hair are cut to create a smooth, wispy look.

Figure 3.4

Thinning shears

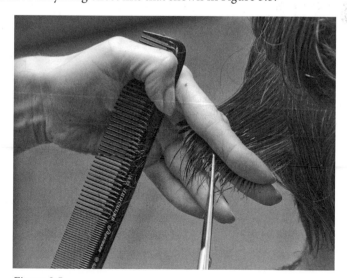

Figure 3.5

An example of a texturing cut

It's important to know these things in order to identify the results in the real world. The techniques don't cross over entirely into the 3D world, but if you can look at the way the hair moves or how it rests, you can learn how to decipher the look in CG.

Digital Hair Basics

Maya Hair is a dynamic system of curve-driven Paint Effects brushes. The system itself is based on NURBS curves; you can add any Paint Effects brush to them. The curves can be used for a variety of things from simulating ropes and chains to tongues and tails.

When you create hair, three nodes are created:

- The hair system node holds the majority of the attributes that define the look of the hair.
- The hair follicle node dictates where the hair is grown from.
- The pfxHair node controls the display quality of the hair. If your system is bogged down by the hair, you can reduce the quality to lighten the load. In addition, the pfxHair node controls the mesh quality if the brush is converted to polygons.

You can use three sets of curves with hair: current, start, and rest position curves. The current curves are graphical representations of what the hair will look like if rendered; you can't directly manipulate them through component editing like NURBS. Start curves and rest curves are NURBS; you can manipulate them as you can any NURBS curve.

Follicles

As in the real world, CG hair is grown from follicles. The follicle controls where the hair is placed on a surface. Each follicle can grow a single curve from it. The curve defines a clump. You can add an infinite number of hairs to the clump. Figure 3.6 shows the default settings for a single follicle.

Figure 3.6

A follicle with hair growing out of it

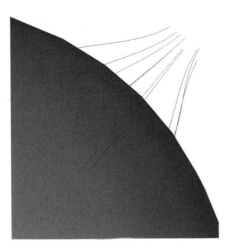

Follicles can be added to polygons and NURBS. You can use three methods to do this:

Adding Follicles to Selected Faces or Points
This is the most straightforward method. You select a group of faces on a polygon object or a surface point from a NURBS surface and add a follicle. NURBS surfaces offer the greatest accuracy. Surface points can be defined anywhere, giving you total freedom to add follicles wherever needed. Figure 3.7 shows a surface point being selected and the subsequent follicle.

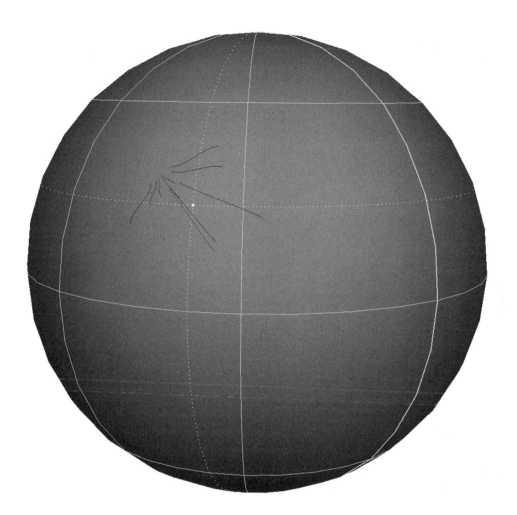

Figure 3.7

You can add follicles anywhere on a NURBS surface.

Follicles can only be added to polygons at the face level. Maya automatically detects your selection and adds follicles to the center of each selected face. For creating a full head of hair, this method is only as good as the face distribution of your geometry. Typically, your geometry will have an uneven number of faces, especially in areas of high or low detail. In addition, the follicles aren't always placed; some are skipped. Figure 3.8 shows that some follicles are missing around the edge of the selection.

Adding Follicles Based on a User-Defined Grid Although the name may imply a flat surface, you can use the grid method to add follicles to any shaped surface. But the follicles must be added to the entire surface, not to components. The grid gives you uniform or random follicle placement across the surface.

This technique also allows you to define passive follicles. When a follicle is *passive*, it takes on the motion of the surrounding follicles, eliminating the need to simulate them.

Figure 3.8

Adding follicles via selected faces can be unreliable.

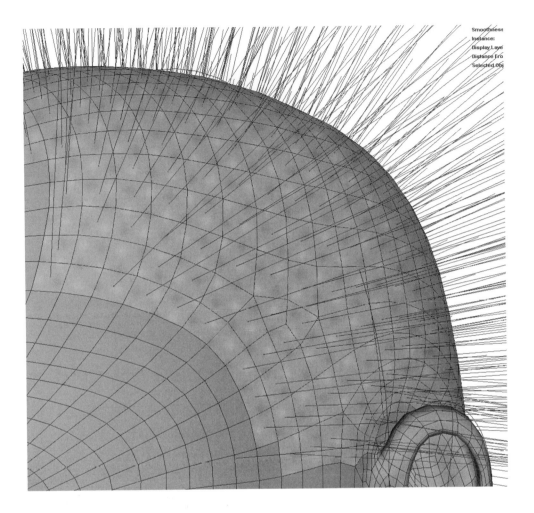

Painting Follicles Directly onto Surfaces Painting follicles offers a lot of flexibility. You define the number of follicles, similar to the grid method, by setting a density value for the U and V directions. Painting adds follicles wherever you paint, but the quantity is restricted by the density values. Increasing the values lets you paint more follicles in the same region onto the same hair system or a different one.

Follicles come with their own attributes. Each can be changed from dynamic to passive or static. Every follicle can override the hair system node attributes. By doing this, you can tailor individual hair tubes; this is similar to painting follicle attributes, but with greater accuracy. The follicle also has a feature that allows you to braid the hair.

Fixed Segment Length is an important feature to note. Using the Segment length changes the way the hair's start curves are sampled. Adjusting this value can create a more natural looking hair simulation by making shorter hairs act stiffer than longer hairs.

The Hair System

The hair system node is the solver and contains the attributes to modify the Paint Effects brush and solver settings. None of these attributes modify the NURBS in the hair system; they only modify the current position curves.

You can adjust the hair system attributes interactively at any point during hair creation or simulation. All the parameters can be keyframed. Most of the attributes are self-explanatory and/or provide enough visual feedback for interpretation. But one attribute can be confusing: Curl.

Curling hair is handled by two separate settings: Clump Curl and Displacement Curl. Clump Curl affects the entire clump or Paint Effects tube. It causes changes around the central axis of the tube, corkscrewing the entire clump. Displacement Curl affects the individual strands of hair within a clump. The width of the hair directly affects the sensitivity of the displacement value. Thicker hair requires a lower Displacement Curl.

Hair clumps can be interpolated between one another. The Clump Interpolation setting fans the ends of the hair clump toward other clumps. Interpolation Range designates the distance at which the hairs will be interpolated; the value is a multiplier against the hair width. Clump Interpolation has a large effect on both curl settings and can diminish their strength. Rendering to see the results is the best way to fine-tune these parameters.

Hair systems are transplantable: you can take a surface with an attached system and apply it to another surface. The follicles can be placed according to proximity or by UVs. You can find several premade hair examples in the Visor; they're set up to be transplanted easily.

Digital Hair Styling

Creating a convincing head of hair is difficult to do. With the hundreds of different styles and techniques available to the hair stylist, just figuring out how a style was created is daunting.

The first step in creating digital hair is determining what the hair should look like. Jack will have what is commonly referred to as a *shag* cut: a multilayered cut with a disheveled appearance. An example and the reference for Jack's hair is shown in Figure 3.9.

The character's head geometry is important, especially if you need to match an actor's hair style. Hair falls differently with gravity based on the shape of the head. If the head doesn't crown properly, the hair doesn't fall properly.

A huge obstacle in working with CG hair as if it were real hair is the amount of hair you're

Figure 3.9

The style used for Jack's hair

dealing with. You should typically have about one-tenth as much CG hair as you'd have real hair based on independently controlled hair curves. Of course, increasing this value improves the look and control of the hair but at a greater computational cost.

It's estimated that a real head of hair has more than 100,000 strands. Blondes have the most, with 140,000 individual hairs. Redheads have the least, with an average of 90,000; and people with dark hair have around 110,000. Men and women both lose hair as they age, with various factors affecting the speed of hair loss.

You can use several parameters to reach the target number of strands. Not all the hairs need to be individually controlled: hair typically moves in groups, so with the exception of that one wild hair, animating is done in sections or globally. Adding 1,000 follicles to your CG character's head provides a good base. From each follicle, you can grow 40 influenced hairs. Then, you can make instances of each of those hairs, allowing you to achieve 100,000+ hairs.

Project: Growing Hair

Ask yourself, where does hair grow on the scalp? It's a good idea to include more area than you think you'll need. You can always move or delete follicles. Painting follicles allows you to get the best follicle placement possible. It's easy to paint anything from a receding hairline to a widow's peak. This first project gets Jack's scalp growing hair and establishes the pipeline to give him a haircut. Follow these steps:

1. Open the scene file hair_v01.ma. The scene contains the Jack character bound and weighted to his skeleton. A texture map illustrating the regions of his scalp has been mapped to his head (see Figure 3.10).

Figure 3.10

The various regions of the head

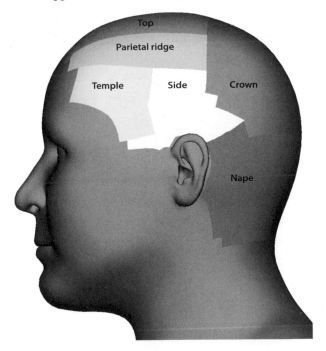

2. Switch to the perspective view. Deselect Strokes and NURBS Curves on the Show drop-down menu. By turning them off, you keep your view from being obscured by curves or clumps of hair. The follicles will be the only visible elements of the hair system when you paint.

3. Choose Hair → Paint Hair Follicles. Change the settings according to Figure 3.11.

   The proper length is based on your character's longest strand of hair. Having the hair at its longest allows you to cut the hair back instead of adding to it. This approach is more intuitive. It also keeps the number of control vertices in each curve at a maximum of 10. The more control vertices you have, the harder it can be to control the hair.

4. Change the Paint Scripts tool settings to match Figure 3.12.

5. Paint a widow's peak of follicles above the character's forehead. You can use Figure 3.13 and the applied texture as a rough guide.

6. Continue to paint follicles all the way around the head. The maximum number of follicles is dictated by the follicle density in the U and V. If you think you need more follicles, you can increase the value and continue to paint. Or, if you're unsure how many follicles you'll need, you can begin with a low value and gradually increase it. Figure 3.14 shows the finished look.

Figure 3.11

Paint Hair Follicle options

Figure 3.12

Paint Scripts tool settings

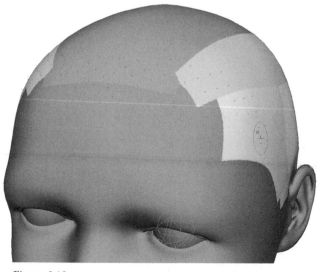

Figure 3.13

Paint follicles to form a widow's peak.

Figure 3.14

Jack's follicles

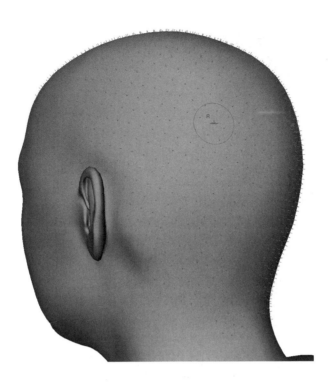

If you paint more follicles than you need, you can hold Ctrl and paint to remove them.

FOLLICLE DENSITY

The human head has more follicles in some areas than others. However, there is no reason to add more follicles in certain areas as opposed to others. You can better achieve small bald or balding areas later by painting a baldness map.

 To check your work so far, you can compare it to `hair_v02.ma` on the DVD.

7. With the follicles placed, you can turn Curves and Strokes back on using the Show drop-down menu in the perspective viewport.

8. At this point, the hair looks crazy (see Figure 3.15). By default, each follicle has 10 hairs growing from it and distributed based on the Clump Width attribute.

Figure 3.15
The default hair

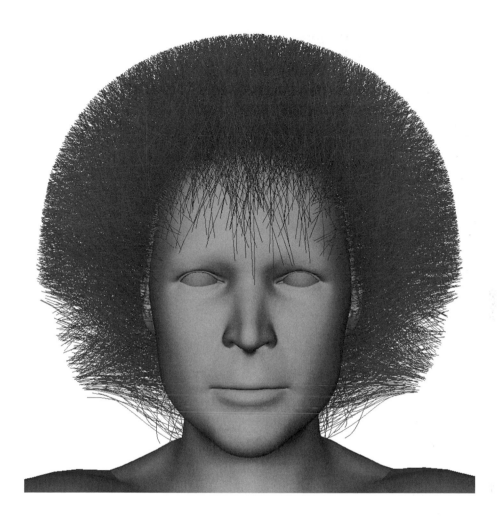

To gain control over this bird's nest, make a single hair grow from the center of each follicle. To do so, open the Outliner and select hairSystem1. Open its Attribute Editor. Change Hairs Per Clump to 1.0, and set Clump Width to 0.0. You now have something more manageable (see Figure 3.16).

ASSIGNING A HAIR SYSTEM

While you're painting, it's possible to inadvertently create a second hair system. This can happen of you back out of the Paint tool and then choose the tool again. You can avoid this issue by choosing the correct hair system before you paint. But if it does happen, there is an easy fix: select the root node to the second set of follicles, and choose Hair → Assign Hair System and then the desired hair system. Now you can safely delete all the nodes associated with the second hair system.

Figure 3.16

A single hair grows from the center of each follicle.

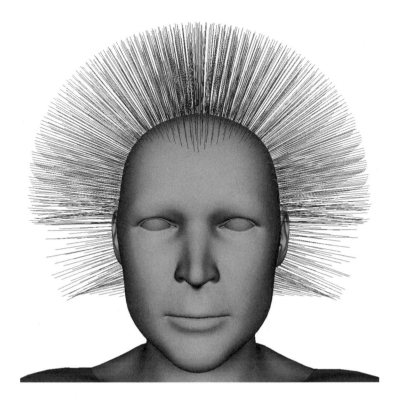

9. Before you get into cutting and styling, it's a good idea to make select sets of groups of follicles. The sets are based on the regions of the scalp shown in Figure 3.10. Press 6 to turn on textures. Jack's head is mapped with an image defining those regions. Change the viewport to a side view.

10. Create a new shelf called JackHairCut.

11. Using the image mapped to Jack's head, create a select set for each area. We'll step through the process for the first set. Choose the Lasso tool from the toolbar.

12. Turn off all the selection masks except Dynamics.

13. Draw a lasso around the nape section of the head to select that region's follicles (see Figure 3.17).

14. Choose Create → Set → Quick Select Set. Name the select set **Nape**, and click Add To Shelf (see Figure 3.18).

15. Continue making follicle select sets for all the head regions. When you're finished, save your scene.

To check your work so far, you can compare it to `hair_v03.ma` on the DVD.

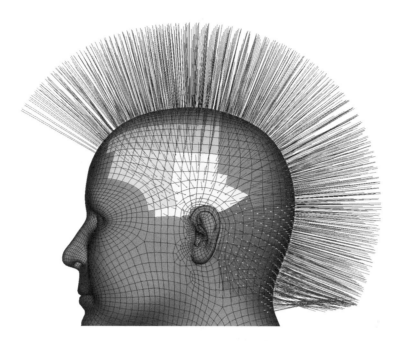

Figure 3.17

Select the follicles in the nape region of the head.

Having shelf buttons makes it easy to select each section. To make working with a large number of follicles manageable, you can turn off their dynamic properties and reverse their direction. Doing so allows you to isolate areas, making it easier to cut and style the hair curves. You can change these settings for an entire selection of follicles through the Channel Box or Attribute Spreadsheet. But doing so can take a while to update and slows the hairstyling process. A more efficient way is to create a MEL script to do the work for you.

Figure 3.18

Create a quick select set for the Nape selection.

16. Open the Script Editor by clicking its icon in the lower-right corner of the interface or choosing Window → General Editors → Script Editor.

17. Press Ctrl+T to create a new tab. Choose MEL for the language.

18. The follicles can't be completely turned off, especially when you're painting values. The first script implies that they're turned off by moving them out of the way and making them rigid. Enter the following in the Script Editor:

```
string $follicles[];
$follicles=`ls -sl`;
for ($selected in $follicles)
{
setAttr ($selected + ".flipDirection") 1;
setAttr ($selected + ".simulationMethod") 0;
}
```

The first line establishes an empty string array. The next line fills the array with your selection. The rest of the script is a loop: it executes a setAttr command on whatever is in the array. In this case, there are two attributes, Flip Direction and Simulation Method. The 1 and 0 at the end of the setAttr commands tells the attribute what to do. The 1 is a Boolean function that turns on Flip Direction. The 0 selects the first of three functions the Simulation Method attribute is capable of.

19. Press Ctrl+A to select the entire script.

20. Make sure the JackHairCut shelf is current. Choose File → Save Script to Shelf. In the pop-up window, enter **Off** for the name. Click OK to add the script to the JackHairCut shelf.

21. Test the script by first clicking the Nape shelf button to select all the follicles in the Nape head region. Click the Off shelf button. The follicles flip, turning into the head and out of sight (see Figure 3.19).

Figure 3.19

The MEL script turns off the Nape follicles.

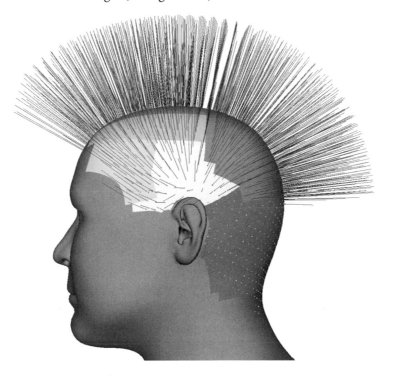

22. To turn the follicles back on, change the script using the following:

```
string $follicles[];
$follicles=`ls -sl`;
for ($selected in $follicles)
{
```

```
        setAttr ($selected + ".flipDirection") 0;
        setAttr ($selected + ".simulationMethod") 2;
        }
```

23. Select the script, and save it to the shelf. Name it **On**.

    To check your shelf and scripts, you can load the `shelf_JackHairCut.mel` file from the DVD. Copy this file to your `\MyDocuments\maya\2011\prefs\shelves` folder. In Maya, open the shelf menu, and click Load Shelf. Navigate to the shelf's location, and choose it.

Hair Length

You can use three tools to change the visible length of hair. The differences among these tools are important to identify. The first is the Scale Hair tool. You can use it on an entire hair system or paint values on individual follicles. The Scale Hair tool scales the size of the hair curve. It keeps the original number of control vertices (CVs) in the curve while shortening the curve's length. Scaling the hair should be reserved for subtle changes or to change the global scale of the entire hair system.

The other two tools are a pair: Trim Hairs and Extend Hairs. Trim Hairs reduces the number of points in the hair curve. Extend Hairs does the opposite by adding CVs to the hair curve. Both of these tools reset the shape of the curve, meaning the curve returns to its original erect state. It's a good idea to cut the hair using the Trim Hairs tool; using it ensures that the number of CVs is kept to a minimum. Having too many CVs can cause instability and oscillation on hair curves.

Project: Cutting Hair

The hair is ready to be cut. It stands perpendicular to the shape of Jack's head. When a hairstylist cuts hair, the stylist grabs sections and pulls them away from the head, extending the hair to its full length. This is done to ensure the proper length. In the CG world, all of the character's hair is fully extended. By using the select sets and MEL scripts you created in the previous project, you can simulate the stylist's technique by working on isolated sections. Follow these steps:

1. Open the scene file `hair_v03.ma`. The scene picks up where the previous project left off.

2. After you cut the hair, you'll want to test it. By making a collision object, you can cause the hair to fall and react naturally. In the Outliner, select hairSystem1Follicles. The hairSystemFollicles node was created automatically when the hair system was first created. Choose Hair → Create Constraint → Collide Sphere.

3. Rename the collision sphere **head_COLLISION**.

4. Use the following transforms to position the collision sphere:

Translate X	0.0
Translate Y	5.60
Translate Z	0.171
Scale X	0.296
Scale Y	0.373
Scale Z	0.385

COLLISIONS

You can use NURBS and polygons to collide with hair, but that can be taxing on your system. When possible, use Hair → Create Constraint → Collide Sphere or Collide Cube. These are implicit surfaces and can be considerably faster to calculate. More important, they don't cause the hair to *chatter* or oscillate when at rest. The downfall with these surfaces is that their shapes can only be scaled. When collision accuracy is vital, you need several implicit collision objects, thus increasing computation time.

5. You need two more collision spheres, one for each ear. Select hairSystem1Follicles, and choose Hair → Create Constraint → Collide Sphere.

6. Rename the collision sphere **l_ear_COLLISION**.

7. Use the following transforms to position the left ear collision sphere:

Translate X	0.296
Translate Y	5.526
Translate Z	0.116
Rotate X	−8.104
Rotate Y	−27.033
Rotate Z	−6.253
Scale X	0.019
Scale Y	0.106
Scale Z	0.064

8. Repeat steps 5 through 7 to create the collision sphere for the right ear. Invert the values for Translate X and Rotate Y and Z to mirror the transforms. Figure 3.20 shows the positions of the collision spheres.

9. Turn off each region of the head except Nape by using the shelf buttons established in the previous project. The Nape area is the only section with hair facing out (see Figure 3.21).

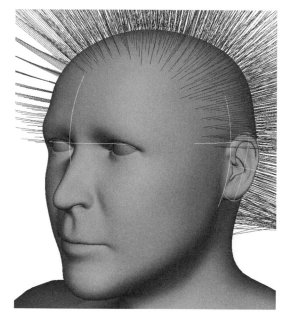

Figure 3.20

Use three collision spheres to make the shape of the character's head and ears.

Figure 3.21

Turn off all the head regions except Nape.

To check your work so far, you can compare it to hair_v04.ma on the DVD.

10. You can now begin cutting the hair. In the Outliner, select hairSystem1.

11. Choose Hair → Paint Hair Follicles. The Paint Hair Follicles window is displayed.

12. Change Paint Mode to Trim Hairs.

Figure 3.22

Settings for the Paint Scripts tool

13. The Paint Scripts tool also opens. Set Paint Operation to Replace with a Value of 0.9. Use Figure 3.22 for the rest of the settings.

14. Make sure the brush size is small, about the size of the distance between each follicle. Even though the other follicles on the head are flipped and their dynamics are turned off, you can still paint their attributes.

The last two rows of follicles around the entire head will remain their full length. Paint the next three or four rows with a value of 0.9.

15. Paint the next three or four rows with a value of 0.8.

16. Paint the remaining follicles with a value of 0.7(see Figure 3.23).

17. Click Play to see the results of your first cut (see Figure 3.24).

Figure 3.23

The back of Jack's hair has been cut.

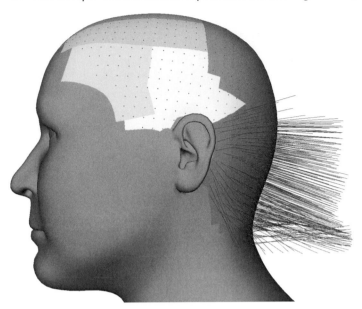

Figure 3.24

Running the simulation is a good way to check the precision of the cut.

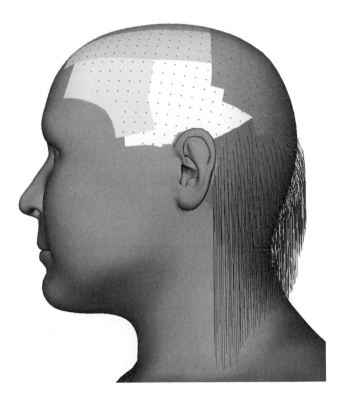

To check your work so far, you can compare it to `hair_v05.ma` on the DVD.

> **PAINTED MAPS**
>
> It's important to visually cut the hair as opposed to painting a texture map. Painting a map doesn't have the accuracy that interactively cutting the hair does. The reason is the shape of the head. If you paint values, you're only painting a ramp that doesn't take into account the shape of the head. Cutting the hair three-dimensionally allows you to see if you need to cut a little more or a little less.

18. Turn off Nape, and turn on Crown.

19. Select hairSystem1. Choose Hair → Paint Hair Follicles. Make sure Paint Mode is set to Trim Hairs. Change Value to 0.7.

20. Paint the last three rows of follicles.

21. Change Value to 0.6, and paint the next three rows. Only do those on the back of the head. Three rows of follicles that wrap around to the side need to be longer.

22. Change Value to 0.5, and paint the rest of the follicles up to the top of the head.

23. Change Value back to 0.6, and paint the sides, increasing in value up to 0.8. Figure 3.25 shows the progress so far.

    To check your work so far, you can compare it to `hair_v06.ma` on the DVD.

    You don't have to worry about getting the hair to the exact value for every strand; it's okay to eyeball it and use your own judgment. The goal is to have the hair shortest on top and gradually reach its full length at the end of the scalp. The important point to keep in mind is that the longest hair goes all the way around the head and isn't just in the back. Therefore, you need to gradually trim the hair from the sides, where it's full length just above the ear, to half its length in the center of the head.

24. To keep from having to back out of the Paint Hair Follicles tool every time you make a selection, you can create a deselect button for the shelf. To do so, hold Ctrl+Shift and choose Edit → Deselect. A new button named Des is added to your shelf. You can now turn

Figure 3.25

Two sections of Jack's hair have been cut.

follicles on and off and deselect your selection without having to leave the Paint Hair Follicles tool.

25. Continue trimming the hairs for the side, temple, and parietal ridge. Use the completed sections as guides for the hair lengths.

26. For the top section of the head, it's easier to flood the region with a value of 0.5. Unfortunately, you can't use the Flood paint option in the Paint Scripts tool; doing so would cause all of the hair to be trimmed to a value of 0.5. Instead, use the Replace option and a larger brush to quickly paint the area. You can be a little sloppy around the forehead, but make sure you paint all the other edges with precision.

27. Set the Replace Value to 1.0. Paint the follicles directly above the forehead. Paint each row, extending the hairs by 0.1 unit (see Figure 3.26).

Figure 3.26

Gradually increase the size of the hair as you work from front to back.

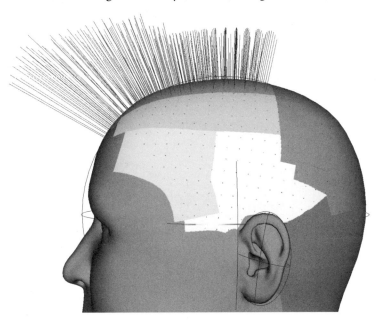

28. Play the simulation to frame 60. The character looks like his hair is wet and combed straight (see Figure 3.27).

29. The hair behind the ear is too long. Go back to frame 1. Paint a value of 0.6 to 0.7, starting from the bottom of the ear and working your way up. When you're finished, the hair should look like Figure 3.28.

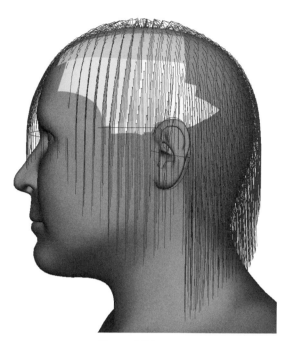

Figure 3.27

The hair simulated to frame 60

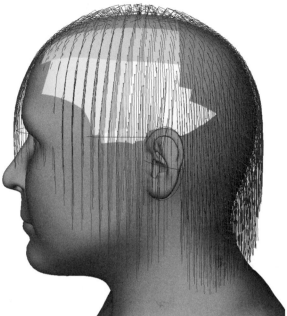

Figure 3.28

Cut the hair behind the ear.

30. Looking at the back of head reveals that the hair is too long and uneven. The hair passes through the geometry, but the problem is obvious in wireframe (see Figure 3.29).

    The hair should almost match the outline of Jack's jaw, which you can see through the wireframe.

31. Shave the V-like follicle pattern around the neckline to 0.4. Use Figure 3.30 for reference.

32. Change Replace Value to 0.7 and paint a few rows along the Nape region directly above the follicles you painted in step 30. Continue painting three or four rows across the nape, all the way to the top of the crown, ending with Replace Value set to 0.4. Use Figure 3.31 for reference.

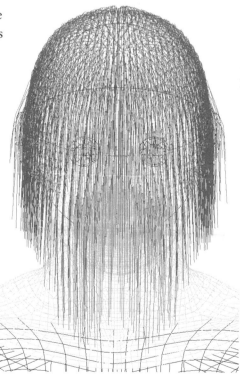

Figure 3.29

The hair is too long around the back.

Play the simulation to frame 60 to check the results. It should look Figure 3.32. This is acceptable.

The hair is still uneven in areas; but remember, you're trimming a CV from the curve. You can't get a precision cut this way. To refine the cut, you'll use the Scale Hair tool in the next project.

To check your work so far, you can compare it to `hair_v07.ma` on the DVD.

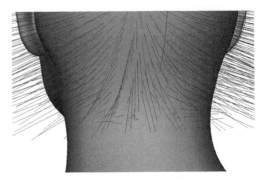

Figure 3.30

Shave the hairs back to a value of 0.4 around the neckline.

A little bit of preparation goes a long way. Setting up shelf buttons to select hair sections and a few simple MEL scripts keeps you focused on cutting the hair instead of constantly toggling back and forth through the interface. It's easy to lose track of the length you just cut. The shelf buttons allow you to check and compare what you've already done, a process that helps simulate real life.

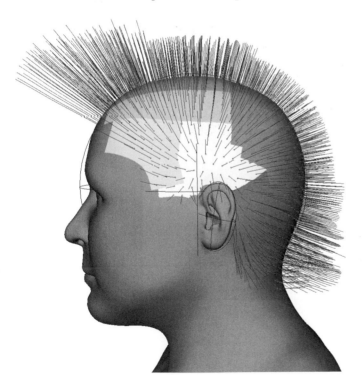

Figure 3.31

Cut the hairs shorter from the start of the nape to the top of the crown.

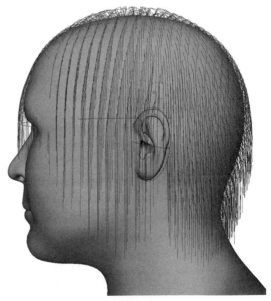

Figure 3.32

Play the simulation to check the length of the hairs.

Project: Hair Styling, Part 1

It's significantly easier to cut hair when it's wet. The weight of the water pulls the hair down, revealing its true length. In Maya, this can be replicated by playing the simulation using its default parameters. Jack has received his first cut and is now ready for styling. This project continues where the previous one left off:

1. Open the scene file hair_v07.ma. The hair in the scene is standing perpendicular to the geometry, and only one strand is being emitted per follicle.

2. Play the simulation to frame 60.

3. In the Outliner, select hairSystem1Follicles.

4. Choose Hair → Set Rest Position → From Current.

5. Set the timeline to the first frame. The hair pops back to its original default pose, or start position. Change the display to see the resting position you just established by choosing Hair → Display→ Rest Position. The hair drops back down to its wet look.

6. You can paint attributes to the rest position curves. Because the hair is in its wet state, you can shape it accurately. Select the hairSystem1 node from the Outliner.

7. Choose Hair → Paint Hair Follicles. Change the options to match Figure 3.33.

8. Painting scale is more creative than trimming hairs. With scale, you can achieve any desired length. As mentioned earlier, you only want to use it for fine tuning. This way, the size of your curve won't become disproportionate to the number of CVs. In the Paint Scripts tool, change to a soft brush with the Scale operation. Set the value to 0.95.

Figure 3.33

Set the Paint Hair Follicle options.

9. You can now interactively trim the hairs to even out the haircut. This may involve scaling and adding painting operations. To make the process easier, create two shelf buttons, one for scaling and the other for adding. Type the following in the Script Editor for the Scale button, and then choose File → Save Script To Shelf:

```
artAttrPaintOperation artUserPaintCtx Scale;
artUserPaintCtx -e -value 0.95 `currentCtx`;
```

Type the following in script editor for the Add button, and then choose File → Save Script to Shelf:

```
artAttrPaintOperation artUserPaintCtx Add;
artUserPaintCtx -e -value 0.05 `currentCtx`;
```

10. Begin painting to make the hair tips smooth all the way around the head. Your goal is to have the hair smoothly change in length. Use Figure 3.34 as reference.

> **ADDITIONAL TRIMMING**
>
> If you find hairs that were left too long or cut too short, you can display the current position curves and use the Trim Hairs or Extend Hairs paint mode to fix them. When you're finished, play the simulation to relax the hair and set the rest position from current. You can then return to the first frame, display your rest position curves, and continue styling.

11. When you're finished cleaning the edges of the hair, it's important to align the rest position curves back to the start position curves. Doing so allows the curves to fall naturally into a relaxed state. Otherwise, the start curves will do their best to match up with the rest curves, potentially causing kinks in the hair. Figure 3.35 shows how the current curve positions have been influenced by the rest curves.

    To get reset the rest curves back to their default position, select hairSystem1Follicles from the Outliner. Choose Hair → Set Rest Position → From Start.

    To check your work so far, you can compare it to hair_v08.ma on the DVD.

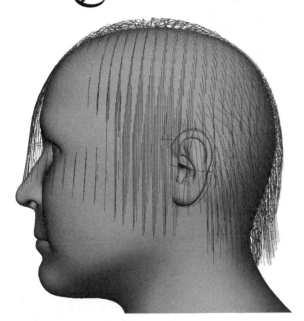

Figure 3.34
Cut a smooth edge around the bottom of the hair.

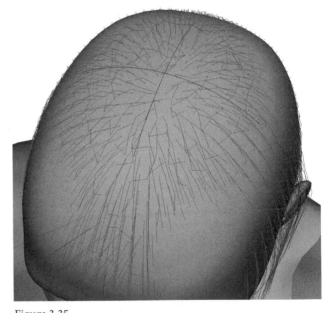

Figure 3.35
The curves no longer fall correctly with the current rest curves.

There are two ways to go at this point: you can add specific shape to the hair or add general properties to the hair tubes. Both methods work, but sometimes the hairstyle lends itself to one or the other. In this case, a shag cut is more random than definitive, so setting the general properties makes more sense. Shaping the hair requires you to be at the first frame of the solver. You can make general property changes at any frame and see the results.

12. Change Hairs Per Clump to 40 and Clump Width to 0.04. Figure 3.36 shows the results.

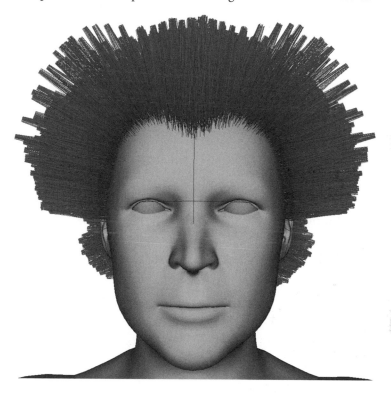

Figure 3.36

Increasing the hairs per clump gives Jack a head of hair.

13. You should set the width of the hair based on the scale of your character. Ultimately, it's what looks best. Jack is built in centimeters, requiring a very small width. Set Hair Width to .001.

14. Open the Collision section. Select Self Collide, and change Repulsion to 0.1. Repulsion causes the hairs to repel each other. With the shag cut, you want the hairs to clump more than they repel. Check your settings with Figure 3.37.

15. Play the simulation to frame 100. You could shape the hair at the first frame. But the hair updates regardless of the frame number, and it makes more sense to see it relaxed on the character (see Figure 3.38).

Figure 3.37

Collision parameters

16. Open the Displacement section. Change Clump to 2.0 and Frequency to 1.0. As mentioned earlier in the chapter, Hair Width has a direct impact on Displacement Curl. If your results seem extreme, you may need to adjust Displacement Curl and Hair Width together. Figure 3.39 shows the results.

17. The shag style has numerous clumps that taper to a point. To achieve this look, set the last key on the Clump Width Scale graph to 0.0 (see Figure 3.40). You can see the results of the graph change in Figure 3.41.

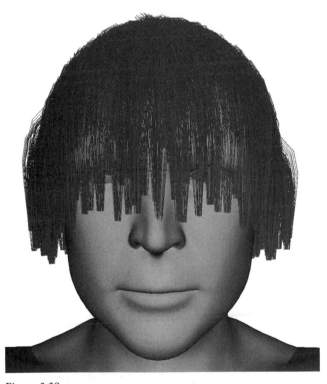

Figure 3.38
The hair relaxed at frame 100

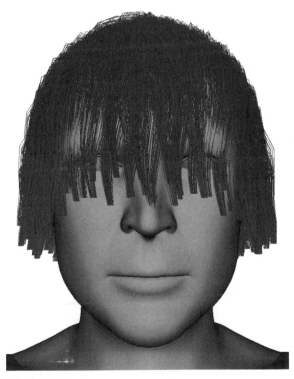

Figure 3.39
Displacement Curl

18. The curl is affecting the entire strand of hair. Instead, you want the hair to come off the head normally and end with curl; this gives the hair a nice wavy look. In the Displacements section, open Displacement Scale. Change the graph to match Figure 3.42. Figure 3.43 shows the results.

   To check your work so far, you can compare it to hair_v09.ma on the DVD.

19. The hair is getting close to the look you're after, but the displacements and additional curl settings have made the hair look too jagged. To fix this, increase Sub Segments in the Clump And Hair Shape section to 3. Compare Figure 3.44 with Figure 3.43 to see the differences.

Figure 3.40
Clump Width Scale graph

Figure 3.42
Displacement Scale graph

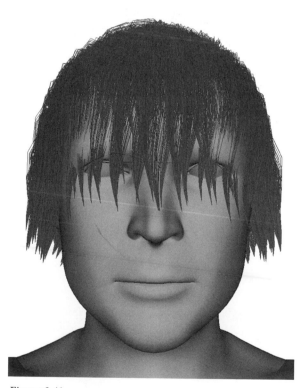

Figure 3.41
Clump Width Scale applied to Jack's hair

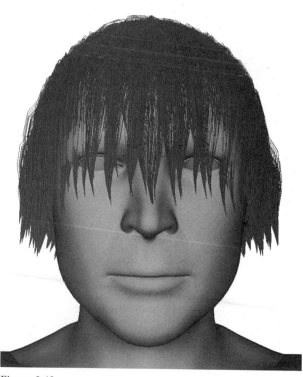

Figure 3.43
Jack's hair looks wavier.

20. The waves in the hair appear wet and styled. To break them up a little, change the Clump Curl graph to match Figure 3.45. The last key is set to 0.8. This twists the hair tube helping to separate the hairs (see Figure 3.46).

21. The hair is thick and bushy. Every strand in each clump ends in the same length. Thinning is the answer to thinning shears and numerous real-world techniques. Increasing this value randomly cuts the ends from individual strands, decreasing the bulkiness of the hair. In the Clump And Hair Shape section, change the Thinning value to 0.6. Figure 3.47 shows the results.

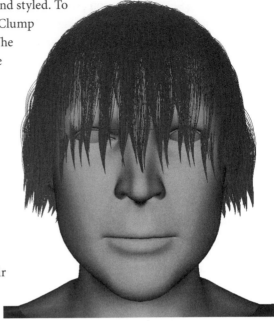

Figure 3.44
Adding subsegments removes the jagged look.

Figure 3.45
Clump Curl graph

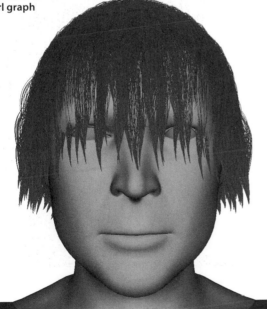

Figure 3.46
The results of adding Clump Curl

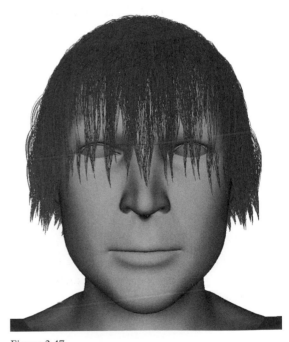

Figure 3.47
Thinning reduces the weight of the hair.

22. Noise is important to any complex placement of objects. When you're dealing with hair, you want to get the right number. Too much noise can make the hair kinked, segmented, and unrealistic. Referring back to the reference material, Figure 3.9, you can see that the randomness of the hair is in the clumps of hair and not in the individual strands.

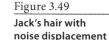

Figure 3.48
Settings for noise displacement

In the Displacements section, change Noise Method to Clump UV. Use Figure 3.48 for the rest of the attributes.

Deriving these settings is a trial-and-error process. Play with the numbers to see what looks best based on the style of hair. Also keep in mind that Displacement Scale controls how much noise the hair ac receives. Figure 3.49 shows the noise applied to Jack's hair.

To check your work so far, you can compare it to `hair_v10.ma` on the DVD.

Project: Hair Styling, Part 2

The general attributes are finished. You can go back and make specific modifications to individual hair strands. The goal is to create the start and resting positions of each curve based on the reference material. Up to this point, you have only modified the tubes or Paint Effects brush. Although this provides a decent general look, the hair curves themselves are pulled straight by gravity. Using a combination of tools and techniques you need to shape the hair curves into the desired style.

Figure 3.49
Jack's hair with noise displacement

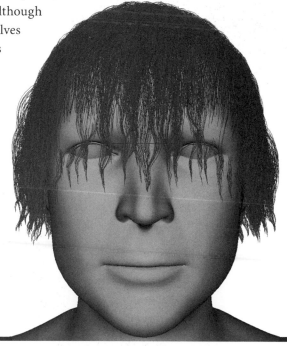

1. Open the scene file `hair_v10.ma`. The scene picks up where part 1 of "Hair Styling" left off. Select hairSystem1, and open its Attribute Editor.

2. Change Hairs Per Clump to 1. This setting makes it easier to see your results and speeds up interactivity.

3. Turn on all the selection masks except Curves.

4. Choose Hair → Display→ Start Position.

5. Select the hairSystem1 node. Choose Hair → Paint Hair Follicles. Use Figure 3.50 to change the Paint Hair Follicle settings.

6. In the Paint Scripts tool, change Value to 0.1. Choose Flood. Flooding the Inclination parameter changes the angle of the hair (see Figure 3.51). The attribute ranges from 0 to 1, with 0.5 being the

default erect position. Values of 0 and 1 lay the hair down to the surface in opposite directions.

7. The hair parts perfectly down the middle, but the part needs to be over the character's left eye. Change Value to 0.9. Paint the hair from the centerline to above the left eye; doing so flips the hair's direction to the other side, moving the part. Use Figure 3.52 as reference.

Figure 3.50

Paint Hair Follicle settings

8. The polarity of the hair is separated by the centerline of the character. By painting Polar values, you can change the inclination's orientation. Polar values start at 0.5. Going up to 1.0 rotates the hair 90 degrees counterclockwise. Painting the Polar attribute is a bit like combing hair.

Change Folliclc Attribute to Polar. Set the paint value to 0.0. Paint the hairs on the right side of the part. Beginning at the forehead, paint 0.0 and gradually work your way to 0.4, stopping at the back of the ear. To brush the hairs on the opposite side of the centerline, use a starting value of 0.5. These hairs are already close to where they should be and only need a value as high as 0.6. Use the smooth brush to clean up (see Figure 3.53).

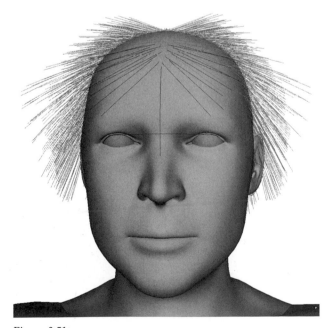

Figure 3.51

Flood the Inclination parameter with a valuc of 0.1.

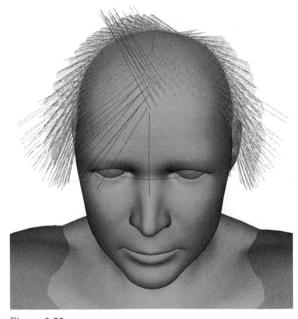

Figure 3.52

Paint the inclination.

9. Paint the Polar value for the left side of the character's head. Begin with a value of 0.9 and work your way to 0.6. Use the smooth brush to clean up (see Figure 3.54).

    To check your work so far, you can compare it to `hair_v11.ma` on the DVD.

    Polar and Inclination establish a good direction for the hair. But playing the simulation destroys all your work. Even though the hairs are combed in the right direction, dynamic forces still have precedence. To counteract the effects, you can have the hair be attracted to the starting curves you just painted.

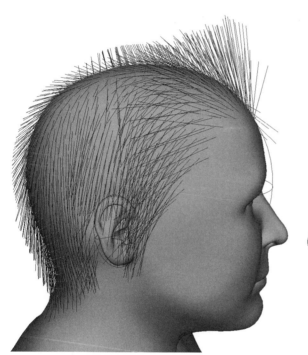

Figure 3.53

Paint the Polar attribute for the character's right side.

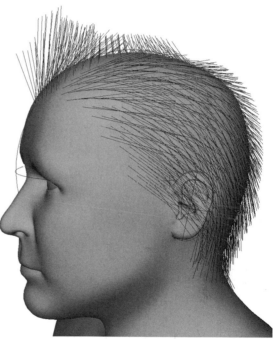

Figure 3.54

Paint the Polar attribute for the character's left side.

10. Choose Hair → Display→ Current Position.

11. Open the Attribute Editor for hairSystem1, and open the Dynamics section. The general direction of the hair is established. You can use the simulation to drop the hair into place as opposed to manually moving each and every CV. Adding Attraction keeps the simulation from erasing the values you painted. Use the settings from Figure 3.55 to change the Start Curve Attract and Attraction Scale settings.

Figure 3.55

Attraction settings

Play the simulation. You can interactively increase or decrease the Attraction values to see what works best. Figure 3.56 shows the hair in a rested position using the attraction settings.

12. Select hairSystem1Follicles. Choose Hair → Set Start Position → From Current. Display the start position curves to make sure all of them have updated. If some appear unchanged, set the position again. Do the same for the rest position curves.

13. Return to the start frame.

14. Choose Hair → Display → Start Position.

15. Select hairFollicles1. Choose Hair → Convert Selection → To Start Curves.

16. Choose Hair → Modify Curves → Lock Length. Locking the length of the curves keeps them from getting distorted. It also makes them easier to style.

17. You can now push and pull the curves to get the exact hair shape. This is the tedious part. It can take a long time to get what you're looking for. Everything done to this point has moved the hairs closer to your target, eliminating a lot of the manual repositioning of the hair's CVs.

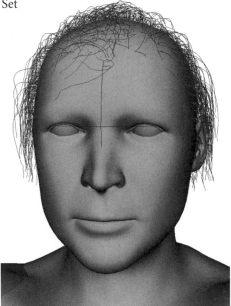

Figure 3.56
The results after simulating

Although it isn't your goal to duplicate the hair from Figure 3.9, that's your reference. Select the hair curve lowest on the forehead. Enter component mode, and choose the last CV. Translate the vertex around to get a feel for the way the hair curve moves. Using Figure 3.57, translate the curve to create the clump over the character's right eye, similar to the reference image.

UNDOING CURVE MOVEMENT

Curve movement can't be undone fully when the curve's length has been locked. When you move a curve, you're moving it from a single or even multiple points. Pressing Undo only returns the points you had selected back to their original positions. Any other points that followed along are updated based on their current position and the undone position of the point you previous moved.

18. A primary goal of manually moving the curves is to pull them out of the geometry and untangle any mixed-up strands. Practice by grabbing an end of a tangled curve and laying it straight.

MOVING HAIR CURVE CONTROL VERTICES

You may find that the CVs get sluggish or unwilling to go where you want them to, the further you get from the hair tip. This is because their lengths are locked, restricting how much motion they have. Moving multiple points instead of a single point can alleviate a lot of this problem.

19. The model in the reference photo has a lot of curled ends on his left side. You can manipulate numerous curves simultaneously to achieve this look. From the character's left profile, select all the hair curves from the back of the ear to the forehead (see Figure 3.58). Make sure you didn't accidentally select any of the right-side curves.

20. Choose Hair → Convert Selection → To Start Curve End CVs.

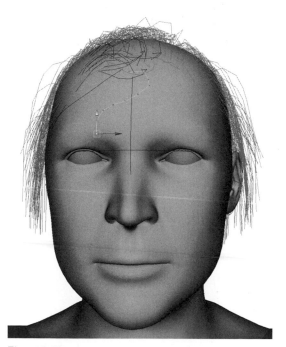

Figure 3.57
Translate the curve's CVs to shape it.

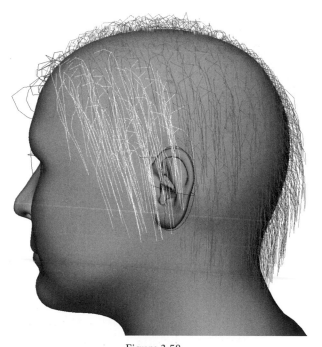

Figure 3.58
Select the hair curves along the left side of the head.

21. Translate the ends in the positive Y and then in the positive X to pull them away from the head with a curl (see Figure 3.59).

22. Add more curl to the hair behind the ears. The hair must be translated in all three axes to get the proper direction. You can also rotate and scale your selection for greater control.

23. Add tip curl to the back of the hair as well. This time, begin by translating in the X and then the Y (see Figure 3.60).

24. Continue around to the right side, pulling the hair out at the ends (see Figure 3.61).

25. Pull the hairs above the forehead one at a time to untangle them and align them to the flow of the hairstyle (see Figure 3.62). Don't be afraid to grab an end and pull it to an extreme. In some cases, pulling the hair in a big loop works well to get it where you want it to go.

RESET CURVE

If you mess up the curve and can't get its shape right, grab the tip and translate it as high as you can above its follicle. Doing so straightens the curve and allows you to start over. You can also try Hair → Modify Curves → Straighten.

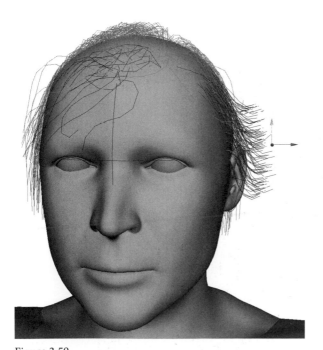

Figure 3.59

Translate the tips to give them a curl.

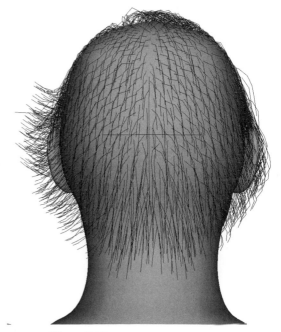

Figure 3.60

Curl the tips on the back of the head.

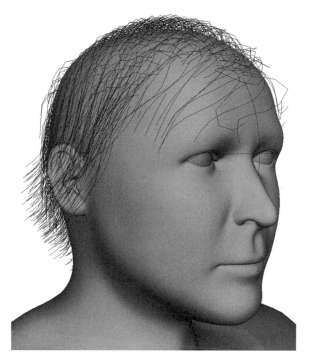

Figure 3.61
Curl the tips on the right side of the head.

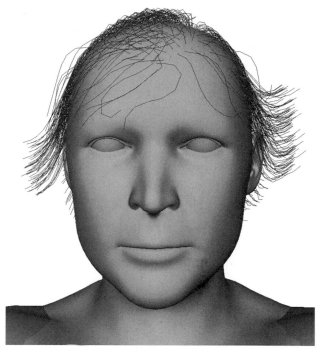

Figure 3.62
Manipulate the hairs above the forehead.

26. When you're finished adjusting the curves, turn your current position curves back on. To see the hair in its entirety, set Hairs Per Clump back to 40 on the hairSystem1 node (see Figure 3.63).

    To check your work so far, you can compare it to hair_v12.ma on the DVD.

27. The next attribute is Bend Follow, which controls the rotation of the hair clump based on the hair's primary axis. Change the value to 0.6 (see Figure 3.64).

28. For the finishing touches, increase the last key on the Clump Width Scale graph 0.1 to give the hair more volume (see Figure 3.65).

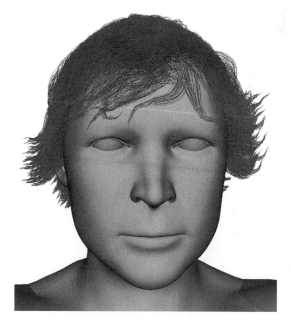

Figure 3.63
The current look of the hair

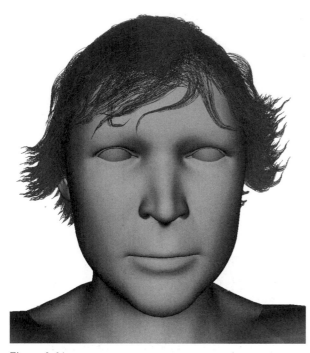

Figure 3.64

Lower the value of the Bend Follow parameter.

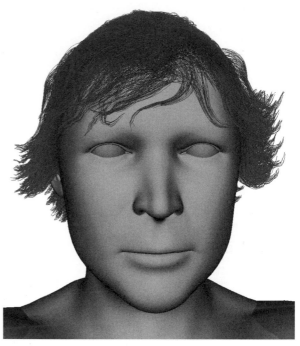

Figure 3.65

Change the last key on the Clump Width Scale graph to 0.1 to add hair volume.

29. The shape of the hair is finished. Playing the simulation causes the hair to fall down and lose its shape. To make it keep its shape, as wavy hair would, you need to increase the Attraction settings. Use Figure 3.66 to change the Start Curve Attract and Attraction Scale settings.

Figure 3.66

Modify the Attraction settings.

Playing the simulation with these settings still lets the hair move but also forces it to maintain its shape. To check your work so far, you can compare it to hair_v13.ma on the DVD.

Project: Hair Coloring

The current color of the hair, which is a dirty blonde, works pretty well for Jack. It needs some fine tuning, though. In the last project of this chapter, you'll modify the Shading section of the hair system node. Before you modify any attributes, you must establish proper lighting. Follow these steps:

1. Open the scene file `hair_v14.ma`. The scene picks up where the previous project left off. Two spot lights have been added to the scene.

2. Lighting setups change from scene to scene. A decent lighting setup to test your shading parameters is mental ray's Physical Sky And Sun shader with two additional spot lights. Open Render Settings, and choose Quality. Choose Production from Quality Presets.

3. Choose the Indirect Lighting tab. Click Create in the Environment section for Physical Sky And Sun. Close the Render Settings window.

4. Two spot lights are already in the scene. To render the hair's self-shadowing properly in an acceptable amount of time, you can use depth map shadows. Select spotlight1, and open its Attribute Editor.

5. In the Depth Map Shadow Map Attributes section, select Use Depth Map Shadows. Deselect Use Mid Distance.

Figure 3.67

Shadows section settings

6. Those settings work for Maya software rendering. For mental ray, open the Mental Ray section, and find Shadows. Change the settings as shown in Figure 3.67.

Figure 3.68

Shadow Map Overrides settings

7. You can now alter the Shadow Map Overrides section. Choose Take Settings From Maya to fill in most of the parameters. Use Figure 3.68 for the rest.

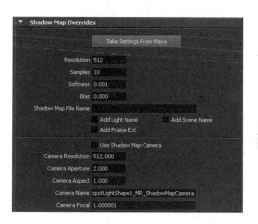

8. Change the Detail Shadow Map attributes based on Figure 3.69.

9. Apply steps 5 through 8 to spotlight2.

10. Render a frame to establish the initial look (see Figure 3.70).

Figure 3.69

Detail Shadow Map attributes

To check your work so far, you can compare it to `hair_v15.ma` on the DVD.

11. The hair looks thick and slightly wet. You're after a lighter, wispier look. Open the hairSystem1's Attribute Editor. Hair opacity and translucency change with hair color: darker colors are more opaque and less translucent, whereas lighter colors are the opposite. Open the Shading section. Change Opacity to 0.5 and Translucency to 0.8. In addition, increase Specular Power to 15. Render the results (see Figure 3.71).

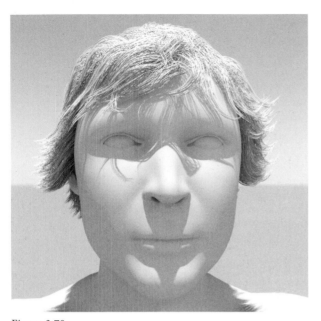

Figure 3.70
The current look of the rendered hair

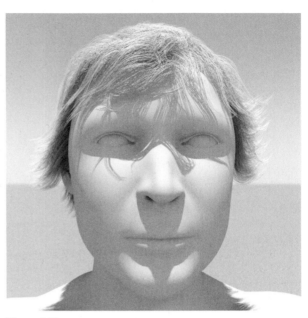

Figure 3.71
The rendered results from the Opacity and Translucency changes

12. Currently, Jack has roughly 1,400 follicles with 40 hairs in each. That gives him 56,000 strands of hair. As stated earlier in the chapter, lighter-haired people typically have 140,000 hairs. Adding this number through Hairs Per Clump and/or more follicles is computationally restrictive. Instead, you can increase the number of visible hairs by using Multi Streaks. The attributes duplicate and offset the current hairs. Use Figure 3.72 for the settings.

Figure 3.72
Multi Streak settings

The Spread values shift the hair away from the original tube. Spread 1 offsets the hairs based on the clump width, and Spread 2 offsets the hairs at the tube's tip. Determining the right amount of spread and direction of the spread can be difficult; rendering is the only way to test the results (see Figure 3.73).

To see the finished hairstyle and to check your work, you can load hair_v16.ma on the DVD.

The hair is finished for now. You'll make final tweaks when you place the character in a scene. Based on the lighting setup, some parameters may need to be changed. This subject is addressed in Chapter 8, "Composition," along with simulating the hair's motion.

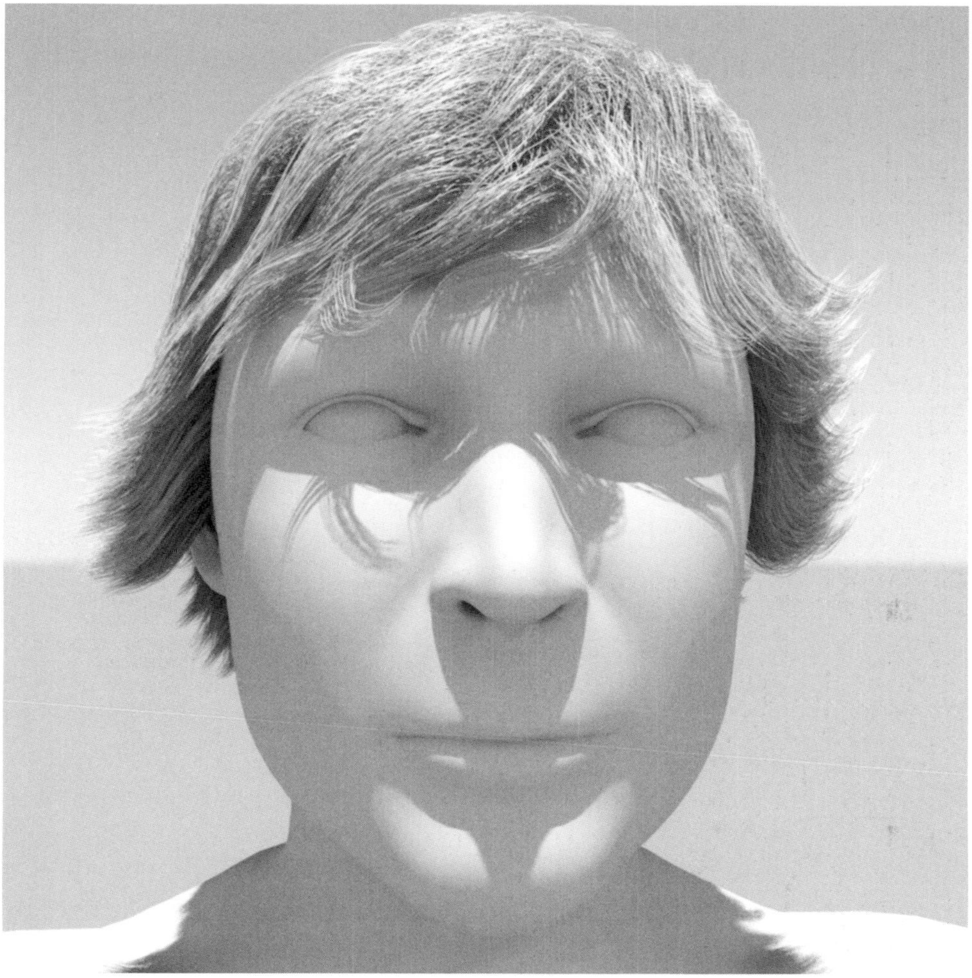

Figure 3.73
The final rendered look

Summary

Creating hair can be tricky and time consuming. It requires an understanding of the look you are trying to achieve. Make sure to do the research and create a plan of attack before starting. Following the order of growing hair, cutting hair, and then styling the hair makes all the difference. Also remember, you can add extra hair without having to add more follicles. The more follicles you have, the harder the hair system is to manage.

CHAPTER 4

Fur

Although the name is a bit deceptive, fur is an essential part of creating a photorealistic character. As the name implies, it's great for covering entire characters. It also excels at creating large fields of grass. In this chapter, however, you'll use it to create eyelashes, eyebrows, and a full beard.

In this chapter you will learn to:

- ■ **Understand the basics of fur**
- ■ **Create a beard**
- ■ **Create eyebrows**
- ■ **Create eyelashes**

Fur Basics

Creating fur is a less intensive process than creating hair. Hair is more hands-on, whereas fur is primarily driven by sliders. Located under the Render module, Fur is actually a shader. When you add fur to a surface, an icon is created to represent it. This is called the *fur feedback node*. The icon updates with the majority of attribute changes but doesn't represent the true look of the fur. Figure 4.1 shows a comparison between the viewport representation and the rendered version.

Figure 4.1

The fur icon doesn't accurately represent fur.

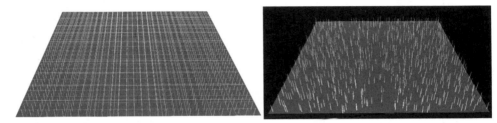

Fur placement is based on the UVs of the surface it's attached to. If your UVs are bad, your fur will be bad. Fur's usage of UVs goes beyond simple placement: it uses them as a starting point for the direction of the fur. If your UVs are divided into multiple shells, and each shell is rotated differently, then the fur will point in different directions when laid flat to the surface. This has no bearing on performance but can be more time-consuming to align.

Prior to applying fur, you define the faces that need it. The UVs of these faces are laid out independently of your texturing requirements, giving you two UV sets. The second UV set is used solely for fur and can be arranged in any manner to best suit the fur. Although you can have as many UV sets as you want, only one UV set can be used with fur. You can easily connect or swap fur to a UV set through the Relationship Editor.

Fur vs. Hair

Fur excels at covering large areas. You can add and render hundreds of thousands of strands efficiently using Maya's software renderer or mental ray. Large patches of fur render more quickly than hair but offer little control when it comes to length. Fur is only shaped based on its base and tip. This means a lot less setup work but limits its usage. Figure 4.2 shows an example of fur being used as grass: more than 500,000 strands of fur are rendered.

Fur has several attributes that can be painted that hair doesn't have. Most of the extra attributes handle what hair does with its curve and follicle. Overall, working with fur can be faster. It's easy to set up, and you can quickly shape it with sliders and numerous noise options.

Figure 4.2

An example of fur grass

You animate fur by keyframing slider attributes or using a hair system to drive it. You add hair to fur as an attractor. The fur is moved by the hair curves based on proximity. Attractor values can be painted as well. Even though fur is limited to base and tip attributes, when it's driven by hair, the entire length of fur is affected and deforms with the curve.

Attribute Maps

In order for you to paint attribute maps, the surface the fur is attached to must have UVs. All the UVs must reside within the 0 to 1 texture space. Fur can be applied to only one UV set per object; therefore, to cover a character, you must put all the UVs in a single set or break the character into separate objects. Figure 4.3 shows an example of a single UV set being used for an entire character.

Figure 4.3

UVs for an entire character

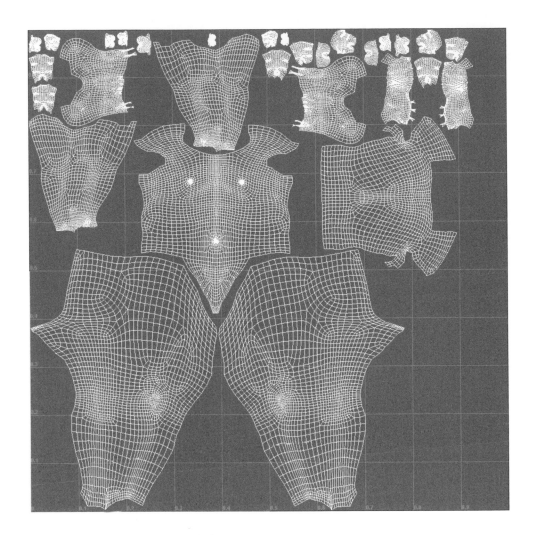

Fur has two separate controls for texture size:

U and V Sample Attribute Located on the fur feedback node. This attribute controls the size of the map to be painted at the time of painting.

Export Width and Height Located in the fur description. This attribute controls the size of the map when it's saved. Let's say you set the fur feedback sample size to 64×64. When you paint, you're painting on a 64×64 texture map. If you set Export Width and Height to 1024 and save the image, the 64×64 texture is blown up to 1024. This of course results in a pixilated image.

Using large sample sizes to paint attribute maps typically results in long refresh times and intermittent crashing, despite your system's resources. Depending on how much fur is on the screen, 256 and 512 are usually the highest sample sizes that you can work with practically.

There are several workarounds to this problem. The first is to use the Maya 3D Paint tool instead of the Paint Fur Attributes tool. Although the fur doesn't update as you paint, you can see the geometry. The second option is to take a UV snapshot and paint on it using a 2D paint program. This method doesn't provide any feedback and forces you to reload your texture in Maya to see your changes. A mixture of both methods is usually employed to complete a fur creation.

When you save a scene, Maya saves the maps into a `Fur Attribute` folder in your project directory. A new version of your fur attribute map is saved every time you save your scene with a new name. It's important to monitor the maps being written to the Fur Attribute folder and keep your fur files organized.

Facial Hair

Hair grows all over the body. It grows the heaviest and fullest on the head. The projects in this chapter deal with Maya Fur and how it pertains to Jack's facial hair: eyebrows, eyelashes, nose hair, beard, and mustache.

Facial hair tends to be thicker than head hair. This makes the hair less manageable, giving it strength to grow where it pleases. Almost all facial hair curls; the longer it gets, the more curl it takes on. Overall, it's richer in almost every attribute, including color (Figure 4.4).

Beards and Mustaches

You should determine beard length early on. It can make the difference between using hair and fur. Analyze your project carefully: the longer the beard or mustache, the more likely it is to require hair. For instance, a handlebar mustache needs Maya Hair.

Any extreme length should use hair instead of fur. But you can mix the two, because the hair shader is very similar to the fur shader. This technique allows you to match the shading flawlessly. In addition, if your character requires a long beard at some point during its lifespan, you can use the two harmoniously to grow length when needed, saving you the time and effort of building multiple setups (see Figure 4.5).

Jack has a full beard. Figure 4.6 serves as the reference. In this section, creating a beard for Jack is broken up into three projects. The first takes you through the process of adding fur. The next modifies the fur attributes and paints specific maps. Finally, you'll shade and render the fur.

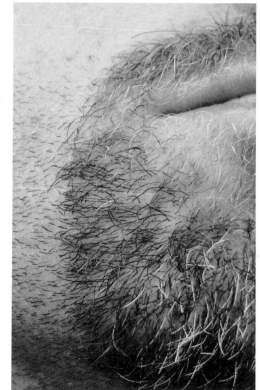

Figure 4.4

An example of facial hair

Figure 4.5

An example for which you would use fur and hair

Figure 4.6

The reference for Jack's beard

Project: Full Beard, Part 1

Jack's beard is your first project, and creating it is broken into three parts. Using Figure 4.6 as reference, you'll use Maya Fur to add the facial hair. The starting scene file is a continuation from the previous chapter. Jack's hair is placed on a layer with its visibility turned off. It's necessary to have it in the scene to match the color as well as a guide for adding sideburns. Follow these steps:

1. Open the scene file `beard_v01.ma` from the `Chapter4\Projects\scenes` folder on the DVD. The scene contains the Jack character bound and weighted to his skeleton. Several layers are set up to keep the scene organized.

2. Fur is needed for the beard, nose hair, eyebrows, and eyelashes. Select the polygons in each of the areas. Use Figure 4.7 for reference.

> **EXTRA FACES**
>
> It's a good idea to always include more than you think you'll need. It's much easier to remove fur than to add fur to undefined areas. The faces on Jack's neck are selected in this project but won't be addressed.

Figure 4.7

Polygon selection for Jack's facial hair

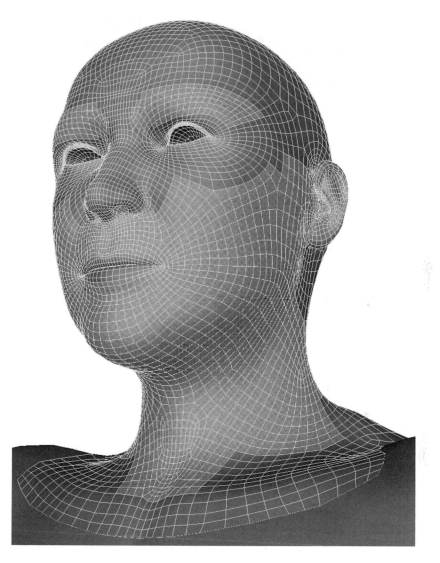

3. Choose Create UVs → Copy UVs To UV Set → Copy Into New UV Set. Change the name of the new set to facialHair (Figure 4.8).

The new UV set is based on the existing UV placement (Figure 4.9). The distribution works for texture. Fur UVs are more demanding.

Figure 4.8

Set the name for the new UV set.

Figure 4.9

The current UV distribution for the facial hair

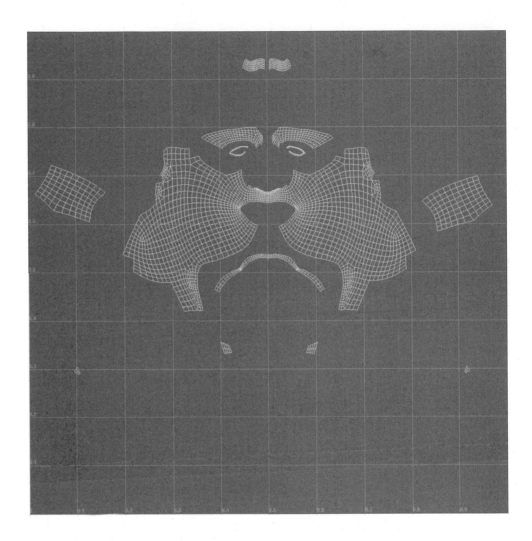

4. Move and sew the neck section and the four small pieces on the bottom (Figure 4.10).

5. Move the pieces together to form a tight group. Scale all the UVs to fill the 0 to 1 texture space.

6. The UVs for the eyelids are too small. Move them to the bottom of the texture space, and uniformly scale them as large as possible (Figure 4.12).

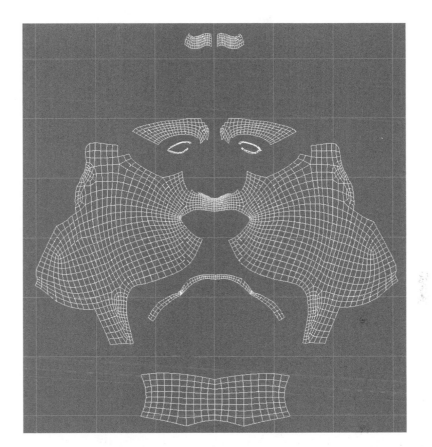

Figure 4.10

Move and sew the smaller pieces together.

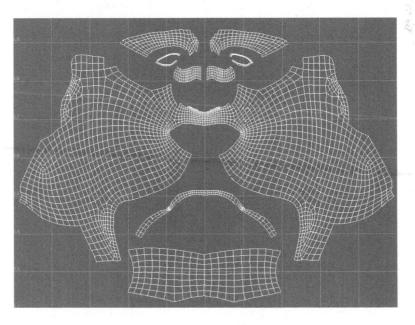

Figure 4.11

Move and scale the UVs.

Figure 4.12

Scale the eyelid UVs.

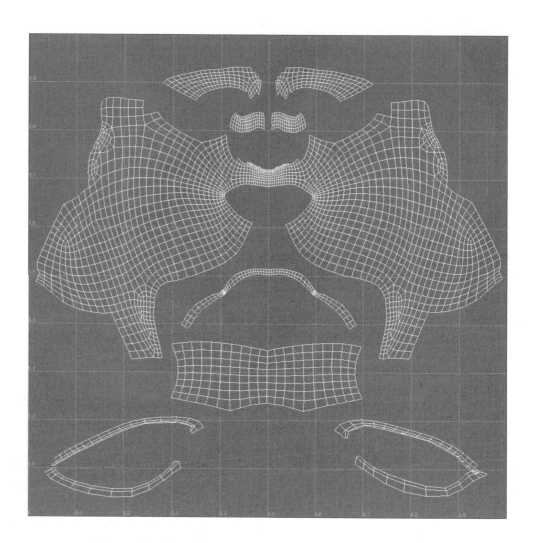

7. The UVs are done. You can now attach fur. Choose Fur → Attach Fur Description → New.

8. The fur is attached and is too large for Jack's scale. Select furDescription1. In the Channel Box, change Global Scale to .034 (Figure 4.13).

   To check your work so far, you can compare it to beard_v02.ma on the DVD.

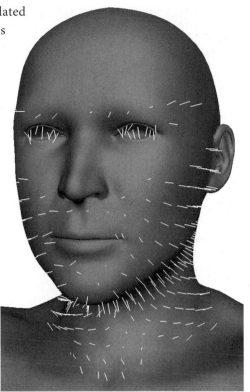

Figure 4.13

Change the global scale of the fur.

9. The beard and nose hairs need to be isolated in their own fur description. You do this by painting baldness maps. You can create attribute maps with the Paint Fur Attributes tool. However, depending on your system's resources, doing so can be problematic. Ultimately, you should use a 2D paint package to perfect the maps. It's a good idea to set up a 2D document early in the process; this makes painting any of the attributes easier to deal with throughout the fur-creation process.

Before you can begin painting, you need to save the UVs to a 2D image. Select head1. In the UV Texture Editor, choose Polygon → UV Snapshot. Change the settings according to Figure 4.14.

10. Load your saved snapshot into Photoshop. You can also load the image beardUVs.iff from the Chapter4\Projects\images folder on the DVD.

11. Use the Magic Wand tool to select the black outside of the UV boundaries.

12. Choose Select → Inverse.

13. Deselect the back of the neck, eyebrow, and eyelash regions.

14. Choose Select → Modify → Expand. Set Expand to 10 pixels (see Figure 4.15).

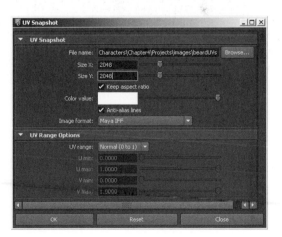

Figure 4.14

UV snapshot settings

Figure 4.15

Expand the selection around the UV groups.

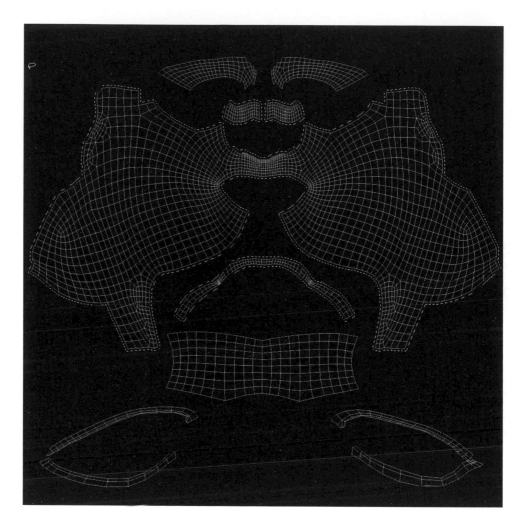

15. Create a group, and add the selection as a vector mask. The mask is created to quickly select the UV boundaries. It's mainly used to fill areas.

16. Move the image of the UVs above Group1. Change its blending mode to Difference. This ensures the UVs are always visible as you paint in grayscale.

17. Create another layer, and flood it with black. This layer provides a backdrop for your attribute maps (see Figure 4.16).

Figure 4.16

The Layers window

18. Hold Ctrl, and click the layer mask image on the Group1 layer to highlight the selection.

19. Create an empty layer under the group. Rename it **Baldness**.

20. Use the Paint Bucket tool to fill the selection with white (see Figure 4.17).

Figure 4.17

Use pure white to fill the selection.

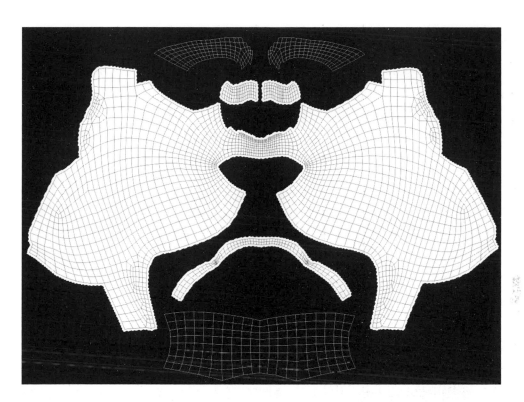

21. Turn off the visibility on the UV snapshot layer, and save the image as beardBaldness.iff. Save the file in the furAttrMap folder of your project directory.

22. You now have a template document and the base for painting your attribute maps. Save the file as Beard1.PSD.

    To check your work so far, you can compare it to beard1.PSD from the Chapter4\Projects\sourceimages folder on the DVD.

Project: Full Beard, Part 2

The baldness map is ready to be applied. In this part of the process of creating Jack's beard, you'll bake the map to the UVs and perfect it using the 3D paint tool. You'll also create additional maps to comb the hair in the proper direction. Follow these steps:

1. Open the scene file beard_v02.ma.

2. Open the Hypershade, and open the Attribute Editor for head_MAT.

3. Choose the Create Render Node icon for Color. Select File, and load beardBaldness.iff.

4. Press 6 to view the map (see Figure 4.18).

Figure 4.18

**current state of the
Baldness map**

5. The baldness texture doesn't look the way it should. Even though the current UV set is facialHair, the texture is using the map1 set. To fix this, choose Relationship Editors → UV Linking → UV-Centric. Connect facialHair to file2; Figure 4.19 shows the connections.

Figure 4.19

**The Relationship
Editor and its
connections**

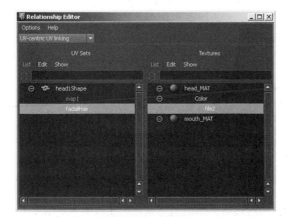

6. Choose Texturing → 3D Paint Tool.

7. Choose the Solid Brush profile, and set the color to black.

8. Paint out the white, leaving only the area of the beard. Use Figure 4.20 as reference.

9. Click the Save Textures button in the File Texture section of the 3D Paint tool. The texture is saved in the `3dPaintTextures` folder of your current project directory.

10. In Photoshop, open the file you saved or load `head1Shape_head_Mat_color.iff` from the `Chapter4\Projects\3dPaintTextures` folder on the DVD. Also open `Beard1.PSD` from the `Chapter4\Projects\sourceimages` folder.

11. Select the Move tool.

12. Hold Shift, and drag the image from head1Shape_head_Mat_Color to open-Beard1. Move the layer into Group1.

13. Soften the edges of the beard where it blends into the skin. Figure 4.21 shows the finished map.

Figure 4.20

Paint the beard.

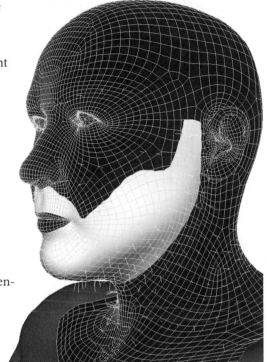

Figure 4.21

Baldness map

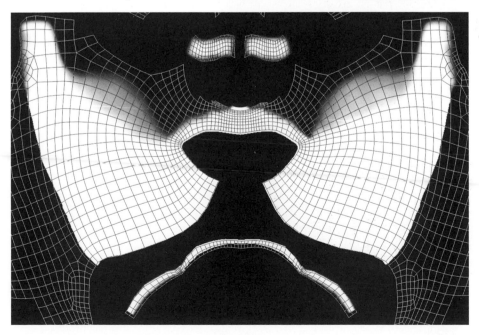

14. Save the image as beardBaldness.iff.

15. Open the scene file beard_v02.ma.

16. Select head1_furFeedback.

17. Open its Attribute Editor, and select FurDescription1.

18. Right-click the Baldness attribute, and choose Create New Texture from the pop-up menu.

19. The Create Render Node window opens. Choose File, and load your beardBaldness.iff file or load beardBaldness1.iff from the Chapter4\Projects\furAttrMap folder on the DVD.

20. Go back to the FurDescription1 tab. Change the Bake Attribute parameter to Baldness, and click Bake. The fur is updated with the new baldness map (see Figure 4.22).

BAKING ATTRIBUTES

Every time you change a map, you need to bake it. You can also update several maps at once by choosing Fur → Update Fur Maps.

---

21. The amount of fur being displayed is too low to determine the accuracy of the painted maps. In the Channel Box, under head1_FurFeedbackShape, change the U and V samples to 256 (see Figure 4.23).

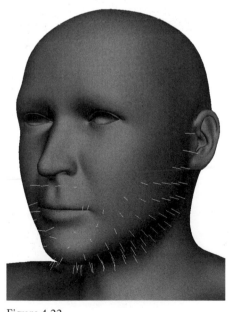

Figure 4.22

The fur is updated with the new baldness map.

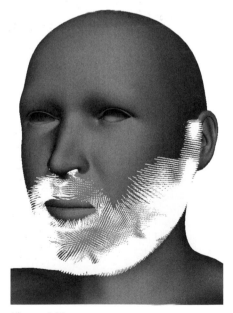

Figure 4.23

Increase the U and V samples.

22. Click FurDescription1 in the Channel Box. Change the Inclination value to .8. The fur angles up (see Figure 4.24). Inclination doesn't control the direction of the fur; it only alters the slope of the fur. The value ranges from 0 to 1, taking the fur from upright to flat with the surface.

23. To get the fur into the proper direction, you need to modify the Polar attribute. Polar is 0.5 by default. Increasing the value rotates the fur counterclockwise; decreasing the value rotates the fur clockwise. Change the value to 0.0 (see Figure 4.25).

24. If your system is capable, it's easiest to paint the polar values by painting the direction. Direction is only available when you paint. When used, it doesn't actually paint a directional map or give you any painted feedback—instead, it paints to the polar map and updates the fur as you paint.

OPTIMIZING PAINT

Turning off Color Feedback in the Display section of the Paint Scripts tool can help prevent Maya from crashing.

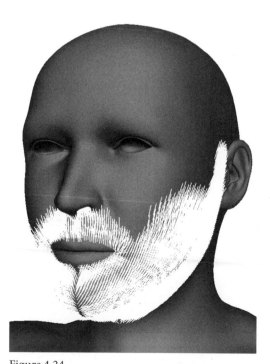

Figure 4.24
Change the Inclination value.

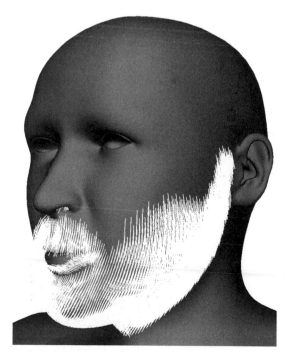

Figure 4.25
Change the Polar attribute's value.

If you have trouble painting using U and V samples of 256, you can downgrade. Remember, doing so dramatically reduces the accuracy of your painted map. Figure 4.26 shows the fur after direction was painted using 256 for the U and V samples. Notice that some areas couldn't be painted.

The directional map was painted using a solid brush. Using the soft brush pushes the fur in all directions until it reaches the appropriate value. This is very difficult to manage, especially across UV shells. Although the solid brush doesn't blend between strokes, it pushes the fur in the exact direction you need it to go. You can blend later on the polar map with the Smooth operation.

25. Another technique is to document the required polar values based on regions of the face. You can do this by scrolling through the range of polar values and making a notation of which values work and where. Figure 4.27 shows an example. These values only work for the left side; the right side would have the opposite values.

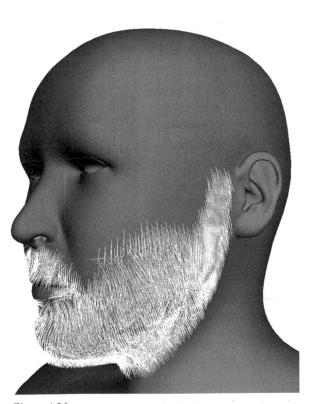

Figure 4.26
The fur after direction was painted

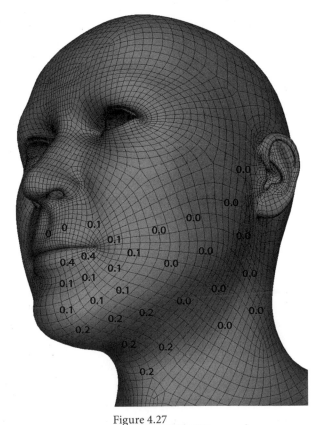

Figure 4.27
The proper polar values for the character's left side

POLAR MAPS

The polar values are mirrored across the surface of the character. If you paint 0.1 for the left side, then the right side needs to be the opposite. Because the Polar attribute originates at 0.5, the opposite value is 0.9.

Using either method, change the direction of the hairs to make a natural-looking beard. This is the part that takes the most amount of time and may require adjusting throughout the process. After you comb all the beard hairs, you can use the Smooth operation to blend the fur together. Be careful to only smooth within the UV shell: smoothing across shells will destroy the flow of the hair. Figure 4.28 shows the efforts of using directional paint to establish the initial flow. Polar values were then painted and smoothed. You can see that there are still a few stray hairs along the edges.

26. To fix the rest of the hairs, clean the polar map in Photoshop. When you're finished, update the map through the Details section of the fur's Attribute Editor. Choose Polar → Maps, and click the polar map's path name (see Figure 4.29).

Click Map Item. Select the polar map through the browser, or load beardPolar.iff from the Chapter4\Projects\furAttrMap folder on the DVD. The final results are shown in Figure 4.30.

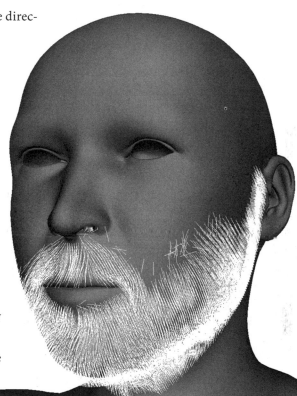

Figure 4.28

The polar values have been smoothed with the Paint Fur Attributes tool.

Figure 4.29

Load the painted polar map through the Attribute Editor.

To check your work so far, you can compare it to beard_v03.ma on the DVD.

To see the actual direction of the fur, you need to render an image. In its current state, not much fur would be rendered—the Density value is too low to see an accurate version of the work you've done so far. Increase the Density attribute in the Fur Description node to at least 100,000. The results are shown in Figure 4.31.

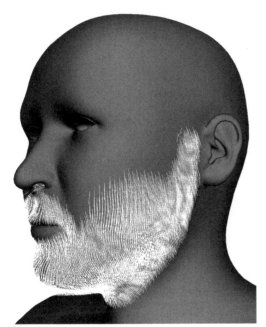

Figure 4.30

The polar map is cleaned up in Photoshop and updated in Maya.

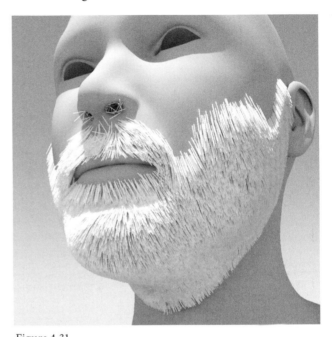

Figure 4.31

The rendered version of Jacks beard.

Painting attribute maps can be a long process and often involves going back and forth between Photoshop and Maya. Most maps are simple to interpret, and you can work with them in Photoshop without having to paint in Maya. The most difficult are polar maps. They're easiest to work with in Maya, by painting the direction and polar values. Painting attribute maps work best if your computer can handle 256 squared maps or higher. Ultimately, you want to take these low-resolution maps and increase their resolution for better detail. Painting at a low resolution establishes basic grayscale values. Therefore, even if your system can only handle 64 squared maps, it still benefits you to paint the basic map in Maya.

Project: Full Beard, Part 3 (Attributes)

So far, you've painted the baldness and polar maps and set the Inclination value. These combined attributes establish the fur's placement and direction. You can now begin adding attributes to get the beard's look. In the next project, you continue perfecting the beard. Follow these steps:

1. Open the scene file beard_v03.ma. The scene picks up where the previous project left off.

2. Every time you save your scene file, the maps are also saved in the furAttrMap folder of your current project directory. The maps are saved based on the map size set in the fur description. This is different from the sample size on the Fur Feedback node, which controls the display and size of the painted map from the Paint Fur Attributes tool.

   Open the Attribute Editor for BeardDescription. Change Map Width and Height to 2048. Keeping the value at 256 causes the maps to be resized every time you save; therefore, when you reopen the scene, the fur looks different, because you lose detail due to downsampling.

3. Choose Fur → Update Fur Maps. The beard now uses the intended size for the painted maps.

PAINTING ATTRIBUTES

If you use the Paint Fur Attributes tool to paint additional maps, the size will be based on the sampling value in the Fur Feedback node. Your painted map will be 256 × 256. You can then load that map into Photoshop to upsample and clean the edges. After you save it, you can reload it into Maya as a 2K image.

4. The first shape-altering attribute to modify is Curl. The curl is broken into the base and tip. Change Base and Tip to 0.3 (see Figure 4.32).

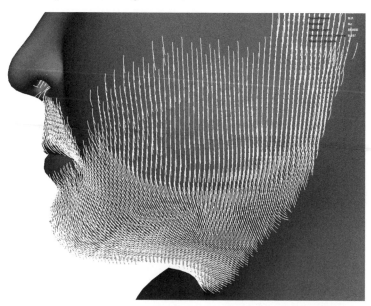

Figure 4.32

Base and tip curl have been added to Jack's beard.

5. Lowering the Curl values below 5.0 has pushed the hairs into Jack's skin. Pull them back out by changing the Inclination value to 0.4 (see Figure 4.33).

Figure 4.33

Alter the Inclination value to raise the fur.

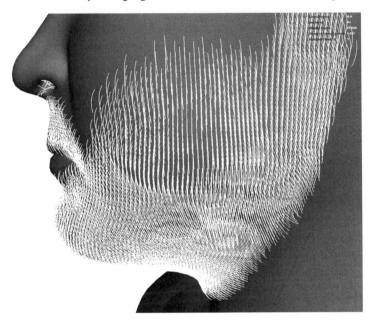

6. Hair never grows the same, especially facial hair. It tends to tangle, twist, and mat due to its coarse nature. Adding noise is a great way to get random growth. Open the Details section; each attribute is represented. Under Inclination, change the values to match Figure 4.34.

Figure 4.34

Add noise to the Inclination attribute.

7. Add noise to Base Curl and Tip Curl, using Figure 4.35 as a guide.

Figure 4.35

Noise attributes for Base Curl and Tip Curl

8. The Scraggle attribute adds crookedness along the length of the fur. A little goes a long way toward increasing the photorealism of the fur. Change Scraggle to 0.1. Add 0.4 to its Noise Amplitude and 25 to its Noise Frequency. Figure 4.36 shows the results on the beard.

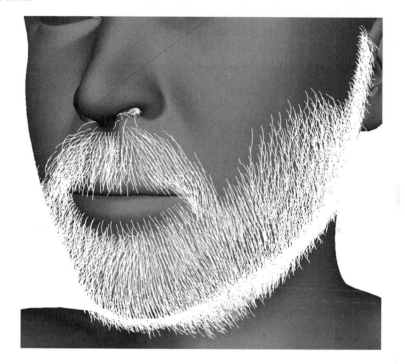

Figure 4.36

Add Scraggle to the beard.

To check your work so far, you can compare it to `beard_v04.ma` on the DVD.

9. Adding Scraggle helps break up the shape of the fur. To create randomness in the direction of the fur, add noise to the Roll and Polar values. Use Figure 4.37 for the settings. Figure 4.38 shows the results.

Polar values rotate fur about its surface axis. This allows you to achieve any angle needed except when you add curl or some other detail-yielding attribute. Polar rotates curled fur in one direction: it doesn't let you change the direction in which the curl is facing. This is where Roll comes in. Roll gives you additional control over the rotation over the surface V axis, allowing you to alter the direction of the curled fur.

Figure 4.37

Noise attributes for Roll and Polar

10. Clumping is another essential parameter to complete the realism of facial hair. You only need a small amount. Change the Clumping attribute to 0.05, and set its Noise Amplitude to 0.1. Figure 4.39 shows the results.

11. With the majority of the attributes set, you can now effectively address the regional length of the beard. The hair above the upper lip hangs too low; paint a length map to reduce it. Also reduce the length under the bottom lip, around the top of the beard, and the nose hairs. Figure 4.40 shows the completed length map, and Figure 4.41 shows the baked map.

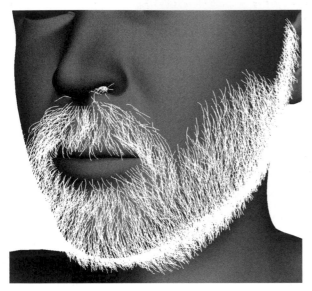

Figure 4.38
The beard fur looks more random.

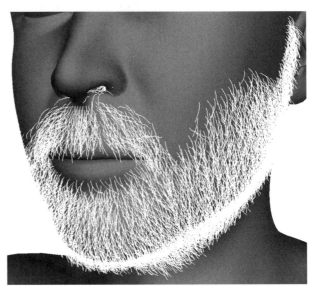

Figure 4.39
Results of adding clumping

Figure 4.40
Painted length map

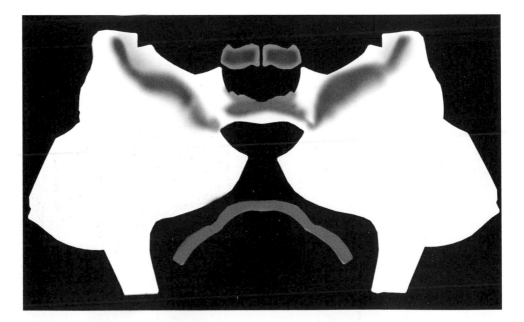

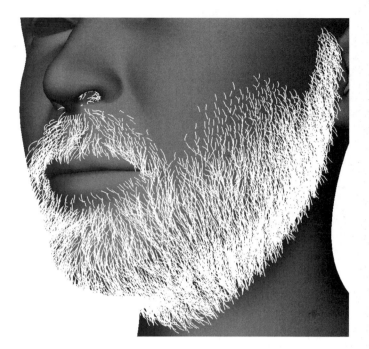

Figure 4.41

The beard with its new length map

MANUALLY ADDING ATTRIBUTE MAPS

Remember, to add an attribute map, you need to right-click the attribute and choose Create New Texture. After adding the texture, you then bake it to the fur.

12. Add noise to the Length attribute using the settings from Figure 4.42. Notice that the recently added length map shows up the under Maps in the Details section.

   To check your work so far, you can compare it to beard_v05.ma on the DVD.

13. You're using the baldness map to mask out portions of the head, to prevent the beard fur description from growing hair in places you don't want. This is an effective technique, but it does prevent you from adding noise to the Baldness attribute through the Details section. Figure 4.43 shows what happens if you try.

Figure 4.42

Noise parameters for the Length attribute

Figure 4.43

An example of noise on the baldness map

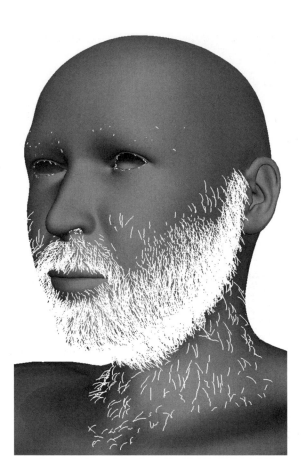

Instead, you must add noise directly to the texture map. Open the baldness map in Photoshop, or load `beardBaldness.iff` from the `Chapter4\Projects\furAttrMap` folder on the DVD.

14. Choose `Filter` → Noise → Add Noise. Use Figure 4.44 for the settings.

15. Save the image and update the Baldness attribute with your texture, or load `beardBaldnessNoise.iff` from the `Chapter4\Projects\furAttrMap` folder on the DVD. Figure 4.45 shows the beard with its updated map.

16. The width of the hair is too thick. Change Base Width to 0.02 and Tip Width to 0.01.

17. To see these results, you need to render. Before you do, increase Density to 120,000 (see Figure 4.46).

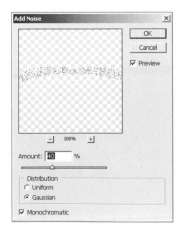

Figure 4.44

Noise settings in Photoshop

Figure 4.45

The beard with noise added to its baldness map

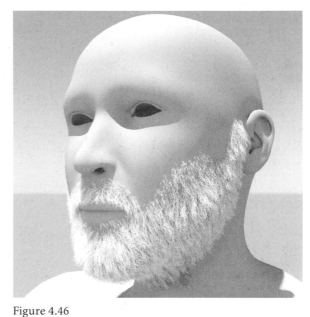

Figure 4.46

The rendered version of the beard

18. A close inspection reveals a bald spot on the upper lip just below the nose (see Figure 4.47). A quick analysis of the baldness map shows that it isn't the culprit. The problem stems from the default equalizer map Maya is using. Equalizer maps help distribute fur evenly across a surface.

Figure 4.47

A comparison of the fur feedback and the rendered version of the beard

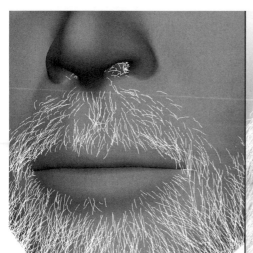

TROUBLESHOOTING FUR

Even prior to rendering, you could determine that the problem wasn't in the baldness or length map. The reasoning comes from the fact that each attribute you've worked on so far has a direct impact on the fur feedback icon in the viewport. If there was an error in one of the maps, it would have shown up before rendering. Therefore, the problem is in the way Maya is distributing the fur.

19. Choose Fur → Fur Render Settings. Change Equalizer Map Width and Height to 2048.

20. Change Default Equalizer Maps to Custom Equalizer Maps. The fur updates after a few moments of processing. The fur feedback now looks like what you see in the render (see Figure 4.48).

21. You can now open the custom equalizer map in Photoshop and fix the problem. The map was being clipped under the nose (see Figure 4.49).

22. Paint the equalizer map below the nose.

23. Increase the levels of the entire map to get its values to be mostly 1.0 or white, by choosing Image → Adjustments → Levels.

24. Push the borders all the way out to the UV shell with the Smudge tool. Figure 4.50 shows the corrected equalizer map.

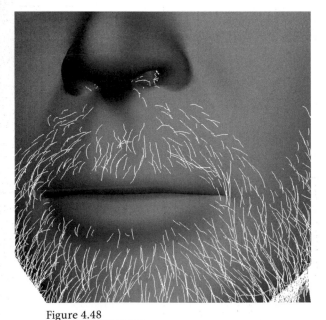

Figure 4.48
The fur equalizer maps have been converted to custom maps.

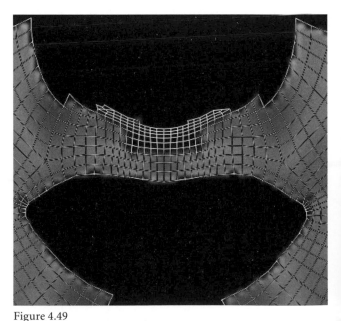

Figure 4.49
The area under the nose is black, causing uneven fur distribution.

25. Save the image and update the maps under the Custom Equalizer section on the fur description node. You can also load `beardEqualizer.iff` from the `Chapter4\Projects\furAttrMap` folder on the DVD. Figure 4.51 shows a render of the beard with its updated map.

    To check your work so far, you can compare it to `beard_v06.ma` on the DVD.

Figure 4.50

New equalizer map

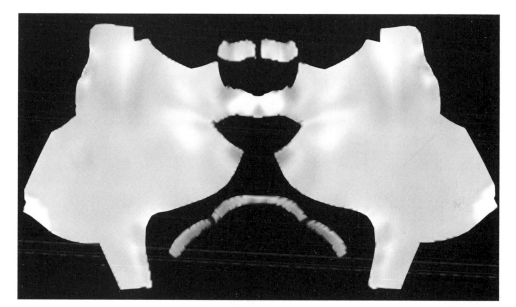

Figure 4.51

The rendered beard

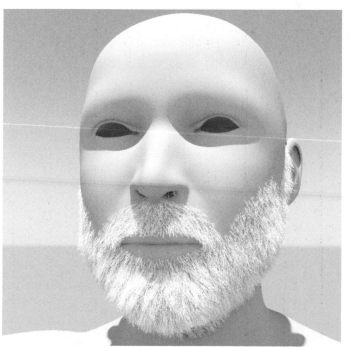

Project: Full Beard, Part 4 (Shading)

The shape and placement of the beard are complete. The last part of the process is shading and lighting. You can use maps for these attributes, but for Jack's beard, it isn't necessary. Using the sliders and noise parameters is enough to achieve the desired look. Follow these steps:

1. Open the scene file beard_v06.ma. The scene picks up where the previous project left off.

2. Open the Attribute Editor for beardDescription.

3. Using the HSV color wheel, change Base Color using the following settings: H 38.0, S 0.5, and V 0.104.

4. Using the HSV color wheel, change Tip Color using the following settings: H 39.0, S 0.5, and V 0.223.

5. Use Figure 4.52 to set the noise parameters for Base and Tip Color. Figure 4.53 shows the rendered results.

Figure 4.52

Noise parameters for Base and Tip Color

Figure 4.53

The beard rendered with color

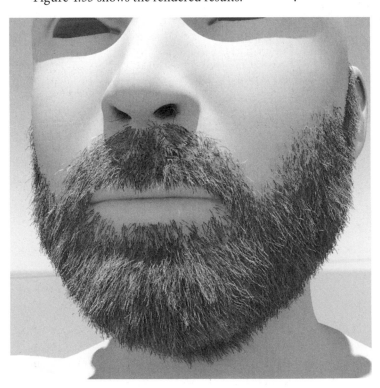

6. Change Base Opacity to 0.9 and Tip Opacity to 0.8.

7. Opacity doesn't change much from hair to hair, but no two hairs are identical. Use Figure 4.54 for the noise parameters.

To check your work so far, you can compare it to `beard_v07.ma` on the DVD.

Figure 4.54

Noise parameters for Base and Tip Opacity

The beard is finished. Figure 4.55 shows the final version. The nose hairs worked out with no effort.

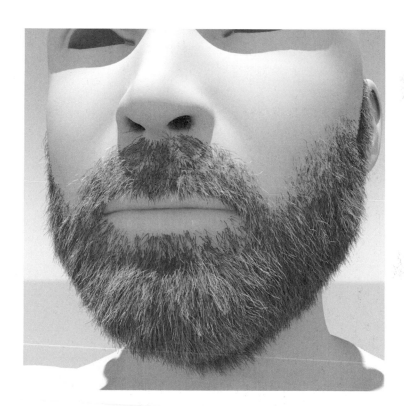

Figure 4.55

The final look of the beard

Eyebrows and Eyelashes

With the beard finished, it's time to move on to the remaining facial hair. The eyelashes and eyebrows are best done with two different fur descriptions, due to the differences in their hair shape. Although it's possible to create them with the same fur description, doing so would require painting individual maps for almost every attribute.

As always, reference material is essential to get the right look. Eyebrows grow differently from race to race and between genders. Before creating them, make sure you have solid references that match your character and aren't generic. Figure 4.56 shows close-up of the eye area to be used for Jack. You can see both eyebrows and eyelashes. Figure 4.57 shows a reference for the top eyelashes.

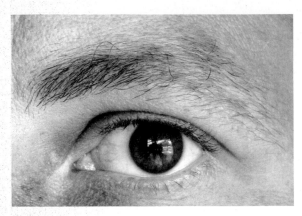

Figure 4.56
Close-up of the eye

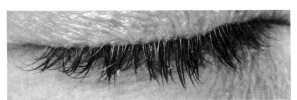

Figure 4.57
Close-up of the top eyelashes

Project: Eyebrows

When you're dealing with eyebrows, Length and Baldness are the two most important attributes. Getting these wrong or right can greatly affect your character's personality. Follow these steps to add Jack's eyebrows:

1. Open the scene file beard_v07.ma. The scene picks up where the previous project left off.

2. Select head1, and choose Fur → Attach Fur Description → New. The new fur description is added and overlaps the beard description.

3. Select head1_furFeedback, and rename it **eyebrow_furFeedack**.

FUR FEEDBACK NAME CHANGES

Sometimes Maya doesn't recognize that you've changed the name of the fur feedback node. When you try to change attributes in the node, Maya comes back with an error stating that it can't find the feedback node using the old name. Saving the scene and reopening it fixes the problem.

4. In the Channel Box, change U Sample and V Sample to 256.

5. Rename furDescription to **eyebrowDescription**.

6. Under eyebrowDescription, change Global Scale to 0.0304 (Figure 4.58).

7. Set Export Width and Height to 2048.

8. Choose Fur → Paint Fur Attributes Tool.

9. Change Fur Attribute to Baldness in the Paint Fur Attributes Tool Settings window.

10. Flood Baldness with a 0.0 value to remove all the fur.

11. Turn on Reflection in the Stroke section in the Paint Scripts tool.

12. Paint an eyebrow using Figure 4.56 as reference. After you paint the basic placement, finish the map in Photoshop. Figures 4.59 and 4.60 show the finished baldness map.

    To check your work so far, you can compare it to eyebrow_v01.ma on the DVD.

13. Interestingly enough, the baldness map also works as the length map. Create a new texture for the Length attribute, and add your baldness map or load eyebrowBaldness.iff from the Chapter4\Projects\furAttrMap folder on the DVD. Figure 4.61 shows the baldness map applied to the Length attribute.

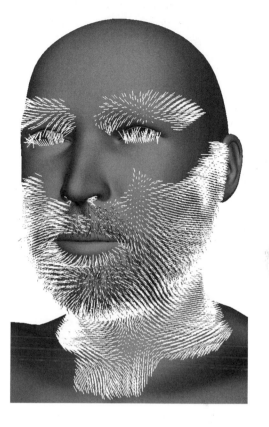

Figure 4.58

Both fur descriptions overlap.

Figure 4.59

Baldness map for the eyebrow

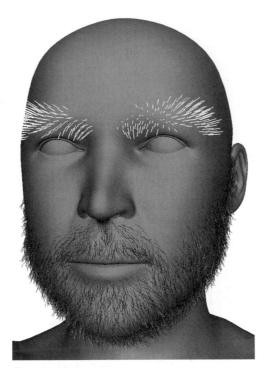

Figure 4.60

Baldness map applied to Jack

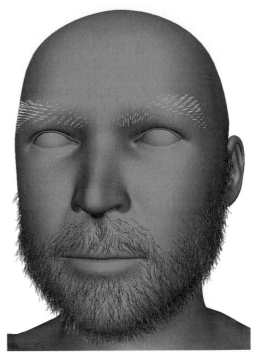

Figure 4.61

New length of the eyebrows

14. Set Inclination to 0.8.

15. Paint the direction or polar values. Polar is more reliable and can be more accurate. Starting at the beginning of Jack's left eyebrow, paint the Polar using a value of 0.35. The brow should taper off with a value of 0.1 (see Figure 4.62).

Figure 4.62

Paint the polar values.

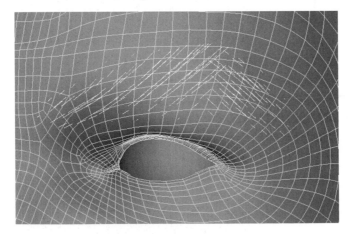

16. Use the Smooth operation to blend the values.

17. Change Brush Opacity and Value to 0.1. Go over the outside edges of the eyebrow to get the hairs to flow properly (see Figure 4.63).

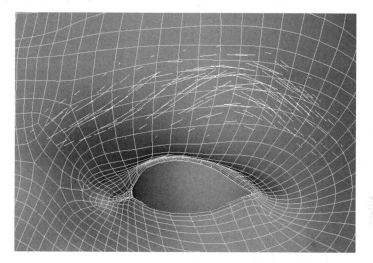

Figure 4.63

Soften the direction of the hair around the borders of the brow.

18. Repeat the process for the right side. Use 0.75 to start with and 0.6 to end.

    To check your work so far, you can compare it to eyebrow_v02.ma on the DVD.

19. Add noise to the Inclination, Roll, and Polar attributes using the values in Figure 4.64. Eyebrow hair grows tightly to the skin, so you should use low values when adding noise to each of these attributes. Always check the inside of the character's head to make sure the hairs aren't penetrating through the surface.

20. Change Base Curl and Tip Curl to 0.4. Set their noise parameters using the values shown in Figure 4.65.

21. Set Scraggle to 0.15 and its Noise Amplitude value to 0.2.

22. Length needs noise as well. Adding amplitude causes the hairs to become too short. But instead of repainting the map, you can increase Map Offset. Figure 4.66 shows the settings.

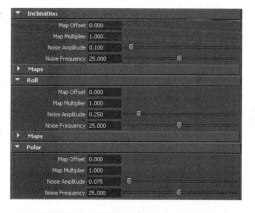

Figure 4.64

Noise parameters for Inclination, Roll, and Polar

Figure 4.65

Noise parameters for Base and Tip Curl

Figure 4.66

Noise parameters for Length

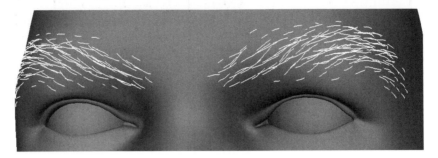

Figure 4.67

Jack's eyebrows

The eyebrows are beginning to look natural (see Figure 4.67). They may appear to be too thick and bushy, but there are still several crucial parameters to change. To check your work so far, you can compare it to eyebrow_v03.ma on the DVD.

23. Using the HSV color wheel, change Base Color using the following settings: H 39.0, S 0.5, and V 0.72.

24. Using the HSV color wheel, change Tip Color using the following settings: H 39.0, S 0.697, and V 0.101.

25. Use Figure 4.68 to set the noise parameters for Base and Tip Color.

26. Change Specular Sharpness to 25 and Specular Color to 0.187. Lowering both of these values keeps the hairs looking dark.

Figure 4.68

Noise parameters for Base and Tip Color

27. Set Base Width and Tip Width to 0.015 and 0.012, respectively. Add 0.005 to each of their Noise Amplitude values.

28. You need to increase Density more than expected, because of how fur is placed. The Density value is for the entire surface and isn't local to the baldness map. Therefore, you need to add fur as though you were covering the entire head. Change Density to 80,000 (see Figure 4.69).

Figure 4.69

Render of the eyebrows

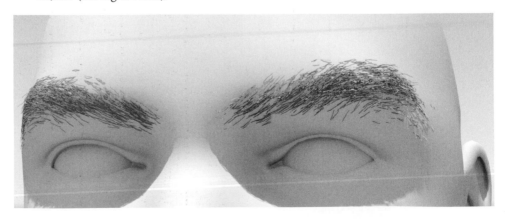

The fur appears thick and bristly—not what you're looking for. Eyebrow hair has a softness to it. Jack's hair had the same problem in Chapter 3, "Hair."

29. Opacity plays a huge part in the look of fur and hair. To achieve a lighter, softer look, change Base Opacity to 0.7 and Tip Opacity to 0.5. In addition, add a little noise (see Figure 4.70).

Figure 4.70

Noise parameters for Base and Tip Opacity

Another render shows that the eyebrows have improved greatly. They now have that soft look (see Figure 4.71).

Figure 4.71

Render of the eyebrows

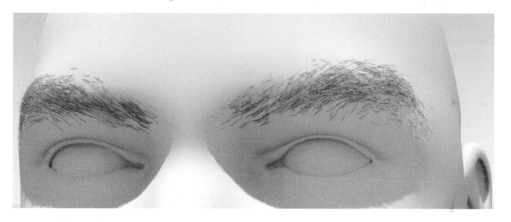

To check your work so far, you can compare it to `eyebrow_v04.ma` on the DVD.

Project: Eyelashes

The last bit of facial hair is the eyelashes. Their construction is similar to that of eyebrows, although they require more painted attribute maps. For the most part, building eyelashes is identical to building the eyebrows. You can follow steps 2 through 12 from the previous project to create the baldness maps (see Figure 4.72). Here are a few tips to consider as you build the rest of the eyelashes:

1. Using a U and V Sample of 512, paint a rough length map. Reduce the eyelash length around both corners of the eye. Leave the middle lashes at their full length. There is no reason to try to paint a final

Figure 4.72

The baldness map is painted.

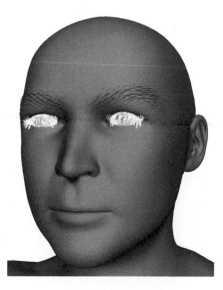

map for the length this soon—you need to establish the direction and curl before the length can be realized. Painting the length now helps reduce confusion from overlapping fur (see Figure 4.73).

2. Eyelashes have a unique curl, making this attribute more valuable than the others. Eyelashes curl up on the top eyelid and down on the bottom eyelid. You can achieve this look solely with the Curl attributes, eliminating the need for Inclination. You need to paint Base and Tip Curl to get the eyelashes to curl in opposing directions. You may have to go back and forth between the Polar attribute to get the proper curl. Figure 4.74 shows the curl without modifying Polar.

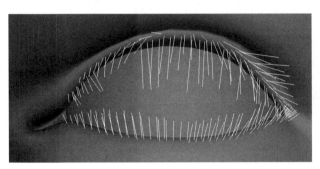

Figure 4.73

The eyelashes after the length has been painted

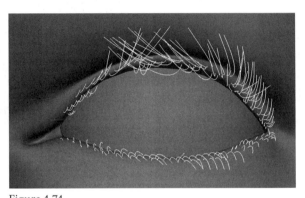

Figure 4.74

Base and Tip Curl have been painted.

3. Take your time with Polar. Each eyelash should be perpendicular to the geometry. Getting the angle right is important; that way, light hits the eyelashes properly (see Figure 4.75).

Figure 4.75

The eyelashes after Polar has been painted

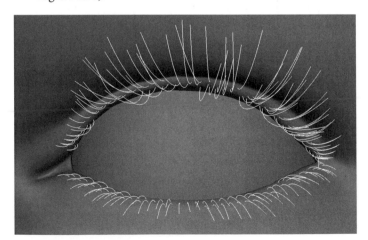

4. Eyelashes tend to clump together in an irregular manner. The Clump attribute pulls the hairs in, toward the eyeball, ruining their placement. Instead, add noise to Roll to create an artificial clumping look (see Figure 4.76).

5. Move the lights around so the eyelashes are no longer in shadow. Doing so helps define the color and specular attributes. Figure 4.77 shows the completed eyelashes.

All the attribute maps are compiled into one Photoshop file. This makes it easier to keep the maps organized and to copy values from one map to the other. You can look at `facialHair.PSD` from the `Chapter4\Projects\sourceimages` folder on the DVD.

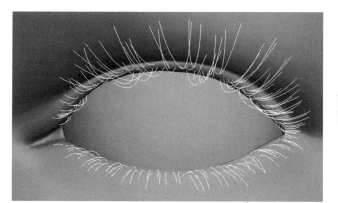

Figure 4.76
Add noise to Roll to clump the eyelashes together.

Figure 4.77
Jack's eyelashes

Summary

Jack's hair is finished. You can see the final results in Figure 4.78. Keep in mind that the current lighting setup is simple and isn't meant to produce photorealistic results; the point so far is to illuminate the hair to identify any problems or mistakes.

To check your work so far, you can compare it to `facialHair_v01.ma` on the DVD.

Figure 4.78

Jack and all his hair

Maya Color Gallery

This gallery features some of the book's images that benefit from being shown in color. Several images in this gallery come from Chapter 8, "Composition." The focus of these images is on the use of subsurface scattering on the character's skin. Each map used with the subsurface scattering shader is shown, as well as the rendered results on the character. To see more of the images from the book in color, please see the companion DVD.

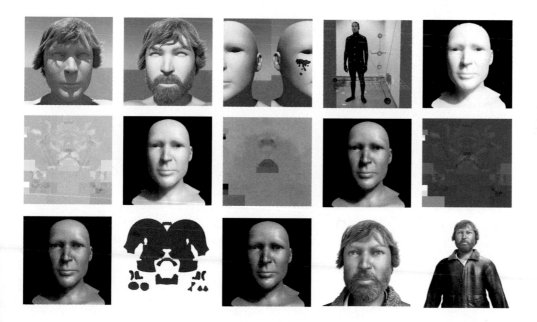

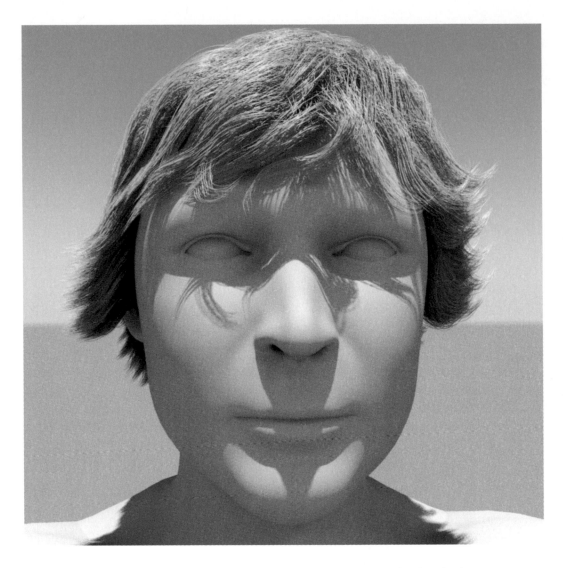

The hair that you create in Chapter 3, "Hair," has been cut, styled, and colored. This image shows the hair in its completed state rendered with mental ray.

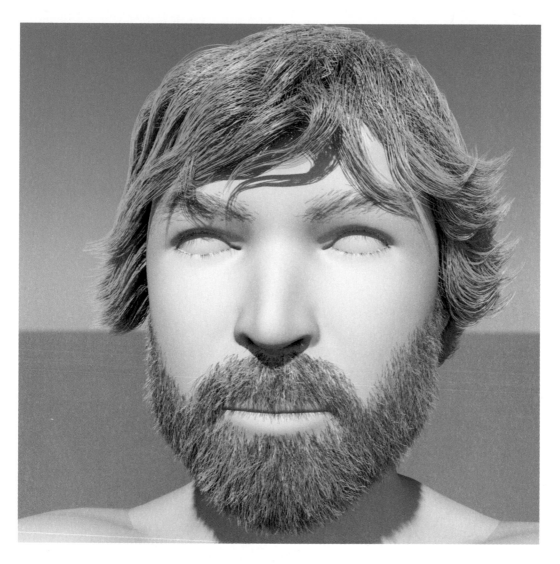

You use fur in Chapter 4, "Fur," to create eyelashes, eyebrows, and a beard.

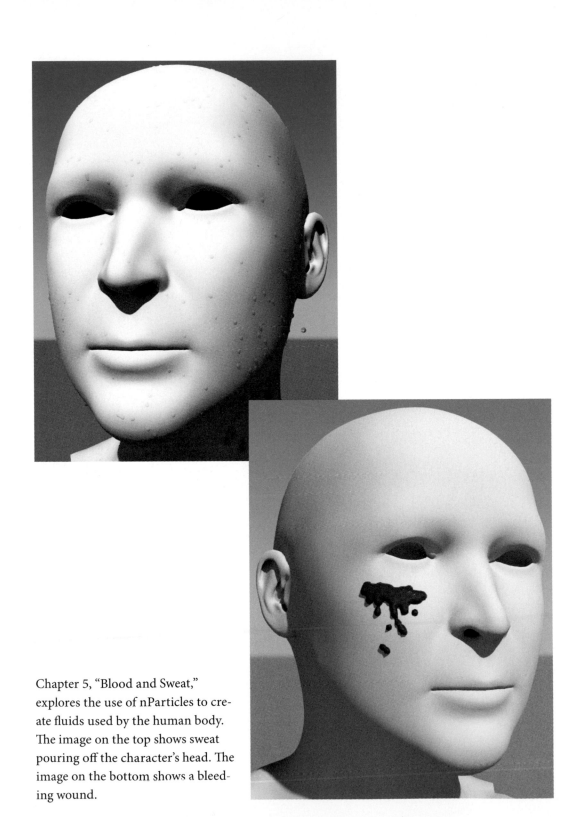

Chapter 5, "Blood and Sweat," explores the use of nParticles to create fluids used by the human body. The image on the top shows sweat pouring off the character's head. The image on the bottom shows a bleeding wound.

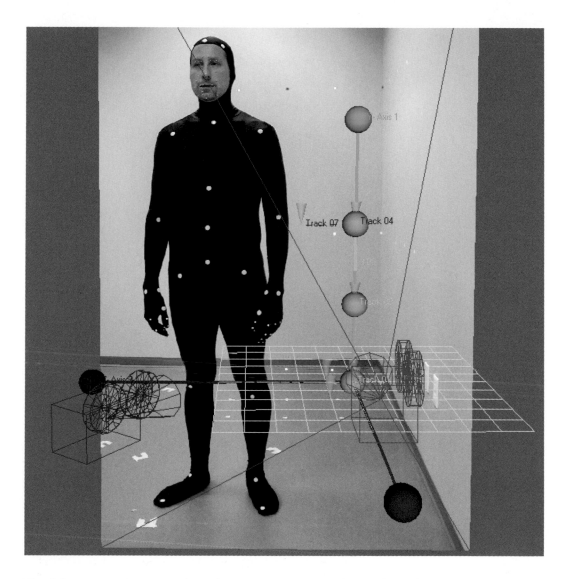

The ability to capture an actor's performance is an essential part of creating a photorealistic character. Chapter 7, "Performance Capture," concentrates on tracking an actor's performance with the help of Autodesk's MatchMover. In this image, a coordinate system has been created using the markers in the footage. The X, Y, and Z axes are color-coded using the same scheme as Maya.

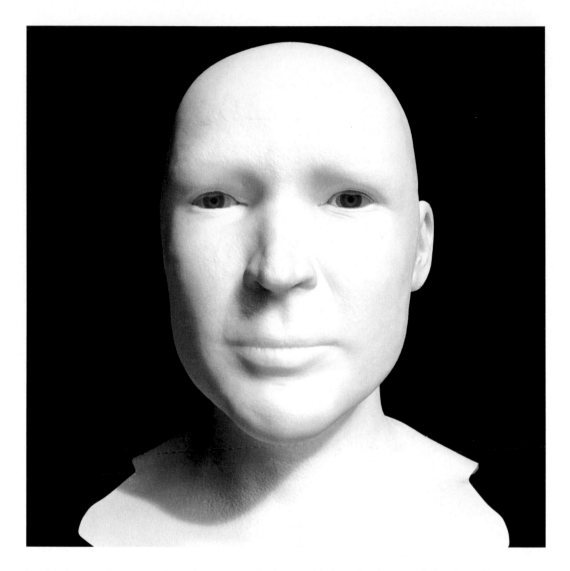

In this image, the misss_fast_skin_maya shader is added to the character's head. Scale Conversion is set to 304.0. Epidermal Scatter Radius and Subdermal Scatter Radius are set to 6.0 and 10.0, respectively. The only maps that have been added at this point are the displacement and bump maps.

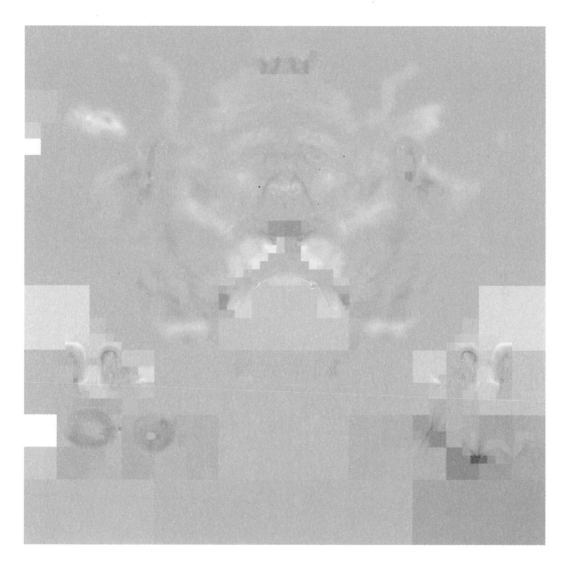

The overall color map includes very few red tones. It should look pale and deathly. Its purpose is to block light coming from the lower layers.

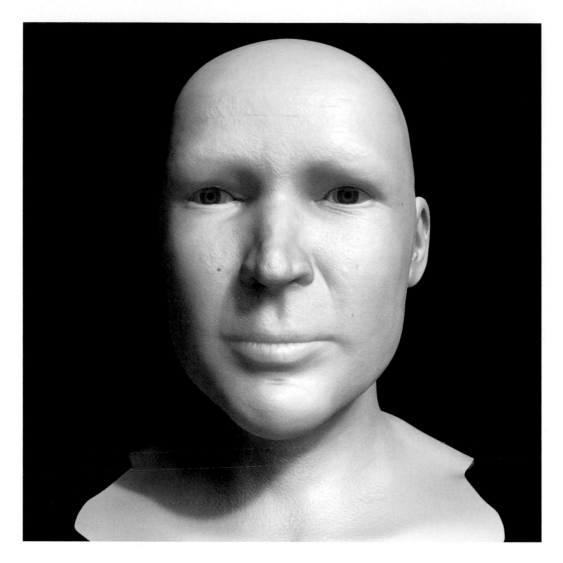

Here are the rendered results of the overall map.

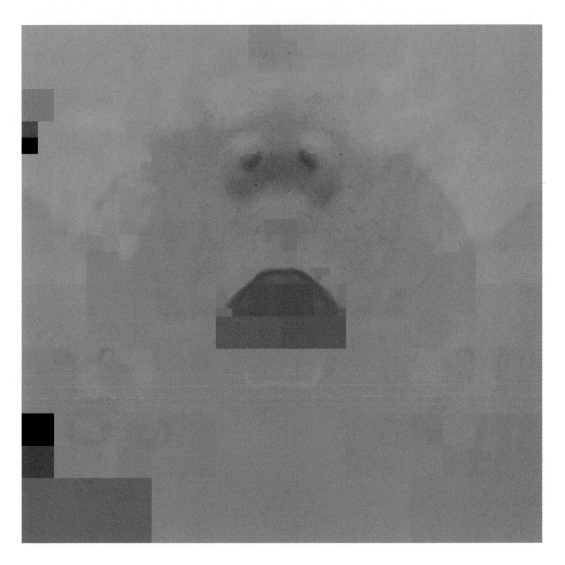

This image shows the epidermal and diffuse maps. The epidermal map is also mapped to the diffuse map. Together, they provide most of the color information in the final render.

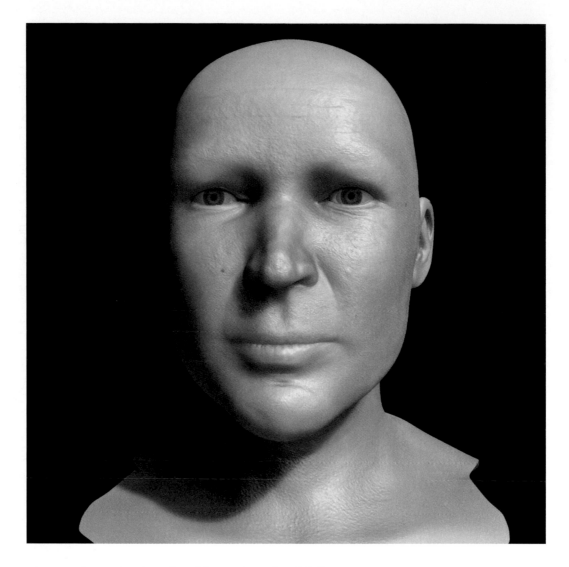

Here are the rendered results of the epidermal and diffuse maps.

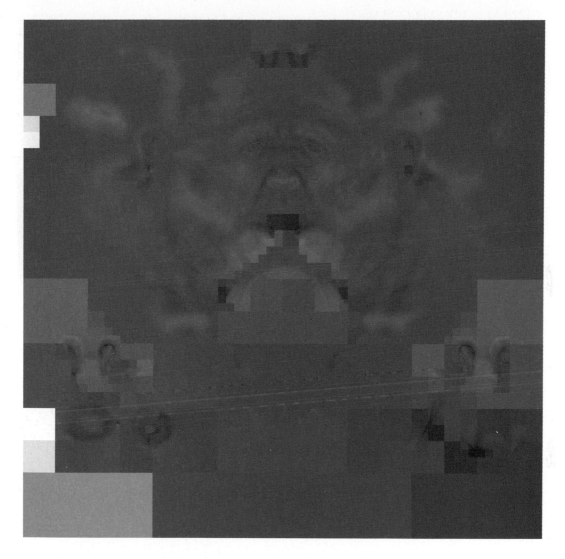

This image shows the subdermal map.

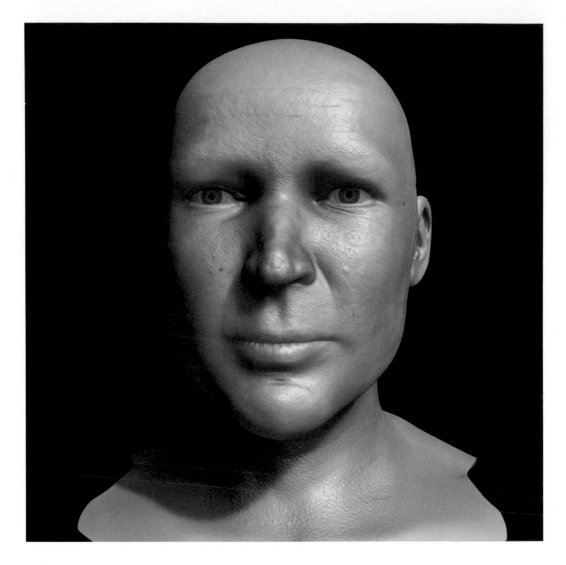

And these are the rendered results of the subdermal map.

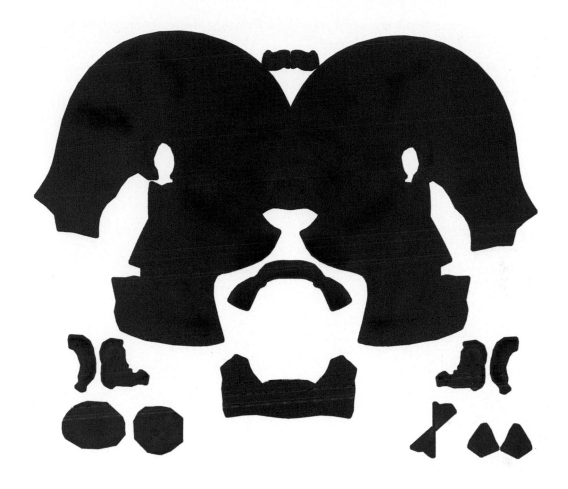

Finally, this image shows the backscatter map.

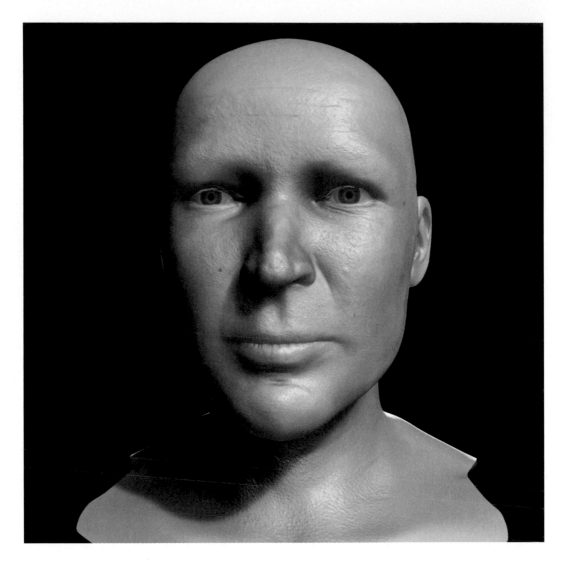

Here are the rendered results of the backscatter map. A ray-traced spotlight has been added behind Jack's left ear to make the backscatter effect visible: you can see the light bleeding through the thin areas of the skin.

This image is a close-up shot of the character. His subsurface scattering shader is complete, along with all of his hair.

And here is a wide shot of the completed version of the character.

Blood and Sweat

The human body produces a variety of substances that contribute to photorealism, beyond hair cells. Blood, sweat, tears, and saliva are essential ingredients to the human recipe. These fluids can often be created with texture. Although effective, textures can be limiting. This chapter explores methods for creating blood and sweat using a three-dimensional approach. The chapter represents a departure from the rest of the book in that the projects here aren't essential to the building of your character; they're bonus effects that your production may or may not require.

In this chapter you will learn to:

- **Create Sweat**
- **Create Blood**

Sweat

Sweat isn't something your character requires all the time. Therefore your character shouldn't have this functionality built into it. It can be easily added for specific shots and doesn't require the character to have any special considerations.

Sweat is released from pores in the skin in an effort to cool the body. As it builds, it eventually takes on enough mass to fall or drip down the skin. For the most part, sweat is water and looks as such. It sometimes takes on a slightly milky color from various oils or lotions put on the skin.

Project: Sweat, Part 1

Jack has been stripped down to his head. Everything that has been done up to this point has been removed for simplicity. In this part of the project, you'll define areas of the face to emit nParticles that will ultimately represent sweat. A nucleus solver, nucleus1, is already in the scene, and its scale is set 0.304. The nParticles you'll create in this project are automatically connected to nucleus1. Follow these steps:

1. Open the scene file sweat_v01.ma. The scene contains Jack's head geometry.

2. Select head1, and choose nParticles → Create nParticles → Emit From Object.

3. Change the emitter type to Surface, and click Create. Jack's head now emits nParticles (see Figure 5.1).

Figure 5.1

nParticles are emitted from the head geometry.

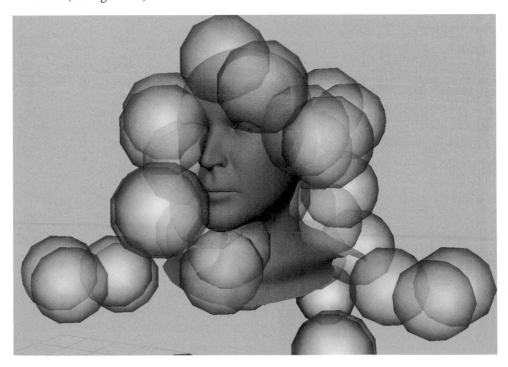

4. Immediately you can see that the nParticles are too large. Select nParticle1, and open its Attribute Editor. In the Particle Size section, change Radius to 0.01 (see Figure 5.2).

5. To get the nParticles to stick to Jack's head, you first need to make his geometry an nRigid body. Then the nParticles will by default collide against it. Select head1, and choose nMesh → Create Passive Collider.

    Watching the simulation shows that the nParticles are definitely colliding with the head geometry. However, they're being trapped inside the head and falling out through Jack's neck opening (see Figure 5.3).

6. The problem is twofold. First, choose nRigid1. Open its Attribute Editor, and find the Quality Settings section. The Trapped Check option is selected, but it has no force. Change the Push Out attribute to 1.0. Playing the simulation reveals that nothing has changed.

    The reason stems from the nParticles colliding with the geometry. Because they're colliding and produced from the same surface, they're immediately being deflected, forcing them into the geometry's interior. You can fix this by increasing Push Out Radius. By default, Push Out Radius is set to 0.011; this number works for the intended end result. To see its effects immediately, increase it to a minimum of .02, which is double the radius of the nParticle (see Figure 5.4).

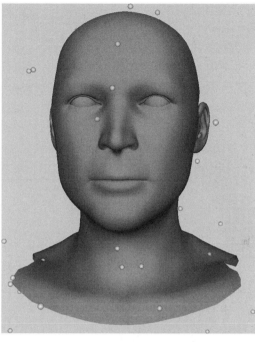

Figure 5.2

The nParticles size is now appropriate.

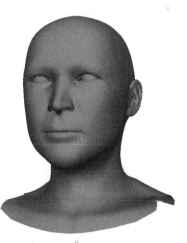

Figure 5.3

The nParticles are colliding inside the head.

Return the value to .011 or leave it at .02. Either value produces the same result.

7. The other part of the solution is to change the nParticle's collision width. You change Collide Width Scale instead of relying on Push Out Radius because the nParticles need to appear flat with the geometry instead of sitting on top of it. Figure 5.5 shows the benefit of using a smaller Collide Width Scale.

    Select nParticle1, and open its Attribute Editor. Open the Collisions section, and set Collide Width Scale to 0.2. Playing the simulation shows that the nParticles are on the outside of the geometry (see Figure 5.6).

To check your work so far, you can compare it to sweat_v02.ma on the DVD.

The nParticles are getting close to the proper motion. But they're traveling too fast—they should stubbornly roll down the face. To get the nParticles to closely follow the contours of Jack's face at the desired speed, you can use the nParticle's collision settings.

8. Select nParticle1. Open its Attribute Editor and the Collisions section. Change Friction to 0.65. This helps a little, but the effects aren't great.

9. Change Collide Strength to 0.15. Lowering Collide Strength on the nRigid causes the nParticles to sink deeper into the geometry's surface. It also appears to have a huge impact on their speed. However, it's the combined collaboration of Friction and Collide Strength that produces the results (see Figure 5.7).

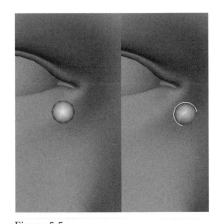

Figure 5.4

The nParticles are no longer colliding with the head interior.

Figure 5.5

A comparison between different Collide Width Scale values

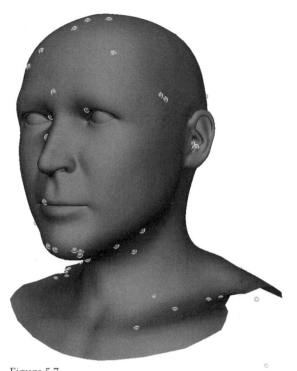

Figure 5.6
The nParticles are outside of the geometry.

Figure 5.7
The nParticles are snug to the surface.

10. At certain points, you want the beads of sweat to drop off the face. You can achieve this by painting collision values on the rigid surface. Select head1, and choose nMesh → Paint Vertex Properties → Collide Strength.

11. Use the Solid brush to paint a value of 0.0 wherever you want the sweat to fall off the face. Typical locations are under the chin, over the brow, and the tip of the nose. Use Figure 5.8 for reference.

PAINTING COLLISION

Painting a vertex map gives you the advantage of speed over using a texture map. It's faster to paint, and painted vertices process more quickly. The sweat simulation isn't very taxing, so you may not notice improved performance. Regardless of whether you use a texture map or a vertex map, you can paint on it while the simulation is running, which will help you greatly in determining how high or low a value is needed to break the nParticles away from the head.

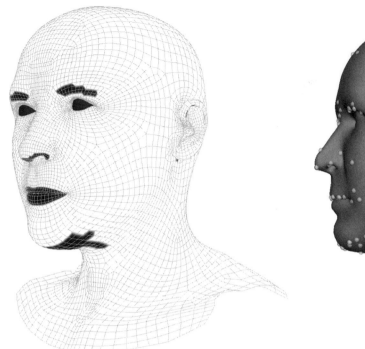

Figure 5.8

The finished Collision Strength map

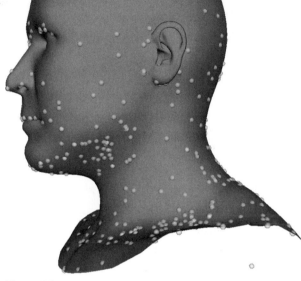

Figure 5.9

The nParticles get stuck around ar0eas painted black.

12. The initial pass on the vertex map isn't enough to cause all the nParticles to fall off at the desired locations (see Figure 5.9). Some get stuck as they lose momentum.

The tricky part about painting the collision properties is figuring out how many vertices you need to paint black to get the nParticle to detach. The nParticles must come within the range of the vertex in order to be affected. This usually results in painting more than you think is necessary (see Figure 5.10).

To check your work so far, you can compare it to sweat_v03.ma on the DVD.

The nParticles are being emitted from areas they shouldn't—for example, from inside the mouth, nose, and eye sockets. You can limit the locations from which they're emitted by applying an emission map to the nParticle emitter. There isn't a paint tool specifically for painting emission maps; you can use the 3D Paint tool, instead.

13. Before you can paint a texture, all the head UVs need to be arranged within the 0 to 1 texture space. Select head1, and open the UV Texture Editor.

14. The UVs are currently arranged in two different sections, as shown in Figure 5.11. Textures are automatically tiled in Maya; therefore, if the UVs are located outside of the 0 to 1 texture space, they receive the same texture as if they were in the 0 to 1 texture space.

    Select all the faces, and choose Create UVs → Copy UVs To UV Set → Copy Into New UV Set.

15. Name the UV set **sweat**, and click Apply And Close (see Figure 5.12).

16. With all the faces still selected, choose Polygons → Normalize in the UV Texture Editor. Use the settings from Figure 5.13, and then click Apply And Close.

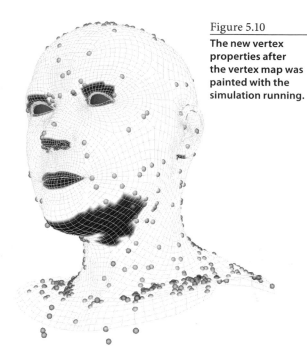

Figure 5.10

The new vertex properties after the vertex map was painted with the simulation running.

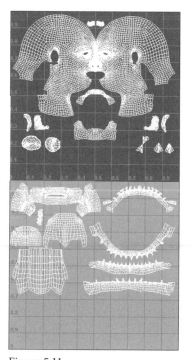

Figure 5.11

The current arrangement for the head UVs

Figure 5.12

Copy Current UV Set Options dialog box

Figure 5.13

Normalize UVs Options dialog box

17. Scale the UVs slightly to move them away from the border. The UVs now fit inside the 0 to 1 texture space (see Figure 5.14).

Figure 5.14

The new arrangement for the head UVs

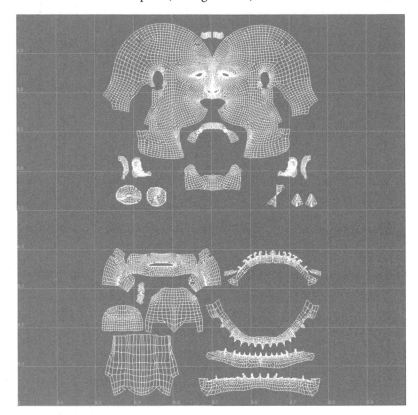

18. You can now paint the emission map. Select head1, and choose Texturing → 3D Paint Tool.

19. The head geometry doesn't have a texture assigned to it, so Maya gives you a warning message. In the 3D Paint tool settings, click Assign/Edit Textures in the File Textures section. Use Figure 5.15 for the options.

20. Set Flood Color to black, and click Flood Paint.

21. Use the Solid brush and a color value of 1.0 to paint the areas that should emit sweat. Flooding the surface with black, instead of the predominantly painted white, allows you to avoid painting the obscured mouth interior. Figure 5.16 shows the painted areas.

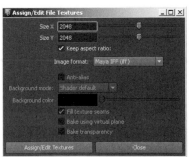

Figure 5.15

Assign/Edit Textures options

22. When you're finished painting, click the Save Textures button in the File Texture section.

23. Find the texture in your 3DPaintTextures folder. Copy the image to your sourceimages directory, and rename it sweatMap.iff.

24. You no longer need the texture connected to the head. In the Hypershade, open the Attribute Editor for body_MAT. Right-click the Color attribute, and choose Break Connection from the pop-up menu.

25. Select emitter1, and open its Attribute Editor. In the Texture Emission Attributes section, click the Create Render Node icon at the end of the Texture Rate attribute. Add a file texture.

26. Load your saved sweatMap.iff file from the sourceimages folder or from the Chapter5\Projects\sourceimages folder on the DVD.

27. Return to the Texture Emission Attributes section for emitter1. Select Enable Texture Rate, and choose Sweat from the UV Set drop-down menu. Figure 5.17 shows the settings.

28. Play the simulation to see the results. Make sure the sweat is emitting where it's supposed to and falling when it should.

   To check your work so far, you can compare it to sweat_v04.ma on the DVD.

Figure 5.16

The black areas represent non-emitting regions.

Figure 5.17

Texture Emission Attributes

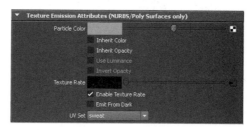

Project: Sweat, Part 2

Sweat doesn't begin as a dripping droplet. Moisture builds into a drop until its weight causes it to fall. This part of the project demonstrates increasing the radius of the nParticle over its age. In addition, you'll add a mia material to the sweat to give it its rendered look. Here are the steps:

1. Open the scene file sweat_v04.ma. Select nParticle1, and open its Attribute Editor.

2. Open the Particle Size section and then the Radius Scale section. Change Radius Scale Input to Age.

3. You can now use the Radius Scale graph to change the nParticle's radius over its age. The first position is its start position. Use Figure 5.18 to set the graph and other values.

Input Max alters the Radius Scale Input value. Increasing it to 5.0 lengthens the time that the nParticle ages. Each integer added is a whole unit of time. The Time

Figure 5.18

Settings for Radius Scale

settings for the scene are 30 frames per second (fps); this translates to the nParticle reaching its maximum radius around frame 150. However, moving the last position on the graph up to 0.5 causes the maximum radius to be reached around frame 75 (see Figure 5.19).

4. With the nParticles starting from nothing, they fall from the surface quickly. They need time to grow before they slide down the face. In the Collisions section, increase Friction to 2.0 (see Figure 5.20).

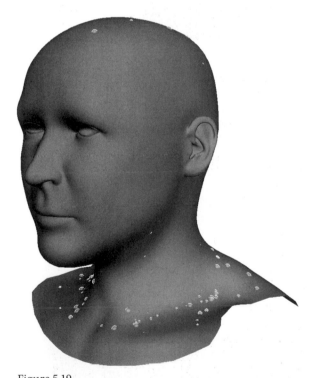

Figure 5.19

The nParticles increase in size over their age.

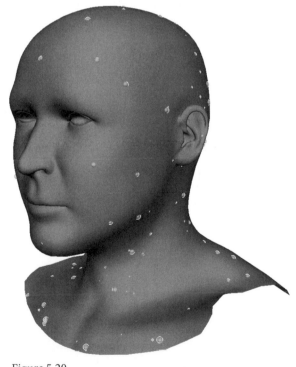

Figure 5.20

Increasing Friction prevents the nParticles from sliding.

5. You want the sweat beads to begin sliding down the face when they fully mature. Altering the Friction Scale graph over the age of the nParticle makes this work. Use the settings from Figure 5.21.

Figure 5.21
The Friction Scale settings

The sweat beads start to slide when the Friction is at 0.65. To get the Friction value to 0.65, set the last position on the Friction Scale graph to 0.325. This acts as a multiplier against the 2.0 Friction value set in the Collisions Sections. . Furthermore, adding a little Friction Randomize value causes some of the nParticles to slide before they're fully grown (see Figure 5.22).

To check your work so far, you can compare it to sweat_v05.ma on the DVD.

6. The sweat needs an attribute to control the amount of sweating. Select head1.

7. In the Channel Box, choose Edit → Add Attribute.

8. The Add Attribute option dialog box opens. Use Figure 5.23 for the settings. Click OK when you're finished, to close the options window.

9. The attribute is added to the head geometry. You now need to connect it to the nParticle emitter. With head1 still selected, choose Window→ General Editors→ Connection Editor. The attributes for head1 are preloaded in the Output section of the Connection Editor.

10. Choose emitter1 from the Outliner.

11. Click Reload Right in the Connection Editor to load the emitter's attributes for the Inputs section.

12. Select SweatRate at the bottom of the left column and Rate midway down the right column (see Figure 5.24). The connection is made; you can close the Connection Editor.

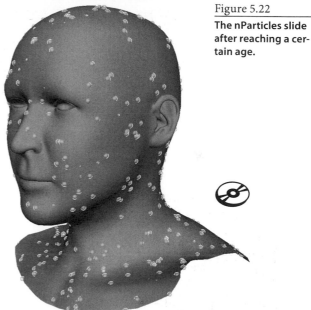

Figure 5.22
The nParticles slide after reaching a certain age.

Figure 5.23
The Add Attribute dialog box

Figure 5.24

Connection Editor

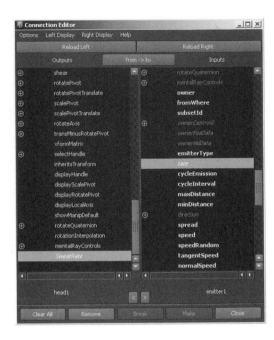

13. Select head1 to test the control. Enter **1000** for SweatRate, and play the simulation. By frame 90, Jack is really sweaty (see Figure 5.25).

14. Finally, you need to add a material to the nParticles. Open the Hypershade.

Figure 5.25

Jack at frame 90

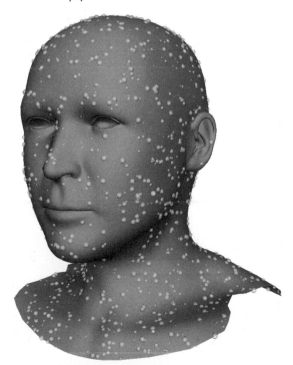

15. Choose Create → Mental Ray Materials → mia_Material.

16. In the mia material's Attribute Editor, choose the Water preset to replace the existing settings.

17. You need to change three settings for the mia material: Diffuse Color, which is white; Diffuse Weight; and Transparency. Use Figure 5.26 to confirm the settings.

    Changing Color and Weight helps give the sweat a slightly milky appearance.

18. Select nParticle1. In the Hypershade, right-click over Mia Material, and choose Assign Material To Selection from the marking menu.

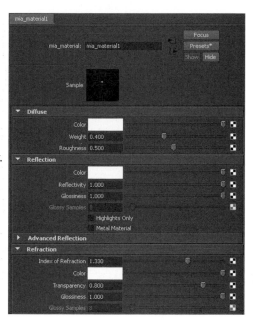

Figure 5.26

Settings for the mia material

The sweat is complete. You can see the finished version in Figure 5.27. To check your work so far, you can compare it to sweat v06.ma on the DVD.

Figure 5.27

The rendered version of the sweat

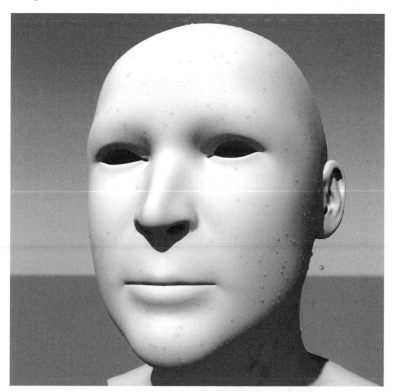

Blood

Computer-generated characters aren't always bleeding. In fact, they rarely ever bleed. Until a few years ago, CG characters were either creatures or part of family entertainment. Dramatic movies have recently progressed into an area where the leading role or pivotal character may be computer generated. This growing trend undoubtedly will call on characters to bleed.

As the saying goes, blood is thicker than water. For computer-generated blood, you need to have a simulation that builds particles from nothing, similar to how you created sweat in the previous project; then, the particles should drip in random streams. The blood needs to stay thick with nParticles to leave a trail.

Project: Blood Drip, Part 1

Blood is similar to sweat, but its consistency is thicker. Like sweat, blood can be created quite well with texture alone. The following project takes you through the process of creating blood that can be interacted with three dimensionally. The pipeline for creating blood is similar to that for sweat, but you convert the nParticles to geometry for an improved rendering appearance. A nucleus node is already in the scene file. Follow these steps:

1. Open the scene file blood_v01.ma. The scene contains Jack's head geometry, stripped of all its elements for simplicity's sake.

2. Select head1, and choose Texturing → 3D Paint Tool.

3. Click Assign/Edit Textures in the File Textures section of the 3D Paint tool options. Use Figure 5.28 for the texture settings.

4. Flood the surface with black, and change the paint's color to white. Use Figure 5.29 for the settings.

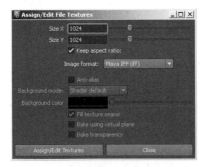

Figure 5.28
Assign/Edit File Textures options

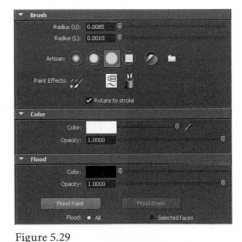

Figure 5.29
3D Paint tool settings

5. Make sure Reflection is turned off, and paint a stroke of varying width across Jack's right cheek. The stroke symbolizes a large open wound. Use Figure 5.30 for reference.

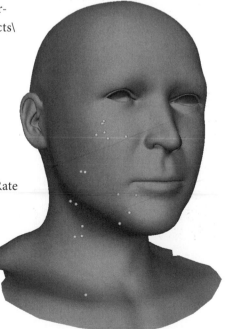

Figure 5.30
The painted wound

6. Click Save Textures in the File Textures section of the 3D Paint tool options.

7. Copy the texture from your project directory's 3dPaintTextures folder, and move it to your sourceimages folder. Rename the image **wound.iff**.

8. Select the body_MAT material, and break the texture connection to the Color channel.

9. Select head1, and choose nParticles → Create nParticles → Emit From Object.

10. Change Emitter Type to Surface. Click Create.

11. Select emitter1, and open its Attribute Editor.

12. Choose Create Texture Node for Texture Rate in the Texture Emission Attributes section.

13. Load the saved wound.iff file from your sourceimages folder or from the Chapter5\Projects\sourceimages folder on the DVD.

14. Return to the Texture Emission Attributes section for emitter1. Select Enable Texture Rate. You can leave UV set to Use Current UV set because the map uses the default set (map1).

15. Emitting from such a small area of the surface requires a large emission rate. Change Rate (Particles/Sec) to 1,000,000.

16. Select nParticle1, and open its Attribute Editor. Change Radius to 0.005 (see Figure 5.31).

    To check your work so far, you can compare it to blood_v02.ma on the DVD.

Figure 5.31
nParticles being emitted from the wound

17. Select head1, and choose nMesh → Create Passive Body. Playing the simulation reveals that the nParticles are trapped inside the head, just as the sweat was earlier in the chapter (see Figure 5.32).

Figure 5.32

The nParticles are trapped inside the head geometry.

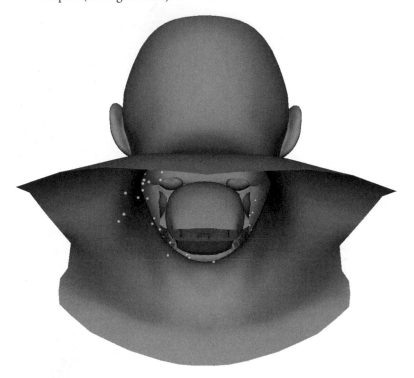

18. Select nRigid1, and open its Attribute Editor. In the Quality Settings section, change the parameters to match Figure 5.33.

19. Select nParticle1, and open its Attribute Editor.

20. Use Figure 5.34 to change the parameters in the Collisions section.

Figure 5.33
Quality Settings

Figure 5.34
Collision settings

Playing the simulation shows the nParticles coagulating at the emission point (see Figure 5.35).You want the blood to pool before it drips.

21. Use Figure 5.36 to establish the Friction Scale over the age of the nParticle. As the nParticle matures, the friction should decrease, causing blood to roll down the face. Set the first position on the graph to 0.4.

    A little randomness helps prevent all the blood from dripping at once. By frame 90, the nParticles should be bleeding (see Figure 5.37).

22. To give the wound a chance to bleed, change Radius Scale, using the settings from Figure 5.38.

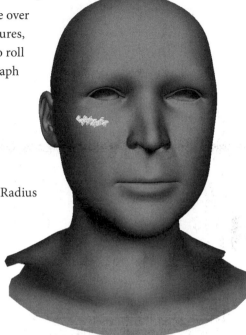

Figure 5.35
The nParticles coagulate.

Figure 5.36
The Friction Scale settings.

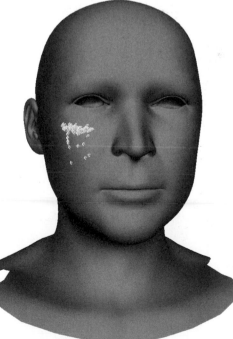

Figure 5.37
The wound starts to bleed before frame 90.

Figure 5.38
Radius Scale settings

The nParticles start small and expand rapidly, like blood rising to the surface (see Figure 5.39).

To check your work so far, you can compare it to blood_v03.ma on the DVD.

23. Currently, the emitter is a steady stream. Blood is pumped by the heart at regular intervals. To simulate this effect, you can add an expression to Emission Rate. Select emitter1. Open its Attribute Editor, and right-click Rate(Particles/Sec). Choose Create New Expression from the pop-up menu.

24. Add the following expression, and then click Create:

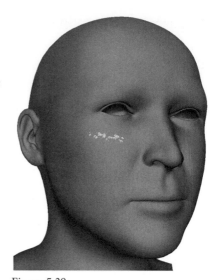

Figure 5.39

The nParticles start small and then grow.

```
emitter1.rate=abs(sin(frame*.01)*1000000)+ 10000;
```

The sin function, or sine wave, is made up of a frequency, an amplitude, and an offset. It creates a steady wave of high and low values. The frequency (frame multiplied by 0.01) determines the distance between waves. Multiplying the frequency by one million gives the wave's amplitude, stating that the highest and lowest points of the wave are positive and negative one million, respectively. You don't want the emitter to go into a negative value—this obviously would prevent nParticles from being emitted until the wave returned to a positive value. Surrounding the frequency and amplitude is the abs function, or absolute. It forces the sine wave to always be positive by causing it to stop at 0.0. You want the emitter to always be emitting something, to keep the blood flowing; therefore, you add 10,000 to the end, giving the sine wave an offset. The nParticles are now emitted at specified intervals (see Figure 5.40).

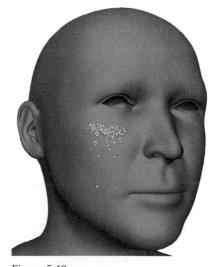

Figure 5.40

The nParticles bleed based on the sine wave expression.

Project: Blood Drip, Part 2

The blood moves properly but doesn't look right yet. The next part of the project converts the nParticles to geometry and a material for rendering:

1. Open the scene file blood_v01.ma. The nParticles are almost ready to be converted into geometry. But an inspection of the simulation reveals a leak of nParticles inside the geometry (see Figure 5.41).

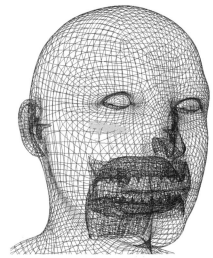

Figure 5.41

The nParticles are leaking inside Jack's head.

The leak is from the nParticles being emitted from overlapping UVs. Again, you need to create a separate UV set specifically for the blood. Select head1, and open the UV Texture Editor.

2. Make sure map1 is the current UV set. Select all the faces within the normalized texture space.

3. Choose Create UVs → Copy UVs To UV Set → Copy Into New UV Set.

4. Name the UV set **wound**, and click Apply And Close (see Figure 5.42).

5. Select emitter1, and open its Attribute Editor. Change its UV set to wound (see Figure 5.43). Playing the simulation again shows that the leak is fixed.

Figure 5.42

Copy Current UV Set Options

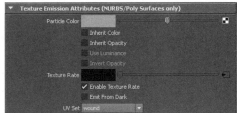

Figure 5.43

Texture Emission Attributes

To check your work so far, you can compare it to blood_v04.ma on the DVD.

6. You can now convert the nParticles. Select nParticle1.

7. Choose Modify → Convert → nParticles To Polygons. polySurface1 is created. Change its name to **bloodGeo**.

8. When nParticles are converted to polygons, their shape node is automatically set to Intermediate Object in the Object Display section (see Figure 5.44).

Figure 5.44

The Object Display section of the nParticles' shape node

Open the shape node's Attribute Editor, and deselect this option to make the nParticles visible.

9. The nParticles ultimately need to be hidden, but it's more advantageous to add them to a layer while you refine the converted geometry. With nParticle1 selected, add it to a layer, and rename the layer **NPARTICLE_BLOOD**.

10. Select bloodGeo, and add it to a layer named **BLOOD_GEO**.

11. Select nParticle1, and open its Attribute Editor. Find the Output Mesh section; these parameters directly affect how the blood geometry is created. Play the simulation to frame 60. With the current settings, no geometry is being created. To make the geometry show up, change Blobby Radius Scale to 200 and Mesh Triangle Size to 0.01 (see Figure 5.45).

12. The blood geometry is obviously too large. The nParticles are small in size, requiring an equivalently small triangle size on the mesh. You should set Mesh Triangle Size in small increments to avoid overloading your system. Decrease it to 0.006.

13. The mesh doesn't change: it's being limited by Max Triangle Resolution. Change Max Triangle Resolution to 500 (see Figure 5.46).

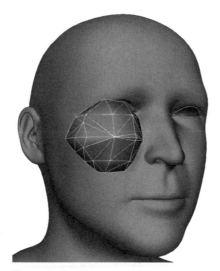

Figure 5.45
The blood geometry is now being created.

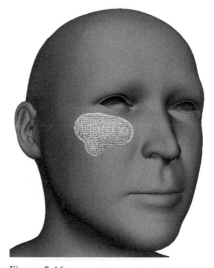

Figure 5.46
The number of triangles in the blood mesh has increased dramatically.

14. You can now alter the size and smoothness of the mesh by altering Threshold and Blobby Radius Scale. Use Figure 5.47 to make the necessary changes.

    In addition, changing Mesh Method helps create a smooth-looking surface (see Figure 5.48).

Figure 5.47

Output Mesh settings

15. The nParticles separate too quickly as they drip down the character's face. Add 0.2 to the Drag parameter on the nParticle node to help slow them down. Figure 5.49 shows the final mesh at frame 90.

OUTPUT MESH PLAYBACK

The output mesh can take a while to process. When you're testing the mesh's look, it's faster to hide the mesh through its layer and play the simulation with the nParticles visible. At the intended frame, you can turn off the visibility for the nParticle layer and the turn on the visibility for the mesh layer. The mesh updates accordingly.

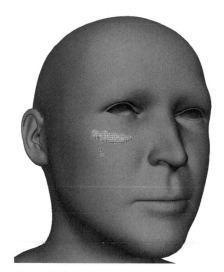

Figure 5.48

The results of the new Output Mesh settings

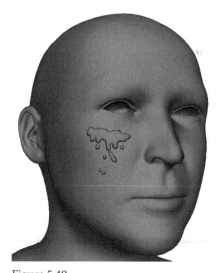

Figure 5.49

The mesh at frame 90

To check your work so far, you can compare it to `blood_v05.ma` on the DVD.

16. With the mesh complete, you can apply a shader to it. Play the simulation to frame 90. Make sure the mesh is visible, and open the Hypershade.

17. Choose Create → Mental Ray Materials → mia_Material.

18. In the mia material's Attribute Editor, choose Glossy Plastic preset to replace the existing settings.

19. Change the color in the Diffuse section using the settings in Figure 5.50.

20. Use Figure 5.51 for the rest of the mia material settings.

Figure 5.50
Diffuse color settings

Figure 5.51
Diffuse and Reflection settings

The blood is finished. The final look is shown in Figure 5.52.

 To check your work, you can compare it to `blood_v06.ma` on the DVD.

Figure 5.52
The rendered blood

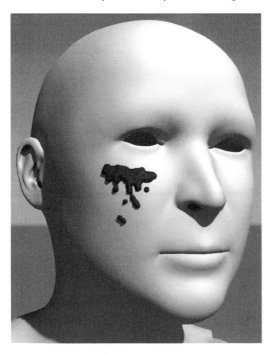

Summary

nParticles are incredibly useful for all types of liquid simulation. They can be emitted from a surface or surface texture and collide with almost anything. In addition to blood and sweat, you can adapt the settings and procedures outlined in this chapter to create saliva, drool, tears, and more.

CHAPTER 6

Clothing

Clothing is difficult to simulate. There is no other way to put it. It's always on the move; it reacts to everything; and it comes in hundreds of different shapes, sizes, and styles. To make matters worse, its motion is primarily dependent on other objects. Translating all this to the digital world requires specifically designed, high-resolution geometry. In this chapter, you'll learn how to build geometry based on clothing type and simulate it to follow fast-moving motion capture.

In this chapter you will learn to:

- **Tailor geometry to fit your character**

- **Build an nCloth Shirt**

- **Build an nCloth pair of pants**

- **Build and nCloth Jacket**

- **Simulate a complete outfit on an animated character**

nCloth Geometry

Figure 6.1

**Uniform geometry
on the right,
as opposed to
unevenly spaced
geometry on
the left**

All the geometry needed for Jack's outfit has been roughed out. It's important to start with basic models. You don't need to add wrinkles, pockets, or other details until the model is fitted to the character through simulation. You'll do most of the critical work and decision making by testing the geometry with nCloth. Converting it back and forth is an essential part of the process to ensure that the geometry functions properly.

You need to understand two principals about building geometry for clothing simulation. The first is polygon uniformity. The more consistent you make the area your faces occupy, the better your simulation. Having irregularly sized polygons alters the integrity of the garment (see Figure 6.1).

Think of each polygon as weighing one pound. When all the polygons are the same size, their weight on top of each other is distributed evenly. If one of the polygons is larger than the others, the weight pushes out unevenly, forcing the polygons to move differently.

The second principal of building geometry for clothing simulation is that adding more geometry is like adding more fabric. This doesn't mean that increasing the resolution of the surface adds more fabric; instead, it refers to increasing the amount of surface area. Although that seems to go without saying, it's important to grasp the ramifications. By adding more fabric, you control how the garment hangs, bunches, or bags. You can take away fabric to create pleats, darts, and tapers (see Figure 6.2).

Digital Tailoring

Figure 6.2

**A pair of pants with
pleats around the
waistline**

Making 3D clothing is primary about the geometry. Simply converting geometry to nCloth isn't good enough. The greater the effort and thought you put into the construction, the better your simulation.

Above all, your geometry needs to fit your character. Sounds simple and obvious, but there is more to it. Clothing fits people properly because it has the necessary amount of fabric in the proper areas. Too much fabric, and the garment is baggy; too little, and it's skin tight. Just right, and it hangs on the body, accentuating the positive and removing the negative. On the other hand, many people wear improper sizes. This means you must also able to fit your 3D geometry to make it intentionally fit poorly. It's an art as much as a science.

When the geometry fits your character, you can convert it to nCloth or take it a step further by dividing it into panels. Clothing *panels* are the individual pieces of fabric that are sewn together to create a complete garment. Dividing the geometry into panels can help make the geometry deform more realistically. Doing so isn't always necessary, but it can make a real difference. Figure 6.3 shows an exploded view of pants separated into individual panels.

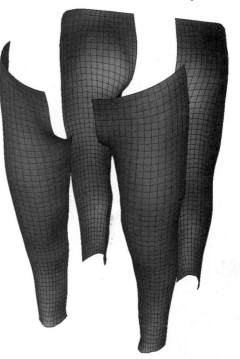

Figure 6.3

A pair of pants divided into panels

Texturing

Textures are immensely important to the garment. To achieve the highest level of photorealism, you should use normal and displacement maps. Normal maps are important for clothing because of the small detail that most clothing has. You can use these maps for stitching and thread patterns. Normal maps don't have to be created through modeling; you can generate extreme detail like thread in Photoshop. You shouldn't use normal maps for things like buttons or seams, which are more prominent. Always model buttons, and create seams with displacement maps.

nCloth supports another type of map called a *wrinkle map*, which is similar to a displacement map. It causes the geometry to be displaced during simulation based on grayscale values. A slider lets you adjust the amount of displacement; the value can be positive or negative. Figure 6.4 shows the settings from the Attribute Editor.

Figure 6.4

Wrinkle map options

Jack's Outfit

Jack is dressed in field pants, a safari shirt, and a bomber jacket. These are shown respectively in Figure 6.5, Figure 6.6, and Figure 6.7.

Figure 6.5

Jack's shirt

Figure 6.6

Jack's pants

Figure 6.7

Jack's jacket

If possible, it's best to purchase the character's clothes—nothing is a substitute for the real thing. Having the clothing gives you the ability to see how they're made, the way they move, and the strength of the materials. In addition, real garments make unbeatable references for painting textures.

Project: Tailoring

Even though you've finished modeling the geometry, you still have to make it fit the character. This may seem redundant, but whatever you model invariably needs alterations. In this project, you'll take up Jack's pants in the crotch and reduce the overall surface area. It's a good idea to start with your character's pants. Establishing the pants first makes it easier to add a shirt over them or tuck in the shirt. Follow these steps:

1. Open the pants_v01.ma scene from the chapter6\ scenes folder on the DVD. The scene contains a weighted version of Jack with his pants, as shown in Figure 6.8.

   The vertices around the waistline of the pants have been positioned exactly where Jack would wear

Figure 6.8

Jack and his pants

his pants. These vertices will be held to his body by a constraint. For now, it's important that they stay stationary.

2. You need to position the pant-leg cuff. Shape the vertices with the transform tools. You can see the final results in Figure 6.9.

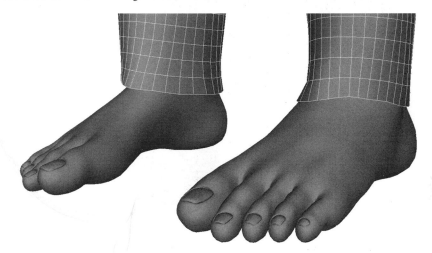

Figure 6.9

The remodeled pant-leg cuffs

3. Select all the vertices of the pants except the border edges (see Figure 6.10).

4. Choose Mesh → Sculpt Geometry Tool. Use Figure 6.11 for the settings.

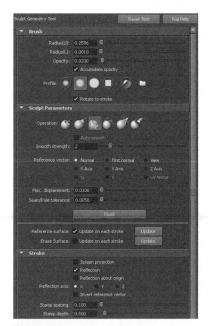

Figure 6.10

Select the vertices on the pants.

Figure 6.11

Sculpt Geometry tool options

5. Use the Smooth brush to reduce the volume of the pants. Only the selected vertices are affected by the sculpting brush, preventing the borders from shifting. It can be difficult to determine how much material you should remove; a good rule of thumb is to reduce the geometry so it touches the skin at its widest points. The space in between should be in a straight line (see Figure 6.12).

6. More often than not, you'll take away more material than necessary, causing penetration. This is part of the process: it's a lot easier to pull the material back out than to meticulously smooth the geometry. Change the brush to Pull, and correct any penetrating vertices. For finishing touches, go over the surface with the Relax brush (see Figure 6.13).

7. Select the pants. Choose Mesh → Smooth, and use the default options. Smoothing the surface is primarily done, because there wasn't enough geometry to get realistic deformations. Another reason is to convert any triangles on the surface to quads, thus helping to balance the spacing of the geometry even further. After you smooth the geometry, it penetrates Jack's skin again (see Figure 6.14).

8. Choose Mesh → Sculpt Geometry Tool, and use the Pull brush to fix the geometry. Figure 6.15 shows the final look of the pants.

To check your work so far, you can compare it to `pants_v02.ma` on the DVD.

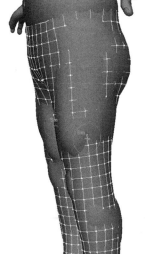

Figure 6.12

Reduce the size of the geometry until it touches the skin.

Figure 6.13

The pants after using the Relax brush

Figure 6.14

Smoothing the geometry causes more penetration.

Figure 6.15

The pants are finished.

9. The pants are ready to test. With the pants selected, choose nMesh → Create nCloth.

10. Before you simulate Jack, you need to set him up as a rigid body. Making him a collision object connects his geometry to the current nucleus solver, enabling you to use constraints to hold the pants up. Select Jack, and choose nMesh → Create Passive Collider.

11. Open the Attribute Editor for nRigidShape1, and change the Thickness parameter to 0.001.

12. Select the nucleus1 tab in the Attribute Editor. Use Figure 6.16 to set the values in the Scale Attributes section.

Figure 6.16
Scale Attributes

SOLVER SCALE

By default, the nucleus solver uses meters to calculate the size of a grid unit. Adjusting Space Scale allows you to increase or decrease the size. Changing Space Scale to .304 alters the scale from meters to feet.

13. Select the pants, and open their Attribute Editor.

14. As with the rigid body, the first thing to establish is the thickness. If the thickness is too large, the geometry will explode quickly. To check the collisions, change Solver Display to Collision Thickness.

    A duplicate surface is displayed around the geometry; it's the same color as the Display Color attribute. This surface represents where collisions take place, essentially giving the geometry an invisible thickness. Figure 6.17 shows a close-up view of the pant-leg cuff.

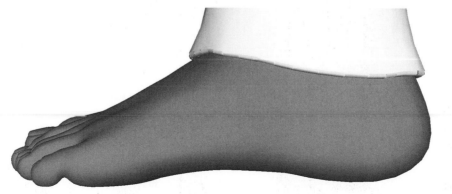

Figure 6.17
The thickness of the pants

15. The thickness is good for now, but you need to address Self Collision Thickness. Change Solver Display to Self Collision Thickness. The display volume is updated (see Figure 6.18).

Figure 6.18

Self Collision Thickness

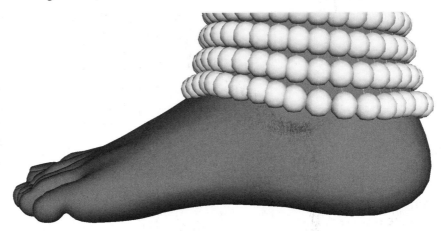

The thickness is represented with spheres instead of the actual surface due to the Self Collision Flag attribute. Change the flag to VertexFace, which is a more complex way to determine collision. In order to make the volume update as well, change Solver Display, and then change it back to Self Collision Thickness.

SELF COLLISION

The VertexFace flag isn't always necessary. In this case, you're primarily using it for its visual representation. Vertex is often suitable and can produce better results. Including too much geometry in the self-collision solver sometimes results in the geometry getting tangled. It's a good idea to begin with Vertex. If you have a collision issue, you can then evaluate which setting would work best.

16. The self collision is too thick. Change Self Collide Width Scale to 1.0. You can also turn off Solver Display.

     This is a good time to save your scene. To check your work so far, you can compare it to pants_v03.ma on the DVD.

17. Select the pants, and click Play in the timeline controls. Stop the simulation at frame 3. Examine the geometry to see if it's being snagged on Jack's geometry. A look around the back side reveals three separate snags (see Figure 6.19).

18. To fix the problem, select the pants, and choose nMesh → Remove nCloth.

19. Use the Pull brush to fix the snags. Turning Template or Reference on for the BODY layer makes the snagged areas more apparent.

20. After you correct the issues, choose nMesh → Create nCloth.

21. Reset Self Collide Width Scale to 1.0 and Self Collision Flag to VertexFace.

22. Play the simulation. The pants should fall down freely (see Figure 6.20).

23. Return to frame 1. A belt is definitely needed. You can create it by adding a constraint. Select the top row of vertices on the pants' geometry (see Figure 6.21).

24. Shift+select Jack's geometry, and choose nConstraint → Point To Surface.

25. Play the simulation again. The effects are more or less the same. This time, the pants stretch until they fall off (see Figure 6.22).

RELAXING THE GEOMETRY

When you're testing attributes, keep in mind that this is the first time the geometry has been simulated. It may move a lot initially and then settle down. The reaction in the first couple of frames isn't an indication of the cloth's overall performance.

Figure 6.19
The geometry is getting snagged on the body.

Figure 6.20
The pants fall freely.

Figure 6.21
Select the vertices around the top border of the pants.

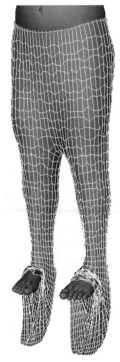

Figure 6.22
The pants stretch too much.

26. At this point, you're only checking the quality of the geometry and not the simulation. To test the geometry, open its Attribute Editor. Select the nClothShape1 tab, and apply the Heavy Denim preset, replacing all the values. Play the simulation again. The results at frame 30 are shown in Figure 6.23.

To check your work so far, you can compare it to pants_v04.ma on the DVD.

At this point, don't worry about the clothing looking good or real, with wrinkles or not. The simulation takes care of that. The pants are made tighter than real pants, compensating for the fact that they will relax. If you model them to the perfect size, they will most likely be too baggy. This ultimately leads to compensating with extremely high attribute values, resulting in a stiff, unrealistic simulation.

When the pants are fitted to the geometry, you can duplicate the pants in their relaxed state and export it to a 3D sculpting package like Mudbox or ZBrush. While sculpting, you only want to add fine detail. Adding modeled or sculpted wrinkles puts them into the garment permanently. This may be necessary sometimes; but for the most part, doing so isn't advantageous. As mentioned earlier in the chapter, you can add specific wrinkles later through a wrinkle map or geometric displacement map.

Figure 6.23

The pants with the Heavy Denim preset

Project: Pants

Now that the pants properly fit the character, it's time to work on their performance. To get the proper motion, you can cut the pants into panels. To do this, you'll remove the nCloth from the geometry. In addition, you'll remove one row of polygons from the top on the pants and refit the belt line to Jack's waist.

Follow these steps:

1. Open the pants_v05.ma scene from the chapter6\Projects\scenes folder on the DVD. The scene is a continuation of the previous project.

2. The panels for the front of the pants are shown in Figure 6.24.

   Using the image as a guide, separate the pants into individual panels. Select the faces for half the geometry from the side view; your selection defines the inner and outer seams of the pants. The inner and outer don't have to match up—you can place them wherever you think is appropriate. Figure 6.25 shows the selection.

3. Choose Mesh → Extract, and use the default options. Delete the history from the new nodes.

4. Switch to the front view, and select half the geometry for the front pants section. Use Figure 6.26 for reference.

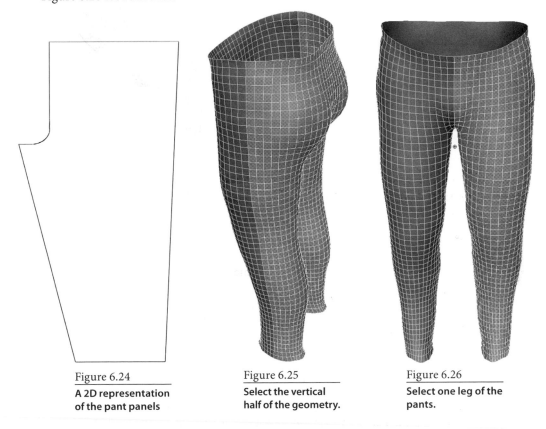

Figure 6.24

A 2D representation of the pant panels

Figure 6.25

Select the vertical half of the geometry.

Figure 6.26

Select one leg of the pants.

5. Choose Mesh → Extract, and use the default options. Delete the history from the new nodes.

6. Repeat steps 4 and 5 for the back panel.

7. You now have four separate pieces of geometry. Select all four, and choose Mesh → Combine. Rename the new node **pants**. You may have to delete an existing node named pants, which is left over from the original geometry.

The pants are back together as a single node. Even though it's one object, the nCloth simulation sees it as four separate pieces because the vertices haven't been welded together. Figure 6.27 demonstrates the results of simulating the object in its current state.

8. Select the pants, and choose nMesh → Create nCloth.

9. To add an artificial belt, select the top row of vertices on the pants. Then, Shift+select the body geometry, and choose nConstraint → Point To Surface.

10. The Point To Surface constraint holds up the pants. To keep the panels together, add component-to-component constraints. The easiest way to do this is through the UV Texture Editor. With the pants selected, open the UV Editor in a separate window.

11. Select all the UVs, choose Select → Convert Selection To Edges, and then choose Select → Select Shell Border.

12. Choose Select → Convert Selection To Vertices.

13. Deselect the vertices along the top of the pants and along the bottom cuff of each leg, leaving the seam vertices selected. Use Figure 6.28 for reference.

Figure 6.27

Each panel is simulated as a separate piece.

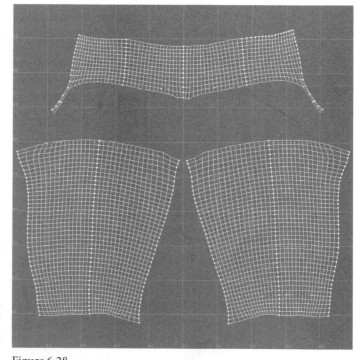

Figure 6.28

The borders of the panels

14. Choose nConstraint → Component To Component (see Figure 6.29).

15. With the constraint selected, change Constraint Method to Weld in the Channel Box.

    To check your work so far, you can compare it to pants_v06.ma on the DVD.

16. Select the pants' geometry, and open its Attribute Editor.

17. Choose the nClothShape1 tab. Replace the attributes with the Heavy Denim preset.

18. Change the Self Collide Width Scale to 3. It's a good idea to always have the self collision larger than the actual thickness of the garment. By keeping it greater, you avoid a lot of interpenetration. This added distance also alters the simulation: it helps make the pants move less by self-colliding earlier when the fabric bunches up.

19. There is no animation on the character; this makes it difficult to evaluate the cloth's performance. Fortunately, you adapted the motion capture of an actor boxing in Chapter 1, "Character Skeletons." The animation has been cleaned up further since then. Choose File → Import, and change the file type to FBX. Choose Import at the bottom of the dialog box.

20. Browse to the chapter6\Projects\FBX folder on the DVD. Highlight Boxing.fbx to load the files options in the window. Change the options to match Figure 6.30. When done, choose Import from the bottom right of the dialog box.

21. Change the range of the timeline to −50.0 through 300.0. Set the current frame to −50.0.

Figure 6.29

Component-to-component constraint

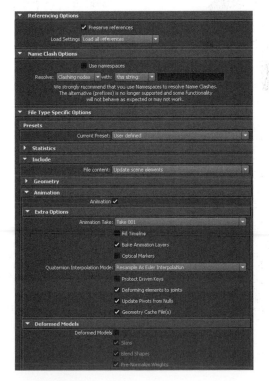

Figure 6.30

FBX import options

22. Select the pants, and open the Attribute Editor. Choose the nucleus1 tab. Use Figure 6.31 to change the Time Attributes settings.

Figure 6.31

Time Attributes section

23. Before you address the garment's material attributes, you need to set the collisions. Select body1, and choose the nRigidShape1 tab.

24. Use Figure 6.32 to set the quality settings.

Figure 6.32

Quality settings for nRigidShape1

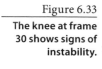

24. Play the simulation with the geometry selected, to test the results. Early into the simulation, you can see the geometry around the knee losing its strength (see Figure 6.33).

Figure 6.33

The knee at frame 30 shows signs of instability.

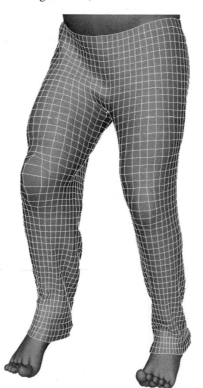

25. When nCloth shows signs of instability, it's typically due to low quality settings on the solver. Open the Attribute Editor for nucleus1, and use the settings shown in Figure 6.34.

Figure 6.34

Solver attributes

26. Create a playblast of the simulation, or watch `pants1.mov` from the `chapter6\Projects\movies` folder on the DVD.

The movie captures frames -50 to 165. Even though the Heavy Denim preset is used for Jack's cotton pants, it works well.

To check your work so far, you can compare it to `pants_v07.ma` on the DVD.

It may seem unnecessary to cut the pants into panels, but let's take a look. Figure 6.35 shows frame 90 from the boxing animation. The pants weren't cut up for this image.

Now, look at Figure 6.36. It shows the pants at the same frame, but in this case they were cut into separate panels. You can also compare the previous animation with this one. Pay close attention to the areas around the seams: notice how the geometry looks like it's pulling on the seam, creating nice ripples in the garment.

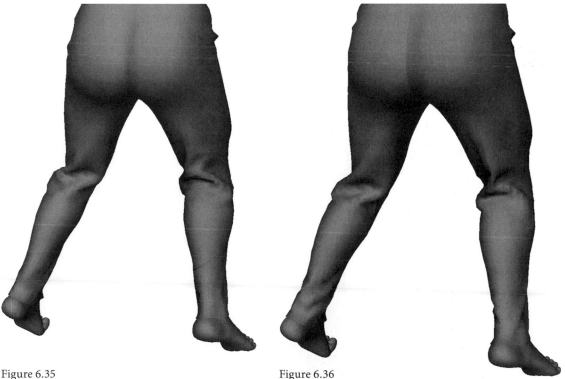

Figure 6.35

Frame 90 of the pants as a solid garment

Figure 6.36

Frame 90 with the pants cut into panels

Project: Shirt

Jack is wearing a long-sleeved shirt tucked into his pants. Over it he wears a heavy jacket. The jacket remains open, exposing the shirt; however, the sleeves are never visible. In this project, you'll add the shirt to Jack's outfit. The shirt has already been fitted and divided into separate panels; to optimize the simulation, the sleeves have been removed. Follow these steps:

1. Open the shirt_v01.ma scene from the chapter6\Projects\scenes folder on the DVD. The scene is a continuation of the previous project. The only addition is the shirt geometry, which is on its own layer.

2. Select the shirt, and choose nMesh → nCloth.

3. Open the nCloth's Attribute Editor. Replace the attributes with the T-shirt preset.

4. The shirt requires numerous constraints to keep it in place. The first one is to keep the shirt tucked into the pants. Select all the vertices along the bottom row of the shirt (see Figure 6.37).

5. With the vertices selected, Shift+select Jack's body. Choose nConstraint → Point to Surface.

6. The next constraint is for the sleeves. Adding the constraint keeps the edges from moving freely. Open edges colliding under other nCloth geometry can cause instability. It's possible to simulate without constraining but not worth the extra effort.

   Select all the vertices around the sleeve openings. Remember, two panels come together across the opening, so there are vertices on top of one another. Figure 6.38 shows the selection.

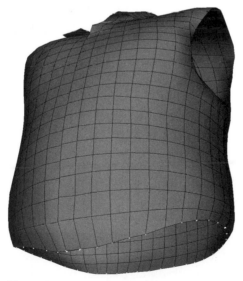

Figure 6.37

Select the vertices along the bottom of the shirt.

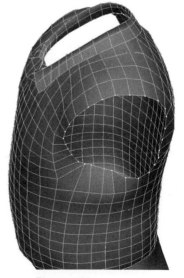

Figure 6.38

Select the sleeve vertices.

7. Shift+select Jack's body, and choose nConstraint → Component To Component.

8. The next constraint keeps all the panels together except the collar. Select the vertices dividing the front and back panels; using the UV Texture Editor can make selecting the vertices easier. Figure 6.39 shows the selection.

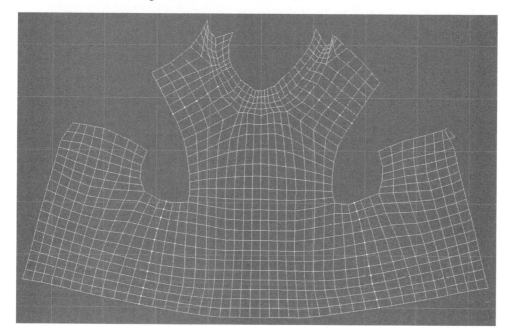

Figure 6.39

The vertices that divide the front and back panels, selected in the UV Texture Editor

9. Shift+select Jack's body, and choose nConstraint → Component To Component.

10. With the constraint selected, change Constraint Method to Weld in the Channel Box.

    To check your work so far, you can compare it to `shirt_v02.ma` on the DVD.

11. Now you need to address the collar. Select the vertices where both panels come together; again, this is easiest to do using the UV Texture Editor (see Figure 6.40).

12. Shift+select Jack's body, and choose nConstraint → Component To Component. Change Constraint Method to Weld in the Channel Box.

13. The collar also requires a constraint. On its own, the nCloth collapses. You could paint higher attribute values to keep the collar's shape, but it's much easier to add a constraint.

    Select all the vertices that make up the collar. The collar is a separate panel and therefore detached from the rest of the model. This allows you to select a single UV and choose Select → Select Shell in the UV Texture Editor (see Figure 6.41).

Figure 6.40

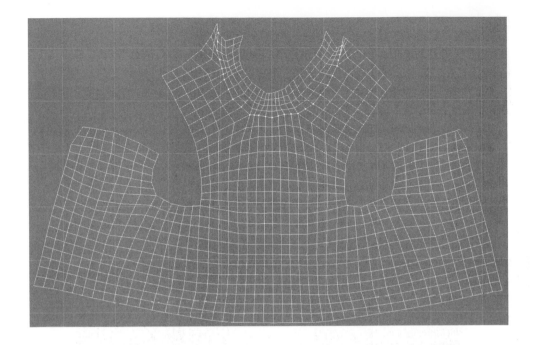

Figure 6.41

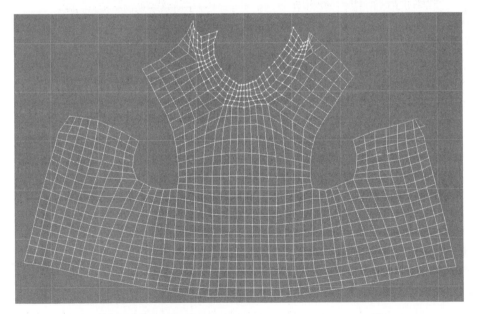

14. Convert your selection to vertices. Shift+select Jack's head, and choose nConstraint → Point To Surface.

15. The last constraint is for the buttons along the front of the shirt. Use Figure 6.42 to make your selection. Make sure you select the vertices from both panels.

16. Choose nConstraint → Component To Component, and change Constraint Method to Weld in the Channel Box. All the constraints are finished; you can see them in Figure 6.43.

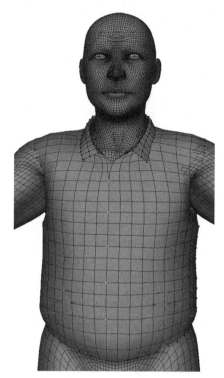

Figure 6.42
Vertices selected for the buttons

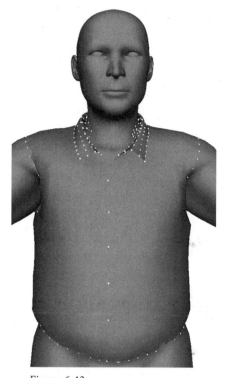

Figure 6.43
The shirt with all its constraints

To check your work so far, you can compare it to `shirt_v03.ma` on the DVD.

17. To test the shirt, turn off the pants. Select the pants' geometry, and open the Attribute Editor. Choose the nCloth1 tab, and deselect Enable.

18. Choose the nucleus1 tab, and change the settings in the Solver Attributes section based on Figure 6.44. These settings are good for the shirt, but you'll need to increase them later in the chapter to handle the jacket.

19. Turn off the visibility on the pants layer.

20. Play the simulation, or watch `shirt1.mov` from the `chapter6\Projects\movies` folder on the DVD.

The shirt solves well enough. The jacket will predominantly cover the shirt, so you don't need to spend much time on it.

Figure 6.44
Solver Attributes section

Project: Jacket

The jacket has been prepared like the shirt from the previous project: it's been fitted and made into panels. But the sleeve vertices have been merged with the body of the jacket. Having the sleeves detached from the body causes the geometry to buckle. This affect is amplified with heavy, thick materials. In this project, you add the necessary constraints to keep the jacket together and assign a material to the garment. Follow these steps:

1. Open the `jacket_v01.ma` scene from the `chapter6\Projects\scenes` folder on the DVD. The scene is a continuation of the previous project. The jacket and its pockets are on separate layers, and the nucleus solver has been adjusted. Substeps is set to 8, and Max Collisions Iterations is set to 20.

2. Select the jacket, and choose nMesh → Create nCloth.

3. Open the Attribute Editor, and assign the Heavy Denim preset.

4. The jacket has numerous seams. You can sew all of them together with a single constraint. Select the jacket, and open the UV Texture Editor.

5. Select all the edges on the jacket, and choose Select → Select Shell Border.

6. Choose Select → Convert Selection To Vertices.

7. All of the panel's border vertices are selected. Deselect all vertices that don't connect to another panel. Figure 6.45 shows the final selection.

Figure 6.45

Selected panel vertices

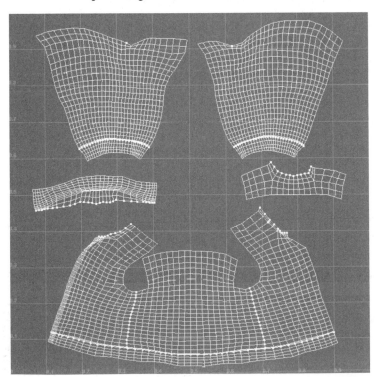

8. Choose nConstraint → Component To Component.

9. Change Constraint Method to Weld in the Channel Box.

10. Currently, the shirt and the jacket collide equally with one another. The jacket needs to be the dominating force because it rests over the shirt. The shirt shouldn't influence the jacket. You can achieve this by placing the shirt on a different collision layer.

    Select the shirt, and open its Attribute Editor. On the nClothShape2 tab, change Collision Layer to 1.

    To check your work so far, you can compare it to jacket_v02.ma on the DVD.

11. Play the simulation for the first 10 frames. Figure 6.46 shows the results.

Figure 6.46

The results of the simulation at frame -40

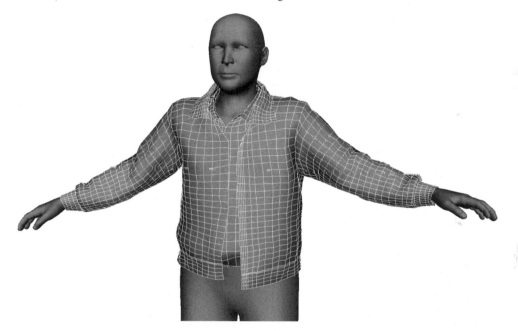

The shirt and jacket are having self-collision problems. The shirt has an open edge on the other side of the buttoned panel. When simulated independently, the edges don't penetrate. When simulated with the jacket, they do. Ignore this issue for now.

12. Play the simulation, or watch jacket1.mov from the chapter6\Projects\movies folder on the DVD.

Regardless of the shirt penetrating itself, it needs a few modifications. Select the shirt, and open its Attribute Editor. On the nClothShape2 tab, change the Thickness and self-collision settings. Figure 6.47 shows all the settings in the Collisions section.

Figure 6.47

The shirt's Collisions settings

13. The jacket looks too big and bulky; you can see it puffing up along the sleeves. Select the jacket, and reduce its Collision Strength value. Figure 6.48 shows the Collisions settings.

To check your work so far, you can compare it to `jacket_v03.ma` on the DVD.

14. Play the simulation, or watch `jacket2.mov` from the `chapter6\Projects\movies` folder on the DVD. Figure 6.49 shows frame 165, the last frame of the saved movie.

Figure 6.48

The jacket's Collisions settings

The jacket is moving well—almost too well. The new collision settings give it the appropriate thickness, but overall it moves too freely and needs to be stiffer. The jacket is stretching too much, resulting in spring-like deformations. It's most noticeable on Jack's left side as he jumps at frame 37 (see Figure 6.50).

Furthermore, the jacket is crinkling around the shoulder area. You need to alter a few settings.

15. Select the jacket, and open its Attribute Editor. Open the nClothShape3 tab.

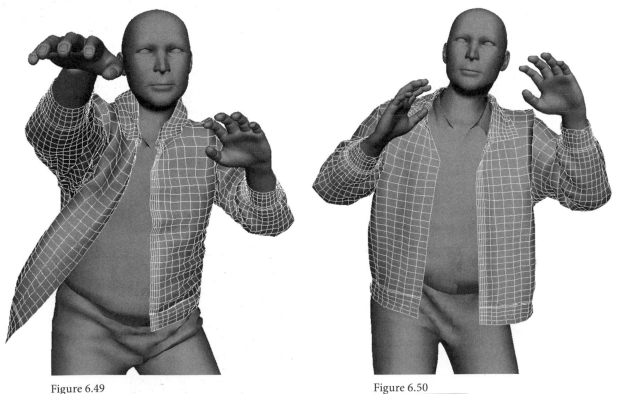

Figure 6.49

Frame 165 of the simulation

Figure 6.50

Frame 37 of the simulation

16. In the Dynamic Properties section, change Stretch Resistance to 100 and Mass to 4.0. Play the simulation again, and evaluate the results at frame 37 (see Figure 6.51).

    The shoulder area has improved. The jacket doesn't slink down as far with Jack's abrupt movements. By increasing Mass, you've given more power to the resistance attributes.

17. The sleeve coming into the shoulder area is still buckling. Change Damp to 1.0 and Stretch Damp to 1.0. Play the simulation again (see Figure 6.52).

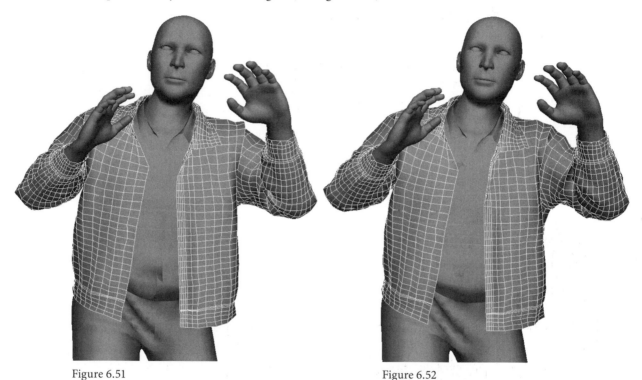

Figure 6.51
Frame 37 of the revised simulation

Figure 6.52
Frame 37 of the simulation after changing the Damp attributes

Now the shoulder area is deforming properly. Check your final settings for the Dynamic Properties section with Figure 6.53.

18. Play the simulation, or watch jacket3.mov from the chapter6\Projects\movies folder on the DVD. The motion of the jacket is good.

    To check your work so far, you can compare it to jacket_v04.ma on the DVD.

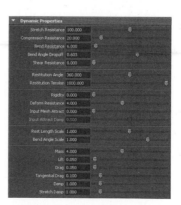

Figure 6.53
Dynamic Property settings

Project: Pockets

Most of the time, you can create pockets through texture. But Jack's jacket benefits from having actual geometry. In this project, you'll take two separate panels—the pocket and pocket flap—and attach them to the jacket. Follow these steps:

1. Open the `pockets_v01.ma` scene from the `chapter6\Projects\scenes` folder on the DVD. The scene is a continuation of the previous project. The jacket and its pockets are on separate layers.

2. Hide the pocket flap. Select the jacket, and make it a Live surface.

3. Select the Pocket node, and snap all the border vertices to the jacket. Leave the top row of vertices (the pocket opening) untouched (see Figure 6.54).

4. Deactivate the jacket as a Live surface.

5. Move the top row of vertices toward the jacket to create a small opening on the pocket.

6. Use the Sculpt Polygon tool to reduce the amount of material in the pocket. Push the vertices close to the surface of the jacket. The Smooth brush works exceptionally well with only the internal vertices selected (see Figure 6.55).

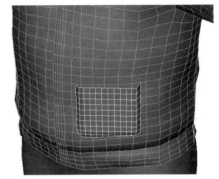

Figure 6.54

Snap the outer edges of the pocket to the Live jacket surface.

7. Unhide the pocket flap. Translate and rotate it to be angled above the pocket, using Figure 6.56 for reference.

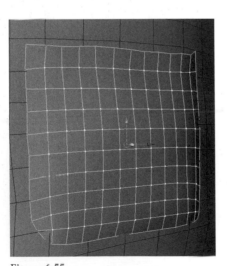

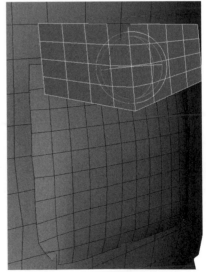

Figure 6.55

Move the vertices of the pocket closer to the surface of the jacket.

Figure 6.56

Move the pocket flap into position.

8. Snap the vertices along the top row of the pocket flap by making the jacket a Live surface.

9. Use the Sculpt Polygon tool to push the rest of the vertices closer to the pocket (see Figure 6.57).

    To check your work so far, you can compare it to pocket_v02.ma on the DVD.

10. Select both panels of the pocket, and choose nMesh → Create nCloth.

11. Select the jacket, and open its Attribute Editor. Choose the nClothShape3 tab.

12. Choose Presets → Save nCloth Preset. Name the preset **Jacket** (see Figure 6.58), and click Save Attribute Preset.

13. Apply the Jacket preset to both pocket panels.

14. Select the snapped border of the pocket, and Shift+select the jacket.

15. Choose nConstraint → Point To Surface (see Figure 6.59).

16. Change Constraint Method to Weld in the Channel Box.

Figure 6.57

Push the pocket flap vertices closer to the pocket.

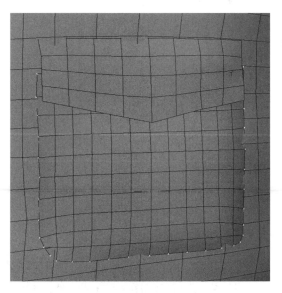

Figure 6.58

Save Attribute Preset

Figure 6.59

Constrain the outside edge of the pocket to the jacket.

17. Select the top row of vertices on the pocket flap, and repeat steps 15 and 16 (see Figure 6.60).

18. Play the simulation to test the pocket. Figure 6.61 shows the relaxed pocket at frame –30.

19. Repeat the procedure for the right-side pocket. To make things easier, you can duplicate the left and mirror it to the other side (see Figure 6.62).

 To check your work so far, you can compare it to pocket_v03.ma on the DVD.

Project: Final Outfit

The jacket is complete. You've tested each element, and they function as intended. It's time to finalize the simulation. To make the simulation run more smoothly, the back of the shirt has been deleted. The geometry won't be seen for this project, so it only complicates the simulation. In this project, you'll make a few final adjustments to the nCloth nodes and prepare the geometry for rendering. Follow these steps:

1. Open the finalOutfit_v01.ma scene from the chapter6\Projects\scenes folder on the DVD.

2. Select the jacket, and open its Attribute Editor. The jacket tends to shift on the character. To reduce its movement and keep it fixed, add 0.1 to Stickiness in the Collisions section of the nCloth.

3. The jacket is bulky and collides with itself to the point of penetration. This has a lot to do with the animation as well. The character's arms bend without taking into consideration the garment's heavy weight and thickness; therefore, the nCloth is pushed inside itself before

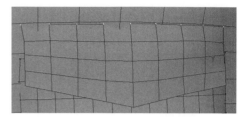
Figure 6.60
Constrain the top edge of the pocket flap to the jacket.

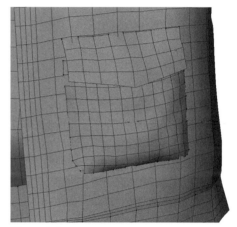
Figure 6.61
The simulated pocket

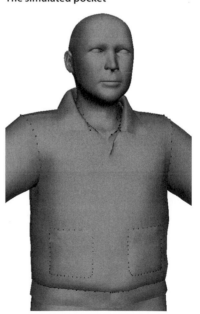
Figure 6.62
The pockets have been attached to the jacket.

collisions have a chance to solve. Select Self Trapped Check in the Quality settings to have the solver identify penetrating geometry and push it back out.

4. The pockets need a few alterations to keep them from conflicting with the body of the jacket. Use Figure 6.63 for the Collisions settings. Make sure you change all four panels making up the pockets.

Figure 6.63

Collisions settings

5. In addition, the pockets flop around and deform too much. Use Figure 6.64 to change the Dynamic Properties settings.

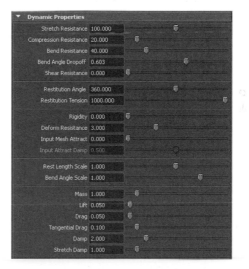

Figure 6.64

Dynamic Properties settings

6. Increase the Solver Attributes values, referring to Figure 6.65.

Figure 6.65

Solver Attributes settings

7. To give the geometry its final look, select each garment and choose Mesh → Smooth. Doing so adds a polySmoothFace history node to each nCloth object. Because it's downstream from the nucleus node, it isn't simulated with the nCloth geometry. Instead, it's deformed by the geometry (see Figure 6.66).

Figure 6.66

The smoothed geometry deforms with the simulation.

To check your work so far, you can compare it to `finalOutfit_v02.ma` on the DVD.

Summary

Jack's outfit is complete. Learning how to successfully build and simulate clothing takes time and practice. To learn more about clothing simulation, check out *Maya Cloth for Characters* (Surrealistic Producing Effects, 2008).

To see the final version of Jack in action, watch `jacket4.mov` from the `chapter6\Projects\movies` folder on the DVD.

Performance Capture

A new age of capturing motion has begun. Almost every part of the human body can be tracked, from fingers to eyeballs. It has become so universal that most home-based game consoles are transitioning to motion-based systems, replacing the need for handheld game controllers. But capturing the data is only half the equation. Getting the data to function as intended is equally as important. In this chapter, you'll learn how to build a motion capture studio, capture data, and apply it to Jack's skeleton. To create the performance capture data you will use Autodesk's MatchMover software. The data is then exported to Maya and applied to the character's skeleton. In addition, you'll create a face rig to accept the captured data and translate it into a driving force for Jack's facial muscles.

In this chapter you will learn to:

- **Build an affordable motion capture studio**

- **Use Autodesk's MatchMover to track an actor's motion**

- **Bring a motion capture performance into Maya**

- **Apply a captured performance to a character**

Motion Capture

Motion capture can be an expensive endeavor. Typical setups are done inside large sound stages, giving actors freedom of movement. Ten to 15 specialized cameras are set up around the room to capture the action from every angle. Special software is employed that can capture marker motion and immediately place it on a skeleton. This type of setup allows immediate feedback, giving you the ability to judge the performance and, in some systems, see the motion on your character.

Capturing motion doesn't have to be sophisticated or expensive. Building your own motion capture studio is possible and affordable. On its most primitive level, motion capture has three elements: the cameras, the actor, and the stage. Each of these elements has minimum requirements; but as long as your capturing needs are flexible, so are the requirements. For instance, if you only want to capture body motion, any camera capable of PAL or NTSC resolution can work.

The system used in this chapter is moderately priced, around $1,500. The majority of the expense is two high-definition cameras. The system can capture body, face, and finger motion. Let's be realistic, though: the motion capture system outlined in this chapter can't compete with a professional setup. It's a manual process, with no feedback or guarantee that the performance is acceptable. With that said, there are things you can do to ensure that your capture session is successful. The following section explains each element and its requirements.

Cameras

Multiple cameras are used to shoot your actor. A minimum of two is required. The more cameras you have, the more complex the movement you can capture. Each camera is positioned to record the movement of the markers from different angles. If a marker is obscured from a single camera's view, you may not be able to automatically track it. This isn't a huge concern, because you can manually add keys until the track is visible again. When you're limited to a two-camera setup, it's essential that every marker be visible to both cameras most of the time. Again, if one camera loses a marker, you can manually fill in the blanks.

With today's technology, the best affordable camera to use is one that is capable of 60 fps at 1080P. An example of the this type of camera is shown Figure 7.1. Although these specifications aren't absolutely necessary, using anything less limits your ability to capture fast motion and full-body performances. Lower resolutions and interlaced video aren't suitable for capturing the body and face at the same time. They work on large body movements—limbs and torso—but don't have the fidelity for fingers and facial motions. Adding more cameras to capture closer angles can offset this issue, allowing lower resolutions. This is okay as long as your actor is relatively stationary.

Our focus is on performance capture, capturing the entire actor's motions from head to toe. Therefore, it's best to have cameras that meet the specifications. Luckily, these cameras are in an affordable price range: around $700 at the time of publication. As new models enter the market, the price should continue to drop, making it possible to expand the number of cameras in your motion capture setup.

Figure 7.1

The camera used to capture the performance shown in this chapter

Actors

Motion capture actors aren't typical actors; nor are they just anyone off the street. They're unique individuals who possess great control over their bodies. Actors need to be able to perform a specific emotion, action, or pose on demand. This is a lot harder than you may think. Your version of being scared may not be what the director has in mind. Therefore you have to change, modify, or tweak the action until it's right. How is that any different from normal acting? In a normal situation, the actor is on a set with real props, costumes, lighting, and atmosphere. On a motion capture stage, nothing contributes to the final look. The entire setup is a solid color, and the lighting is flat. The stage is as sterile as an operating room. Everything is raw and exposed.

Most people have an extremely difficult time envisioning what will become of the performance they're watching on a motion capture stage. Watching a well-known actor is a little different. They know how to perform as they would normally in a live-action situation. Therefore, you recognize the performance. You subliminally pick out motions and gestures unique to the actor. You accept them and mentally place them in a situation you have seen before.

The real difference is for the actor. During motion capture, they're covered from head to toe in a special suit covered with little white balls. Some actors are apprehensive or have complete disdain toward the process because it can interfere with their acting abilities.

The Suit

For high-fidelity capturing, it's best to wear a solid colored, tight-fitting uniform. Typically, a black or blue unitard is used; these can be purchased from dance or theatre supply shops. They usually run about $80. Wearing a solid color provides a large degree of contrast between the markers and the actor. An example is shown in Figure 7.2.

The suit needs to be tight fitting so the markers don't get lost if the fabric bunches or folds. This can also cause the markers to shift position. In addition, the looser the fabric is, the more opportunity it has to reflect light. This can cause hotspots or glares, making it difficult to track marker positions.

Figure 7.2

The unitard

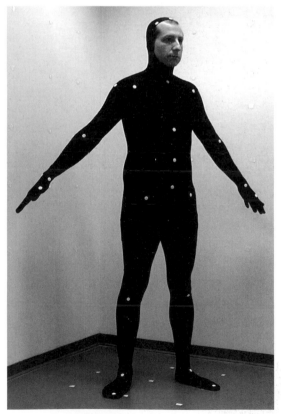

An inherent problem with this setup is that it doesn't accommodate the altered motion that results from wearing a bulky outfit. This isn't as big an issue as it once was: several software packages, including Maya, allow you to retarget or offset motion capture data. Although it still doesn't accurately depict the true motion, it does retain the integrity of the captured motion.

Markers

Marker position varies based on the motion capture setup. Professional systems use specific marker placements to ensure that the actor can be calibrated with their custom skeleton. The setup in this chapter doesn't require specific locations. The reason is that you have to create a skeleton every time you capture a performance. Although doing so provides a lot of flexibility, it also creates varying data. There is no consistency between captures, so you have to manually calibrate every time.

Markers that protrude off the actor are best. Begin offset from the surface makes them more visible using fewer camera angles. You can use almost anything as long as it sticks to the actor and stands out against the actor's uniform. Velcro is a great material to start with; it's highly versatile and is sold in a large assortment of shapes and colors. Three-quarter-inch Velcro coins are used on the motion capture suit in Figure 7.3.

The coins have a sticky back that lets you attach them to the uniform and reposition them. They aren't meant to adhere to fabric, so they may fall off. A spot of hot glue attaches them permanently. You should only use the soft side of the Velcro—the rigid side easily pulls and tears weak, stretchy fabrics. If you're using a unitard or a spandex type material, remember to be careful when placing the coins you don't want the stiff Velcro to damage the suit. Figure 7.4 shows the Velcro coins on the suit.

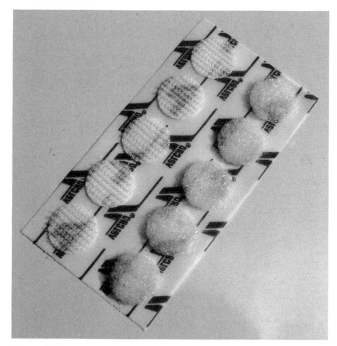

Figure 7.3
A close-up of Velcro markers

Figure 7.4
Tracks point of the body

Finger markers require smaller objects. They must not extend too far; otherwise they can inhibit the actor's performance. Most craft stores sell small half-moon–shaped beads (see Figure 7.5). Like the Velcro coins, they have their own adhesive and can be temporarily placed on fabric (see Figure 7.6).

Place markers on each knuckle and on the fingertips, on both sides of the hands. This allows you to track

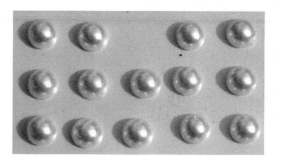

Figure 7.5
A close-up of the beads used on the hands

the fingers through a full range of motion. However, even with markers on the front and back of each hand, the markers may be obscured if you use a two-camera setup. In this event, the markers need to be keyframed manually or interpolated when they're obscured.

Figure 7.6

**Tracks point of
the hands**

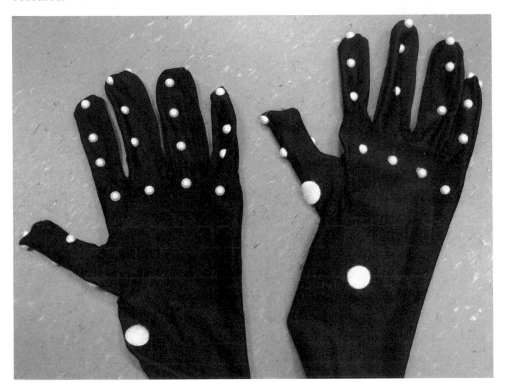

Face markers are the most difficult. White or silver plastic beads are glued to the actor's face. You can use spirit gum or liquid bandage for glue. Anything lightweight and shiny can work as a marker, but the size is critical. Too small, and the markers won't read on camera; too large, and they can bleed into one another. Figure 7.7 shows the beads used for this book.

Place the face markers based on human anatomy. You should have at least one marker for each defined muscle of your face rig. If you can use more, do so. You can never have too many for tracking purposes, but you can certainly have too few. Of course, covering every inch of your actor's face isn't practical either. Figure 7.8 shows the position of the markers to be glued to the actor's face.

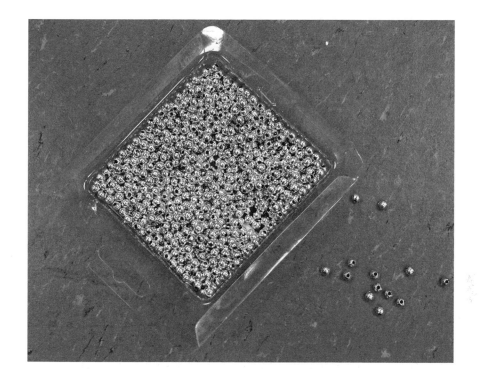

Figure 7.7

A close-up of silver beads used on the face

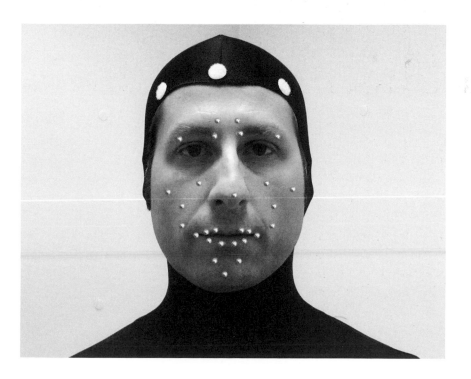

Figure 7.8

The markers of the face

The Stage

The stage varies based on your script requirements. You must judge how much space you need. Full performance capture with only two cameras limits your actor's range of movement. The smaller the actor's face is in frame, the harder it is to track the markers.

In addition to considering your space requirements, you need markers that can be tracked around the stage. Figure 7.9 shows the basic setup.

Figure 7.9

The stage

The markers can be almost anything; simple colored stickers are used in this setup. They're placed on all the visible walls and floor. Use colors that read well on camera and have a high contrast to your background color. You can find fluorescent colored coding labels at most office supply stores. They can be any shape but should be less than an inch (see Figure 7.10). Although only seven markers are required to build a three-dimensional space, you should place as many environment markers as you can.

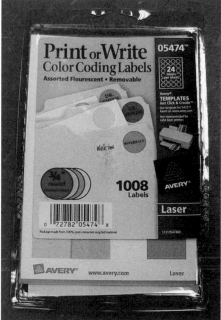

Figure 7.10

Colored stickers used for wall markers

The room you choose should be a solid color that contrasts with your actor and their markers. The stage should be evenly lit to avoid hot spots or dark shadows. If the lighting is too hot, it can wash out a white marker.

Make sure you have a minimum of seven track points in both camera angles. As mentioned, it's best to have many more—you never know what markers your actor will obscure. Having to reshoot because you couldn't define the coordinate system is a frustrating experience.

Capturing Motion

During your capture session, make sure the action stays within the camera views. Because only two cameras are used in this chapter, the stage area is limited. Communication with your actor is essential when you're dealing with a limited setup. With two cameras, the actor won't have a lot of space to move in.

Be sure to do several practice runs to ensure good framing. If your field of view is too large, the face and hand markers may be too small in the frame to track. In addition, make sure the cameras are stable and locked down— you don't want them to move even the slightest bit during a performance.

The day of the shoot, take actual measurements of the room and from marker to marker. You'll enter these measurements into the software to calculate the 3D space. You can typically get away with a single measurement that defines the distance between two markers. However, you can never be too sure which markers will work for you; it's best to gather as much data as possible.

Project: Body Tracking

After you record a performance, you must convert the video into three-dimensional data. To do this, you import the footage into Autodesk's MatchMover. In this project, you'll import footage of a motion capture performance and track each marker in 3D space. Follow these steps:

1. Open Autodesk's MatchMover 2011. In the toolbar, make sure the interface is set to Full.

2. Choose File → Load Sequence or its icon from the toolbar. Navigate to the chapter7\
   projects\MatchMover\sourceimages\Camera1 folder on the DVD. Select the first frame,
   and use Figure 7.11 for the rest of the options.

Figure 7.11

**Load Sequence
options**

3. Repeat the procedures from step 2 to load the camera2 sequence.

4. Use the Display tools on the toolbar to change the viewport to Two Side By Side (see
   Figure 7.12).

Figure 7.12

**Two Side By
Side view**

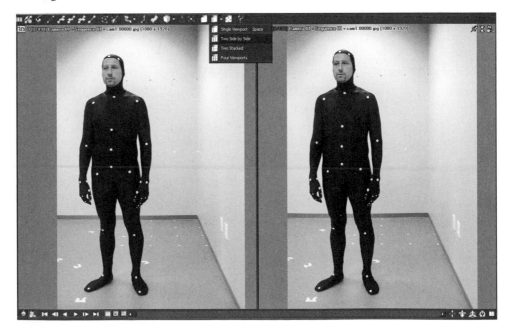

5. Both sequences are loaded into MatchMover. At the first frame, the viewports only show Sequence 01. Sequence 02 is displayed directly after Sequence 01. You can see it update at frame 496. The sequences need to be synchronized to play at the same time.

   Make sure you're at frame 0. Choose Sequence 01 from the Project window. Its parameters are now displayed on the opposite side of the screen in the Parameters window. In the Synchronization section, select Synchronized At Frame (see Figure 7.13).

6. Select Sequence 02 from the Project window, and synchronize it as well. The two sequences already match up and have the same number of frames. Therefore, they don't require an offset in order to synchronize. They're both set at frame 0.000.

Figure 7.13
Select Synchronized At Frame in the Synchronization parameters.

7. To have them sync in the viewports, click the camera icon in the upper-right corner. The icon is highlighted in yellow when activated.

8. The two cameras are synchronized and show the first frame of each sequence. The left viewport shows Camera 01 or Sequence 01 and the right Camera 02 or Sequence 02. If either is incorrect, click the camera name at the top of the viewport to change cameras (see Figure 7.14).

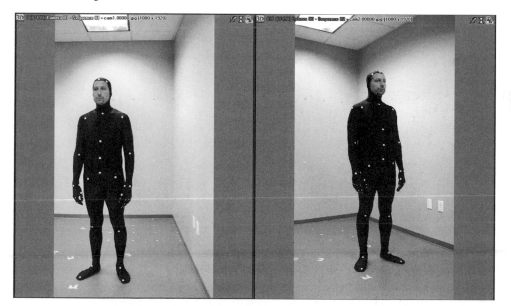

Figure 7.14
The two sequences are synchronized.

9. Some of MatchMover's default settings don't work well for this project. Choose Edit → Preferences, and switch to the 2D/Auto Tracking tab. Deselect Smart Prediction and Automatic Key Insertion (see Figure 7.15).

Figure 7.15

2D/Auto Tracking preferences

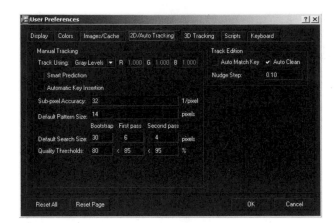

To check your work so far, you can compare it to `bodyTrack_v01.nmf` on the DVD.

10. The first set of points to establish are the coordinate system and camera tracking points. A minimum of seven tracking points are required: they provide MatchMover with the necessary information to build a 3D environment from the two sequences. Choose 2D Tracking → New Track or click the New Track icon on the toolbar.

11. Left-click and hold on the tape closest to the corner of the room. A magnified view of the area is displayed. Move the tracking point to the center of the tape. Do this in both viewports (see Figure 7.16).

Figure 7.16

Add a tracking point.

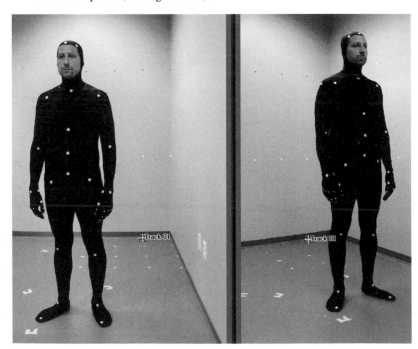

12. Add three more tracking points to the floor. Use Figure 7.17 as a guide.

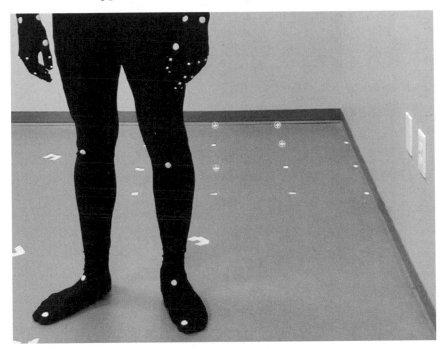

13. Add three tracking points on the walls. For each of these, place the tracking point in the middle of the marker. Use Figure 7.18 for reference.

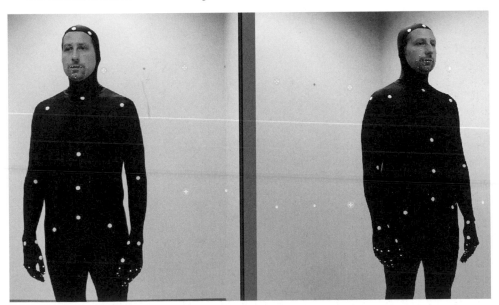

14. Each point needs to be tracked to the footage. Select Track 01 from the Project window. Choose 2D Tracking → Track Forward or click its icon on the toolbar. You can also press F3 as a keyboard shortcut.

    The Tracking window below the workspace shows the track's progress. Green indicates a solid track; yellow to red indicates that the track has slipped or lost its positions. If the software completely loses the track you'll get a message that the quality is too low.

15. Track the rest of the points. All the points track without errors.

     To check your work so far, you can compare it to bodyTrack_v02.nmf on the DVD.

16. With seven points tracked in the scene, you can solve for the camera. Choose 3D Tracking → Solve For Camera, or click its icon on the toolbar. Progress bars appear at the bottom of the screen. When the camera finishes solving, the grey dots next to your track points should be all green, indicating a good track.

17. In order for the actor to be tracked properly, you must establish a coordinate system. MatchMover creates one automatically, but it works best if you create your own. Right-click the Coordinate Systems folder, and choose New Coordinate System.

18. In the Parameters window, set the options shown in Figure 7.19.

Figure 7.19

Coordinate System parameters

The parameters create an origin for the world. The actual origin doesn't make much difference—the goal is only to extract the motion. The placement of that motion is handled in Maya.

The Distance parameter is the number of units from the designated track points beneath the parameter. It's best to get accurate measurements from the motion capture stage. The units are arbitrary and can describe feet, meters, and so on.

ENTERING COORDINATE SYSTEM PARAMETERS

You must apply the coordinate system before you click another element. The Parameters window doesn't retain the values entered until you do so. If you need to identify a tracking point, you can hover over the track in any viewport to reveal its name.

---

19. Change the Axis 1 settings to match Figure 7.20.

20. Enter the Axis 2 settings from Figure 7.21, and then click Apply Coordinate System.

Figure 7.20

Axis 1 parameters

Figure 7.21

Axis 2 parameters

21. To check the coordinate system, switch a viewport from 2D to 3D by clicking the 3D icon in the upper-left corner. Figure 7.22 shows the 3D space.

Figure 7.22

The coordinate system

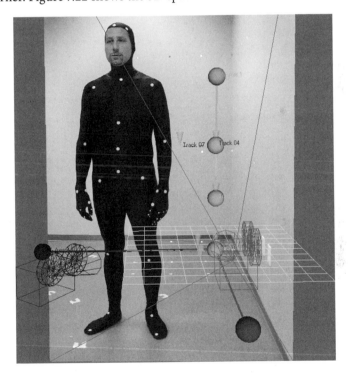

22. To keep the tracking points organized, right-click the Point Tracks folder in the Project window. Choose New Group. Rename the group **Coordinates**.

23. Select the seven point tracks, and drag them to the Coordinates folder. Click the – sign next to the folder's name to close it.

24. Right-click the Point Tracks folder, and create another group. Rename the group **ActorBody**.

25. Change the Motion parameter to Non-Rigid Motion (Motion Capture). All the track points added to this group will have these settings.

   To check your work so far, you can compare it to bodyTrack_v03.nmf on the DVD.

26. Right-click the ActorBody group folder, and choose New Track. The tracking point is automatically added to the group. Place a chest track point on the upper-right corner of the marker below the actor's neck. Doing so helps avoid confusion with the hand markers that get close to that chest marker at frame 900. Figure 7.23 shows the positioning.

Figure 7.23

Add a track point to the actor.

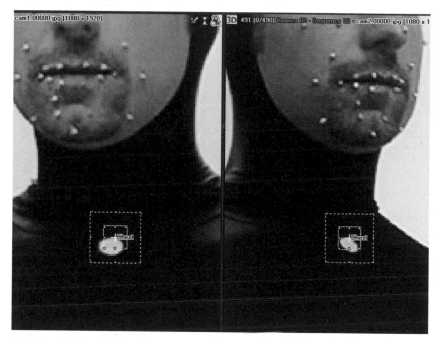

27. Add the following track points to both sequences. You can place the points centered within each marker:

   L_Foot

   R_Foot

   L_Ankle

   R_Ankle

   L_Knee

   R_Knee

   L_Clavicle

   R_Clavicle

Run Track Forward on each of them as you go. This gives you a total of nine points tracked. Use Figure 7.24 for reference.

Figure 7.24

Nine tracking points are placed.

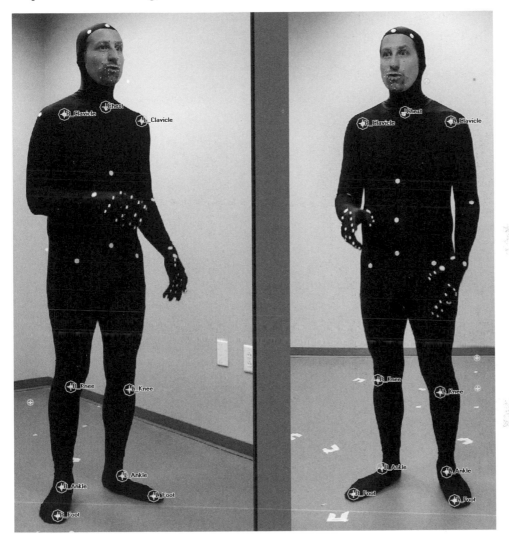

28. Solve for the camera to check the validity of the tracks. If the tracks are good, the grey dot next to each point will turn green in the Project window.

29. All the tracks are good except for the left and right clavicles. The right clavicle gets obscured at frame 285 in Sequence 01: the actor's right arm goes in front of it for about 14 frames. To correct it, go to frame 298, where the marker is visible again.

30. Select the R_Clavicle point track from the Project window. Place the track in Sequence 01 to create a key at the current frame. The Track window updates with a black dot.

31. Click Track Forward to solve the point from the current frame to the end of the sequence.

32. Go to frame 284, and choose 2D Tracking → Interpolate Track or click its icon on the toolbar. The gap between frames 281 and 304 is filled: MatchMover guesses the track point's position through the empty space.

33. Repeat the procedure for the L_Clavicle. It loses its track starting at frame 773.

To check your work so far, you can compare it to bodyTrack_v04.nmf on the DVD.

34. Add a track point to the sternum, and track it forward.

35. The sternum does well until the right arm crosses it during Sequence 02. Add keyframes to frames 769, 831, 841, 878, and 889. When you add a key, any solved path is cleared after the key (see Figure 7.25).

Figure 7.25

The space after the key is cleared.

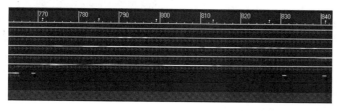

36. You can now start to solve the gaps in the track. Go to frame 769, where the arm goes above the sternum marker. Shift+click in the Track window to highlight frames 769 through 831. Click Track Forward to fill in the gap (see Figure 7.26).

Figure 7.26

The space is filled.

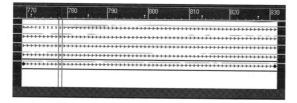

37. Shift+click to select frames 841 to 878. These frames can be tracked. Click the Track Forward icon.

TRACK SELECTION

Selecting a portion of the track isolates it, permitting only that section to be solved. Often, a portion of the track is selected without your realizing it. This prevents you from solving the current track or a new one. To clear your selection in the Track view, Shift+right-click.

38. Shift+click to select frame 889 to the end of the sequence. Click Track Forward.

39. The areas where the hand obscures the marker can be interpolated. Because most of the track is solved already, clicking the Interpolate icon fills in the blanks.

40. Press F9 to solve the camera.

41. Add a track point to the left hip marker. Click Track Forward.

42. The track does well in Sequence 01 up to frame 360. At frame 361, the L_Hip point jumps to the thumb marker (see Figure 7.27).

    Reposition the track point at frame 361 to create a new keyframe, and clear the rest of the solve.

43. Go to frame 379. Add another key to the track point (Figure 7.28).

44. Select frames 361 to 379, and click Interpolate Track. Check the solve by scrolling through the frames. The path looks great: the hand marker passes by, and the hip stays with the actor's motion (see Figure 7.29).

45. Go to frame 379. Click Track Forward to solve the rest of the frames. Remember to deselect your selection in the Track view prior to tracking forward.

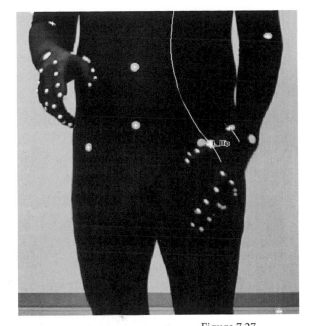

Figure 7.27

The hip track point has jumped to the thumb marker.

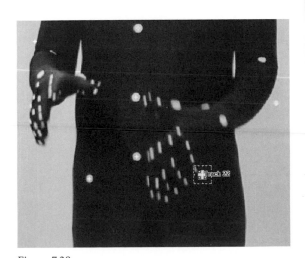

Figure 7.28

Add another key to the hip after the hand has passed over it.

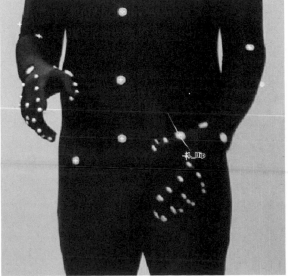

Figure 7.29

The corrected hip path

46. Press F9 to solve for the camera. When the solve is finished, the track turns green in the Project window.

47. Several of the hand points get obscured throughout the capture. There are markers on the front and back of each hand—if the back gets lost, move the track point to the front. For instance, look at frame 395 (see Figure 7.30).

    A small amount of the thumb marker on the front of the hand is still visible. In a few frames, it vanishes. Add a key at frame 390 to the front thumb marker.

48. Scroll forward in the sequence until the opposite thumb marker—the one on the palm side of the hand—is roughly in front of the other. Make an educated guess of where this would be; frame 404 looks good. Add another key (see Frame 7.31).

49. Interpolate between frames 390 and 404.

50. You can now add a key to the palm-side thumb marker at frame 490 (see Figure 7.32).

Figure 7.30

The upper-right thumb marker is about to be obscured.

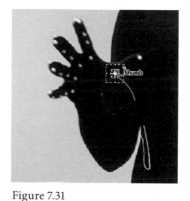

Figure 7.31

The two thumb markers overlap.

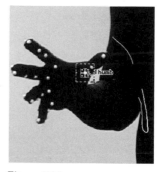

Figure 7.32

Add a key to the thumb marker.

51. Go back to frame 404. If you track forward, the thumb marker immediately jumps to the adjacent marker farther up the thumb. This happens because the tracking point's search zone is too large. With the track point selected, change all four of the Search Zone values to 10 in the Parameters window (see Figure 7.33).

Figure 7.33

Change the Search Zone values for the thumb.

> **ALTERING KEY PARAMETERS**
>
> When you change the Search Zone or other tracking key parameters, they only affect the keyframe you're on. All the previously established keys still have their original values. Any frames you add after making a change retain the changes in the key.

52. Select frames 404 through 490, and track forward.

53. Another method for tracking points is to add keyframes to all the frames right before the track gets lost and then interpolate each of these areas. When you're finished, click Track Forward to complete the entire segment. The interpolated sections are skipped and not re-solved.

54. Complete the rest of the body track points by using the methods outlined in the previous steps. If you feel confident enough, you don't have to solve the camera after each track—you can wait until you're finished. At the end, you'll have 23 tracks.

55. Inspect each track. Make sure there are no red areas. If you have red bars, check the section frame by frame. Add keys, and resolve the red areas.

> **MISSING MARKERS**
>
> Sometimes markers disappear and never return. In these cases, you need to add keys by guessing where the marker is. The goal is to add enough keys to allow MatchMover to interpolate from key to key. It doesn't matter if your key sits on top of another marker in the scene, because you aren't going to have MatchMover solve the track.

To check your work so far, you can compare it to `bodyTrack_v05.nmf` on the DVD.

Project: Face Tracking

The process for tracking the markers on the face is no different than tracking the markers on the body. However, it can be more difficult due to the markers' small size. In this project, you'll look at techniques for tracking the small markers:

1. Open the scene file `faceTrack_v01.nmf` from the `chapter7\Projects\MatchMover\scenes` folder on the DVD. The scene picks up where the previous project left off.

2. Create a new point tracks folder in the Project window, and rename it **ActorFace**.

> **GROUPS**
>
> Groups make it easy to organize numerous tracking points. In addition to keeping the displayed number limited in the Project window, they also limit the number of points shown in the Track window. Furthermore, each group can be hidden, making your workspace less cluttered.

3. Change the Motion parameter to Non-Rigid Motion (Motion Capture) in the Parameters window.

4. The jaw marker is the easiest marker to track. Create a track point for the jaw in Sequence 01 and Sequence 02. Use Figure 7.34 as a guide.

Figure 7.34

Add the jaw track point to both sequences.

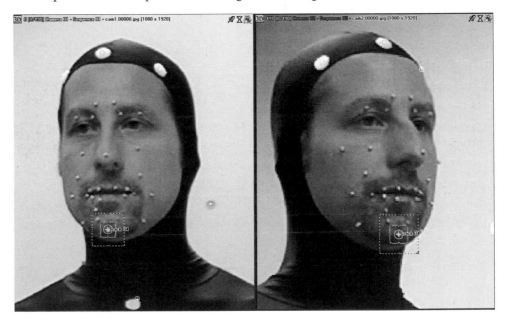

5. Click Track Forward to solve the point. The jaw track is good in Sequence 01 but stops due to low quality in Sequence 02.

6. After the sequence stops, move to the next frame and place the point at that frame.

7. Click Track Forward to continue the solve.

8. Repeat steps 6 and 7 until the track point is completely solved.

9. Add another track point to the R_Mentalis in both sequences (see Figure 7.35).

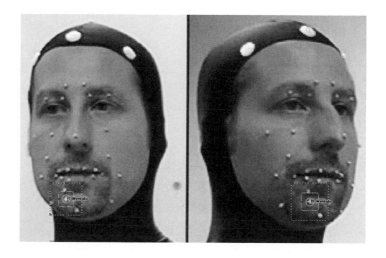

Figure 7.35
Add the R_Mentalis track point.

10. Change the track point parameters for Sequence 01 using Figure 7.36 as reference. Sequence 02 can keep the defaults.

     Decreasing the Pattern Zone and Search Zone values helps keep the track point from jumping or drifting off the marker. Selecting Use Colors changes the solver from using only contrast to using contrast and color, which slows down the solver calculations. By checking coefficients, you can specify a color. White is the default and works with the white markers. Using coefficients speeds up the solver again.

Figure 7.36
Track point parameters for the first key

11. Sequence 02 requires several keyframes throughout the segment. Continue to add keys and track forward until the point is finished.

     To check your work so far, you can compare it to `faceTrack_v02.nmf` on the DVD.

12. Add another track point to the corner of the mouth for Sequence 01 (see Figure 7.37). Rename the point **R_ZygomaticusMajor**.

13. Change the tracking key's parameters based on Figure 7.38.

14. Track the point forward. The solve makes it to about frame 30.

15. Ctrl+click the timeline at the frame immediately following the solved portion of the track.

16. Place another key at frame 100 (see Figure 7.39).

Figure 7.37
Add the right zygomaticus major track point.

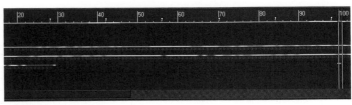

Figure 7.38
_____

Tracking Key parameters

Figure 7.39
_____

Add a key at frame 100.

17. Choose 2D Tracking → Track Bidirectional or click its icon on the toolbar. The solver goes forward and then backward to solve the point (see Figure 7.40).

Figure 7.40
_____

**Bidirectional
tracking**

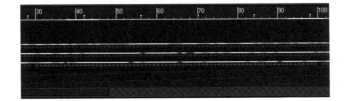

18. Add another key at frame 200, and repeat the procedure. If the bidirectional track fails, add another set of keys between the existing solved track. Use forward and/or backward tracking to complete the track.

19. Continue the R_ZygomaticusMajor track. When you're finished with Sequence 01, complete Sequence 02.

20. Using the variety of methods outlined, finish the rest of the tracks for the face. There are 30 tracks in all. Figure 7.41 shows the finished tracks.

EYELIDS

The eyelids are tracked as well, although no markers distinguish them on the actor. Place a key on the brightest edge of each eyelid, upper and lower. This technique works well because there is a high degree of contrast between the eyeball and the skin.

To check your work so far, you can compare it to `faceTrack_v03.nmf` on the DVD.

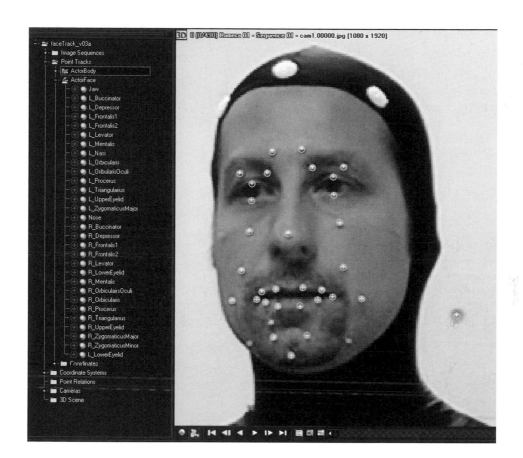

Figure 7.41

The finished track points

Project: Finger Tracking

Finger tracking is the most difficult because the markers tend to disappear or move too quickly. This project walks you through tracking the index finger. You'll use a few different strategies to get the best track in the shortest amount of time. Follow these steps:

1. Open the scene file `fingerTrack_v01.nmf` from the `chapter7\Projects\MatchMover\` scenes folder on the DVD. The scene picks up where the previous project left off.

2. Create a new point tracks folder in the Project window, and rename it **ActorFingers**.

3. Change the Motion parameter to Non-Rigid Motion (Motion Capture) in the Parameters window.

4. Change the workspace to a single viewport with Sequence 01. Use the spacebar for the keyboard shortcut, just like in Maya.

5. Create a new track point under the ActorFingers folder.

6. Go to frame 47. Place the track point on the tip of the finger, as shown in Figure 7.42.

7. Change the Tracking Key parameters to match Figure 7.43.

8. Use Track Backward to solve to the beginning of the sequence.

9. Click Track Forward.

10. The track makes it to about frame 210 before it slips off its marker.

11. Add a key to frame 0, and click Track Forward.

To check your work so far, you can compare it to fingerTrack_v02.nmf on the DVD.

12. Check the track by Ctrl+clicking to scroll through the timeline. Go to the end of the track.

13. Reposition the track point to create another key. Track forward.

14. The track makes it to frame 253. Add a key at frame 254.

15. Change the Tracking Key parameters to match Figure 7.44.

16. Go to frame 263, and add a key.

17 After 263, the hand moves up quickly, causing the marker colors to streak. The track will definitely fail through this section. Click Track Forward to solve for the previous frames.

18. The track does okay between frames 254 and 263. It starts to drift around frame 258. Instead of adding a key, Shift+select frames 258 and 263. Click Track Backward. The section now looks good.

19. Go to frame 289, and a key.

20. You can do the rest of the fingers using the same techniques. For the most part, adding a key for every frame is the answer. Luckily, only 20 or 30 frames aren't trackable.

Figure 7.42

Add a track point to the end of the index finger.

Figure 7.43

Tracking Key parameters

Figure 7.44

Tracking Key parameters for frame 254

21. The body and face tracks are already solved for. To include the finger or any other additional tracks, you don't need to re-solve the camera. Instead, you can keep the current tracks locked and add new ones. Re-solving the camera can cause all your old tracks to be altered. Choose 3D Tracking → Extend Camera Fixed.

> To check your work so far, you can compare it to `fingerTrack_v03.nmf` on the DVD.

Tracking all the points can be a time-consuming process. It definitely makes you think about the benefits of a professional setup that maps the actor's motion directly to a skeleton. Here are a few tips to keep in mind when you're tracking points.

- Place the track point on the brightest pixel.
- If the marker being tracked is close to other markers, reduce the tracking pattern and search zone.
- If your track point slips during a sequence but only for a few frames, let the track finish. When it's finished, use Track Backward to correct the bad frames.
- Start wherever the marker is most prevalent. You don't have to start at a sequence's first frame.
- If a track point is obscured for long periods of time, place a key every tenth frame and interpolate between the keyframes.

> You can look at the finished scene file by opening `fingerTrack_v04.nmf` on the DVD.

Exporting to Maya

After your actor is tracked and your camera is solved, you can export the motion to Maya. MatchMover exports directly to Maya ASCII, making the process extremely simple. Choose File → Export, and change File Type to Maya (.ma). Figure 7.45 shows all the settings.

Figure 7.45

The Export Option window

Each tracked point is displayed as a locator in Maya. The cameras, their associated sequences, and groups of tracked points are all exchanged between the two software packages. The cameras and footage are of no use in Maya for this project and can be discarded. Figure 7.46 shows actor's tracked points isolated in Maya.

Project: Building a Skeleton

Tracking markers on an actor is the longest and most difficult part of capturing a performance. The last step in the process is to convert the captured data into a skeleton in Maya. The following project takes you through the process:

1. Open the scene file capture_v01.ma scene from the chapter7\ Projects\Maya\scenes folder on the DVD. The scene contains the exported performance data from MatchMover (see Figure 7.47).

2. Select rzCamera1 and rzCamera2, and delete them.

3. The tracked points have the same hierarchy from MatchMover. Find the Coordinates group, and delete it.

Figure 7.47

The exported scene from MatchMover

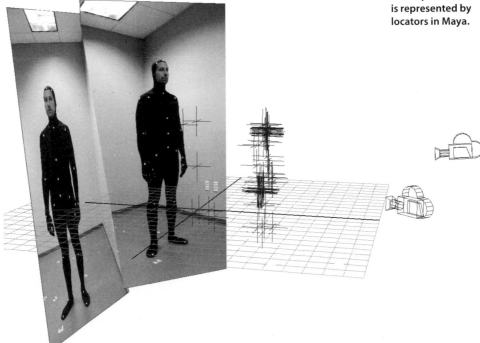

Figure 7.46

The exported data is represented by locators in Maya.

4. Select all the locators under the ActorBody group. Change their scale to 0.1 (see Figure 7.48).

5. Select all the locators under the ActorFace group. Change their scale to 0.02 (see Figure 7.49).

6. Select all the locators under the ActorFingers group. Change their scale to 0.05.

7. Select the locators from all three groups. In the Channel Box, break the connections for the visibility channel.

8. Draw a joint to connect each of the body locators. Build the skeleton as you would a human character, snapping the joints to the locators. The left shoulder couldn't be tracked, so you can skip the right shoulder. Figure 7.50 shows the completed skeleton.

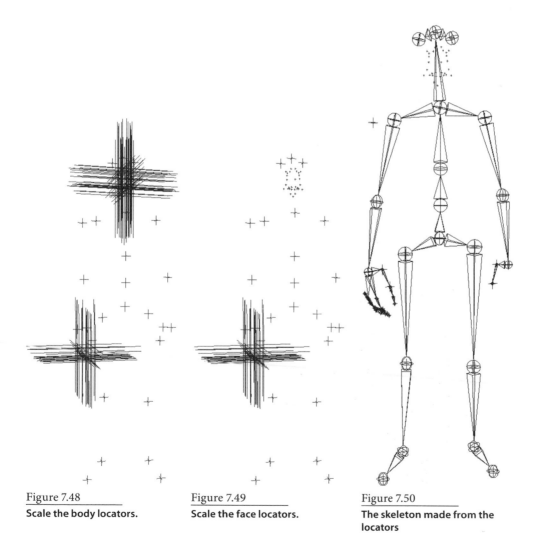

Figure 7.48
Scale the body locators.

Figure 7.49
Scale the face locators.

Figure 7.50
The skeleton made from the locators

To check your work so far, you can compare it to `capture_v02.ma` on the DVD.

9. Create a joint from the chest to each of the face joints. It's easiest to create a single joint and repeatedly duplicate it, snapping to each locator (see Figure 7.51).

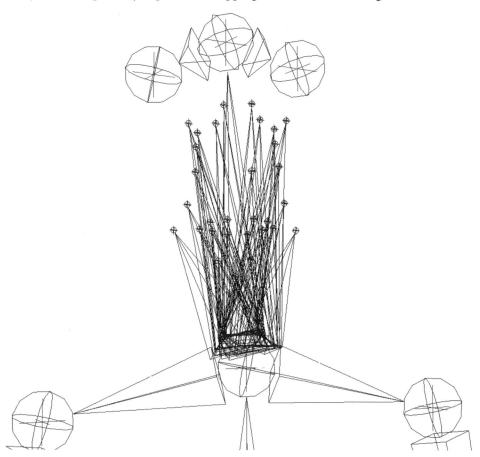

10. Rename each joint based on the locator it's snapped to.

11. Each joint is point-constrained to a locator. Shift+select the locator and then the joint. Choose Constrain → Point, and use the defaults.

   Play the performance. The fingers are a bit wobbly and have a few pops in their motion. Proceed with the conversion process; you can tweak the animation later.

12. Import the scene file `jack_skeleton.ma` from the `chapter7\Projects\Maya\scenes` folder on the DVD. The scene contains a weighted version of Jack.

13. Group the motion capture locators and constrained skeleton under a single name, and rename it **mocap_GRP**.

14. Move the group node's center pivot to the root joint of the constrained skeleton.

15. Snap mocap_GRP to root_JNT (Jack's root). The two skeletons are shown in Figure 7.52.

16. The motion capture skeleton is larger than Jack. Rotate and scale the mocap_GRP node to fit Jack's approximate size. There is a proportional difference between the two. Scale mocap_GRP uniformly to match the shoulders. Figure 7.53 shows the results.

   To check your work so far, you can compare it to capture_v03.ma on the DVD.

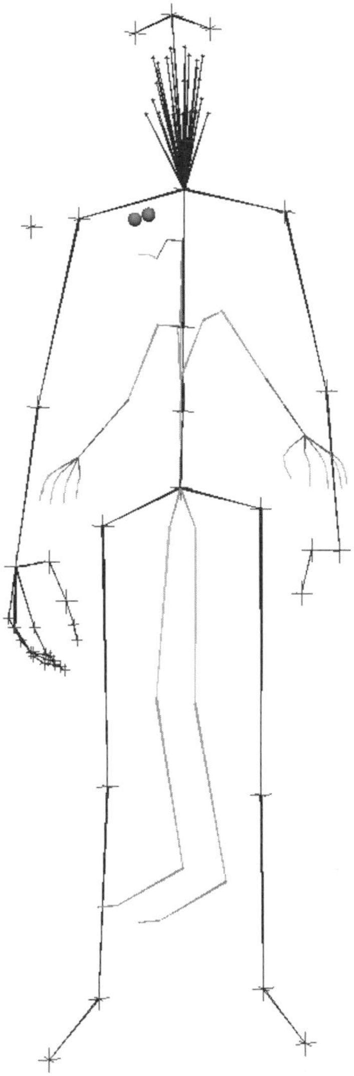

Figure 7.52
The roots of the two skeletons are snapped together.

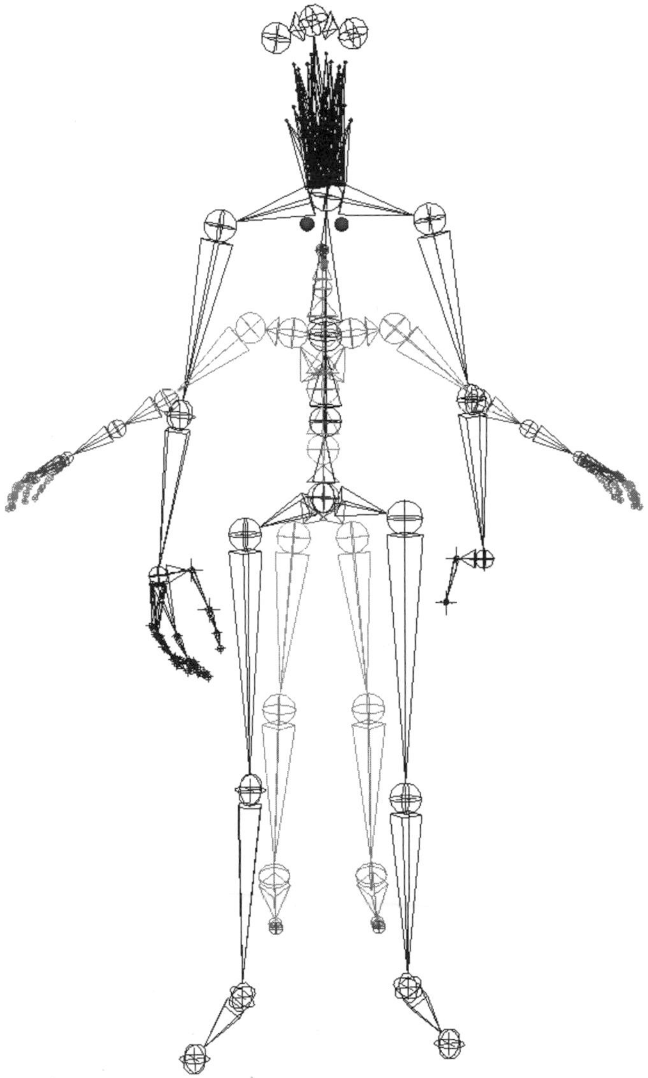

Figure 7.53
The two skeletons overlap.

Calibrating the character to the motion capture skeleton comes next. This part of the process requires your best guess. You want to have Jack's character match the pose of the actor from the original captured performance. You don't want to match the joints' orientations one to one—doing so would bend Jack's joints unnaturally because the markers weren't positioned in the exact center of the actor's joints. So, you manually pose the 3D character to come as close as possible to the actor's position while still retaining the character's natural look.

17. Jack's root joint is the only joint that can match the motion capture skeleton. Shift+select root_MOCAP and root_JNT.

18. Choose Constrain → Point, and use the default settings.

19. Choose Constrain → Orient. Use the default settings, but select Maintain Offset.

20. Jack is standing in an appropriate upright position. His spine doesn't need to be adjusted. Add a single chain IK handle from root_JNT to spine1_JNT.

21. Point-constrain the IK handle to abdomen_MOCAP. Use the defaults with Maintain Offset selected.

22. Repeat steps 20 and 21 for the next two joints, ending with the chest.

23. Jack's clavicles are too high. Rotate both of them 15 units in the positive Z.

24. Add IK handles, and constrain them.

25. To align the right shoulder, you can use an orient constraint. Shift+select R_clavicle_MOCAP and shoulderRght_JNT, and choose Constrain → Orient. Use Figure 7.54 for the settings.

Figure 7.54

The Orient Constraint tool options

26. Delete the orient constraint you added in step 25.

27. Add an IK handle from shoulderRght_JNT to elbowRght_JNT.

28. Point-constrain the handle to R_elbow_MOCAP.

29. Orient elbowRght_jnt to R_elbow_MOCAP. Add an IK handle. Constraining the IK handle in its current position causes the arm to rotate further than desired; you can see an example of this in Figure 7.55.

30. You need to move the IK handle to the wrist joint in order for it to move properly. To do this, choose Modify → Evaluate Nodes → Ignore All.

31. Select the IK handle, and snap its pivot only (keyboard shortcut D) to the wrist joint.

32. Choose Modify → Evaluate Nodes → Evaluate All. Play the performance again to see the difference (see Figure 7.56).

33. Constrain the handle to R_hand_MOCAP.

34. Continue constraining the rest of the skeleton with the exception of the hands.

    To check your work so far, you can compare it to capture_v04.ma on the DVD.

35. For the most part, Jack's bones are rotating in the Y and Z. The X rotation isn't being influenced by the motion capture. Several joints need to capture the rotation of the X axis. The wrist is one of those joints. You need to make a few additions made to the mocap skeleton in order to get the correct rotational information. To help make things easier, add root_MOCAP to a new layer and turn off its visibility.

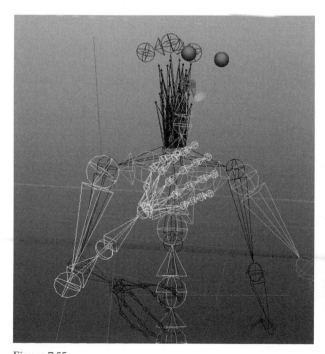

Figure 7.55
The elbow bends too much.

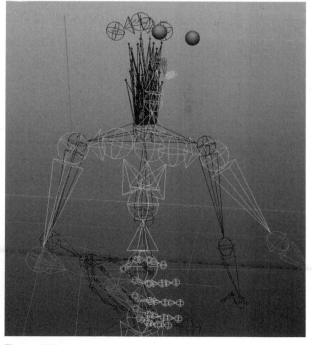

Figure 7.56
The elbow now bends correctly.

36. Add all the existing IK handles to the SKELETON layer, and turn off its visibility.

37. The only elements visible in the scene are the performance locators. The first axis to extract is *X*. Create a two-bone skeleton, snapping the root to the rzTracker_R_pinkyProximal locator and the end bone to the rzTracker_R_middleProximal locator. Figure 7.57 shows the setup. The mocap skeleton is turned on just for reference.

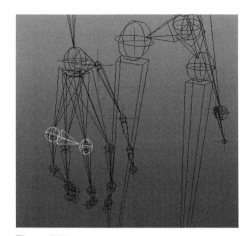

Figure 7.57

Create a two-bone skeleton across the hand.

38. Rename the two bones starting with the root **R_wristX_JNT1** and **R_wristX_JNT2**.

39. Orient them using the settings from Figure 7.58.

40. Add an SC IK handle to the skeleton.

41. Point-constrain R_wristX_JNT1 to rzTracker_R_pinkyProximal. Use the default settings.

42. Point-constrain the IK handle to rzTracker_R_middleProximal. Use the default settings. Having the handle constrained to the locator causes the root of the chain to rotate.

43. Shift+select R_wristX_JNT1 and radiusRght_JNT. Add an orient constraint based on the options shown in Figure 7.59.

Figure 7.58

Orient Joint Options window

Figure 7.59

Orient Constraint Options window

If you play through the performance, you can see that the right arm rotates in the *X* axis properly. Figure 7.60 shows frame 250.

44. Now you can address the *Y* and *Z* axes. Draw a joint from rzTracker_R_Hand to rzTracker_R_middleProximal.

45. Rename the two bones starting with the root **R_wristYZ_JNT1** and **R_wristYZ_ JNT2**. The default orientation of the joints is good.

46. Add an SC IK handle to the skeleton.

47. Point-constrain R_wristYZ_JNT1 to rzTracker_R_Hand. Use the default settings.

48. Point-constrain the IK handle to rzTracker_R_middleProximal. Use the default settings. Figure 7.61 shows the setup.

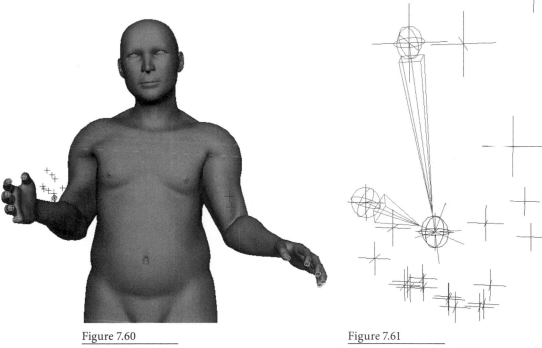

Figure 7.60
Frame 250 of the performance

Figure 7.61
The current progress of the wrist

49. Turn on the visibility for the SKELETON layer.

50. Shift+select R_wristYZ_JNT1 and wristRght_JNT. Choose Constrain → Orient. Use Figure 7.62 for the settings.

Figure 7.62

Orient Constraint Options window

Figure 7.62

Orient Constraint Options window

51. The wrist now rotates properly but needs to be calibrated to the performance. Select radiusRght_JNT. In the Channel Box, select radiusRght_JNT_orientConstraint1. Change its Offset X value to –35.0.

52. To calibrate the Y and Z axes, select wristRght_JNT. In the Channel Box, select wristRght_JNT_orientConstraint1. Change Offset Y to 11.0 and Offset Z to 172.0.

   To check your work so far, you can compare it to `capture_v05.ma` on the DVD.

Using the techniques from this project, you can finish connecting and calibrating the Jack's skeleton. You can also look at the finished version `capture_v06.ma` from the `chapter7\Projects\Maya\scenes` folder on the DVD.

Summary

Capturing a performance is a long and complex process. If you're new to motion tracking, it can be even more daunting. Like most things, the more you do it, the more you understand it, ultimately leading to a more refined process. Here are a few suggestions that can improve your system.

- Do a quick capture of your actor prior to building your character. You only need two photographs of the actor in the motion capture suit. From these, you can construct a 3D skeleton. You can then use that skeleton for the proportions of your character.

- Add additional markers to limbs. You can use four markers around each knuckle, elbow, wrist, knee, and ankle.

- Use different colored markers on the fingers to help distinguish them.

- Add additional lighting to highlight the face and hands to make the markers stand out more.

- The more cameras, the better!

   Some markers may not track well or at all. Do your best to interpret the markers motion. If you can't track the marker, you can always correct the motion in Maya at a later point. As long as most of the markers track, the performance will show through.

CHAPTER 8

Composition

Creating a photorealistic character utilizes every aspect of Maya. Throughout the book, you have used the tools to create individual elements of the Jack character. Each element works as an isolated asset. Bringing it all together taps Maya's true power and flexibility. This final chapter takes you through the process of assembling Jack and rendering his performance.

In this chapter you will learn to:

- **Connect motion capture data to muscles**

- **Connect skin to muscle**

- **Simulate skin**

- **Render the character with subsurface scattering**

Connecting Data

You can deal with the facial performance-capture data in several ways. You can use it to drive blend shapes or a bone's transformation. Either is acceptable and can produce good results. However, your goal here is to go beyond this and add the realism of simulated muscles and skin. Using the performance data as a trigger enables you to re-create this effect.

Before you activate the muscles, you add the body's motion to the character. The data can be copied or imported from an FBX file onto the character. After you apply the data to the character, it may require some cleanup. Check the Graph Editor to make sure the curves don't have any single-frame spikes.

Jaw Data

The jaw requires two sets of data. The first is Y translation to replicate the relaxing of the buccinator muscle, causing the jaw to drop or open. Next is the rotation in the Z. The jaw motion is extracted and attached to the upper palate joint's translate Y and rotate Z. This gives you a good base for creating realistic lip syncing.

Project: Jaw Motion

The jaw is critical to speech and deserves extra attention to transfer its motion to Jack. You need to take its motion from the performance capture and apply that motion to Jack's skeleton for both translation and rotation. The following project takes you through the steps:

1. Open the jaw_v01.ma scene from the chapter8\scenes folder on the DVD. The scene contains Jack's character skeleton and motion capture data (see Figure 8.1).

2. Select all of the face motion capture joints, from jaw_MOCAP to R_levator_MOCAP.

3. Highlight the Translate X and Y attributes in the Channel Box (see Figure 8.2).

4. Choose Edit → Keys → Bake Simulation, and set the tool options using Figure 8.3. Click Bake.

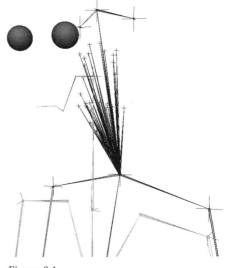

Figure 8.1

The elements in the scene file

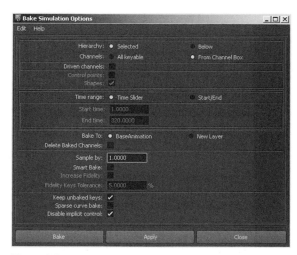

Figure 8.3

Bake Simulation Options

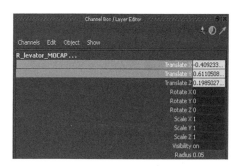

Figure 8.2

Channel Box with highlighted channels

5. Parent the face joints to skull_JNT.

6. Delete everything in the scene except the root_JNT hierarchy. Doing so effectively frees Jack's skeleton from all of its constraints and allows it to move under its own keyframes.

7. Change the Translate Z value to 0.5, pushing the face joints forward (see Figure 8.4).

    To check your work so far, you can compare it to jaw_v02.ma on the DVD.

8. Draw an SC IK handle from upperPalate_JNT to tongue1.

9. Rename the IK handle **jawIK**.

10. Shift+select jaw_MOCAP and jawIK.

11. Add a point constraint using the options shown in Figure 8.5.

12 Select upperPalate_JNT, and highlight the Rotate Z attribute in the Channel Box.

13. Choose Edit → Keys → Bake Simulation. Use the same settings as in step 4.

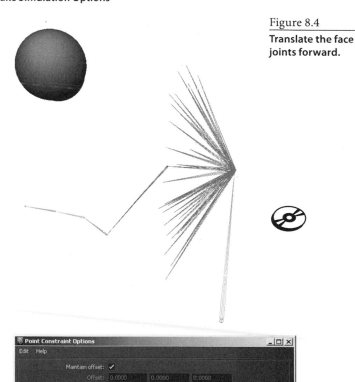

Figure 8.4

Translate the face joints forward.

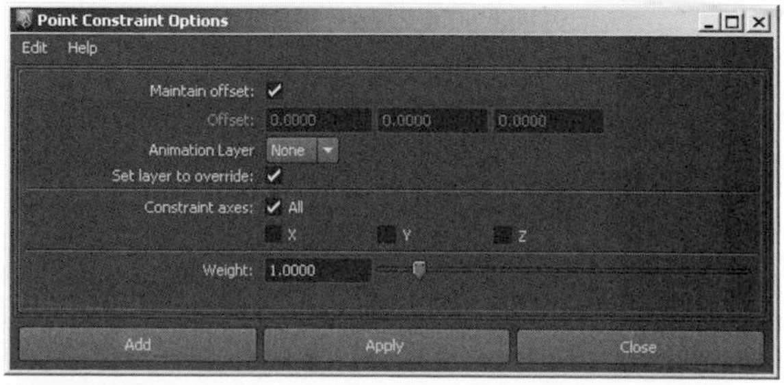

Figure 8.5

Point Constraint Options

14. Delete jawIK. The upper palate joint now rotates in the *Z* axis. This gives the jaw its proper rotation, but it still lacks its dropping motion.

15. Shift+select jaw_MOCAP and upperPalate_JNT.

16. Add a point constraint using the options shown in Figure 8.6.

Figure 8.6

Point Constraint Options

17. Select upperPalate_JNT, and highlight the Translate Y attributes in the Channel Box.

18. Choose Edit → Keys → Bake Simulation. Use the same settings as in Step 4.

To check your work so far, you can compare it to jaw_v03.ma on the DVD.

The jaw motion is now transferred. You can watch the motion by opening jaw1. mov from the chapter8\Projects\movies folder on the DVD. The jaw actually moves too much—you can see in Figure 8.7 how it moves into the skull.

A little of this is necessary, especially because the character starts with his mouth slightly open. In the next project, you'll copy the jaw motion to another skeleton and add a utility node to increase or decrease the jaw's motion.

Project: Importing Jaw Motion

The actor's performance was captured at 60 frames per second, but the final scene is to be rendered at 30 fps. When you import the captured motion of the jaw into a scene set at 30 fps, the keyframes are automatically adjusted. This project copies the jaw motion from the previous project to another skeleton. After it's transferred, you use utility nodes to control the motion's intensity. Follow these steps:

1. Open the jaw_v04.ma scene from the chapter8\scenes folder on the DVD. All of Jack's motion has been added to his skeleton except for the jaw joint.

2. Choose File → Import, and browse to chapter8\scenes\jaw_v03.ma. Click Import.

3. The entire skeleton and the facial joints are brought into the scene. The only data needed is the translation and rotation from the upper palate joint. Select upperPalate_JNT from under the jaw_v03_root_JNT hierarchy.

4. Make sure you're at the first frame of the animation. In the Channel Box, right-click the Rotate Z attribute, and choose Copy Selected from the pop-up menu.

5. Select upperPalate_JNT from under the root_JNT hierarchy.

6. In the Channel Box, right-click Z Channel, and choose Paste Selected.

7. Repeat steps 3 through 6 to copy the translateY.

8. Delete the entire jaw_v03_root_JNT hierarchy.

   To check your work so far, you can compare it to jaw_v05.ma on the DVD.

9. Select upperPalate_JNT, and choose Window → Hypergraph:Connections.

10. To control the jaw's motion, you need to add a few utility nodes between the animation curve nodes and the upper palate node. In the Hypergraph, choose Rendering → Create Render Node.

11. Choose Utilities at the left side of the Create Render Node window, and click multiplyDivide at right (see Figure 8.8).

12. Middle-click upperPalate_JNT_translateY1, and drag to the multiplyDivide node. Choose Other from the pop-up menu. The Connection Editor is displayed.

13. Use Figure 8.9 to connect the two nodes. Keep the Connection Editor window opened after making the connections.

14. Select upperPalate_JNT_translateZ1, and choose Reload Left in the Connection Editor.

15. Connect the output to inputZ.

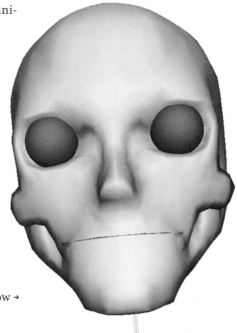

Figure 8.7

The jaw penetrates through the skull.

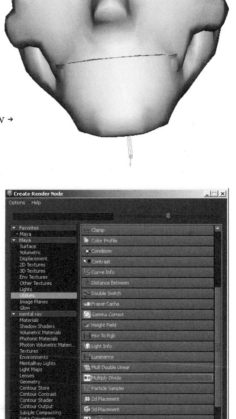

Figure 8.8

Create Render Node window

16. Middle-click the multiplyDivide node, and drag to upperPalate_JNT. Choose Other from the pop-up menu. The Connection Editor is updated.

17. Connect outputY to translateY and outputZ to the rotateZ. Figure 8.10 shows the connections.

Figure 8.9

Connect the output of the animation to the inputY.

Figure 8.10

Connect the output of the utility node to upperPalate_JNT.

18. Open the multiplyDivide node's Attribute Editor. Change the settings to match those of Figure 8.11.

 To check your work so far, you can compare it to jaw_v06.ma on the DVD. You can also watch jaw2.mov from the chapter8\Projects\movies folder on the DVD.

Figure 8.11

The multiplyDivide settings

Muscle Data

The muscles in the character's face have been connected to a Volume Curve field to control their contraction. You animate the face by adding a value to the field's magnitude. Understanding the role each muscle plays in the human face enables you to animate the character with anatomic precision.

The motion capture data extracted from the actor's performance in Chapter 7, "Performance Capture," is used to control the muscles' contraction. You connect either the *X* or *Y* axis to the magnitude of a muscle's field via a remap utility node. When the value of the motion capture data increases, so does the magnitude of the field. This in turn causes the muscle to contract based on the preestablished motion you set up in Chapter 2, "Face Rigging." In effect, you're causing the muscles to fire, similar to neurons firing in the human brain.

Project: Muscle Calibration

So far, you've created hair, clothing, and even sweat. Now it's time to convert the performance motion into muscle motion. This project takes the data from the facial performance capture and uses it to trigger the left and right zygomaticus muscles to tighten. Here are the steps:

1. Open the muscleCalibration_v01.ma scene from the chapter8\scenes folder on the DVD. The scene contains the essential components to demonstrate the muscle calibration process (see Figure 8.12).

2. Shift+select L_zygomaticusMajor_MOCAP and L_zygomaticusMajor_FIELD.

3. Choose Window → Hypergraph:Connections. You want to change the output from the motion capture data to values that can be used to drive the magnitude of the muscle's field. This can be accomplished by using a utility node.

4. In the Hypergraph, choose Rendering → Create Render Node.

5. Choose Utilities on the left side of the Create Render Node window, and click Remap Value at right (see Figure 8.13).

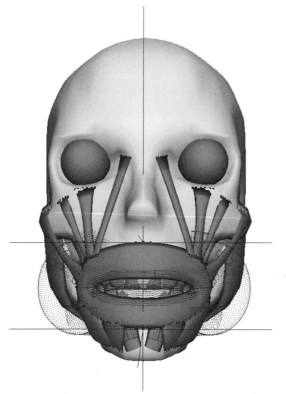

Figure 8.12

The scene elements

Figure 8.13

Create Render Node window

6. Middle-click L_zygomaticusMajor_MOCAP, and drag it to the newly created remapValue1. The Connection Editor opens.

7. Connect the output of translateY to inputValue (see Figure 8.14).

8. Middle-click remapValue1, and drag it to L_zygomaticusMajor_FIELD. Choose Other from the pop-up menu. The Connection Editor opens.

9. Connect outValue to magnitude (see Figure 8.15).

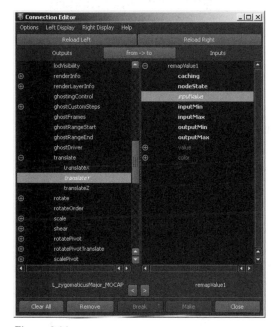 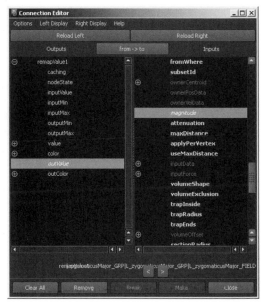

Figure 8.14

Connect translateY to inputValue.

Figure 8.15

Connect outValue to magnitude.

10. Open remapValue1's Attribute Editor. You only need to change the Input and Output Ranges. Input Min and Input Max are the highest and lowest values you want to remap. For all the facial muscles, the minimum is the value from the first frame of motion. In this case, it's .589. Input Max is derived from the highest absolute value in the direction of the muscle's motion. For the left zygomaticus major, the value is .728. You can see this easily in the Graph Editor shown Figure 8.16.

11. The Output Min value is always 0.0 to keep the muscle in its relaxed, neutral position.

FLEXED MUSCLES

If your scene starts with the muscle already flexed, you can set the magnitude input value to reflect this. You will, however, have to simulate the scene to get the muscle in its starting position.

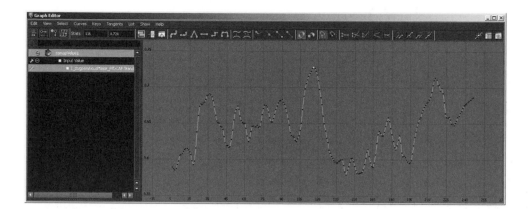

Figure 8.16

Use the Graph Editor to find the Input Max value.

12. Set Output Max to the highest magnitude desired. For instance, if you tested the muscle as demonstrated in Chapter 2, and it took a value of 100 for the magnitude to pull the muscle into its fully flexed position, then you would use 100 for the Output Max value. Figure 8.17 shows the settings used for the zygomaticus muscle's remap value.

13. Repeat the procedure for the right side. The values of the remap input and output ranges are shown in Figure 8.18.

Figure 8.17

Input and output ranges for the remapValue utility node

Figure 8.18

Input and output ranges for the right side remap utility node

14. With motion applied to the muscles, you can now adjust their nCloth attributes. Use the following numbers to update both zygomaticus major muscles:

Damp	0.0
Stretch Resistance	30.0
Compression Resistance	1.0
Bend Resistance	50.0
Stretch Damp	0.0

15. Muscle moves fast. Their reaction to the motion capture data needs to be quick. To achieve proper muscle speed, it's essential to increase the Time Scale attribute on the nucleus solver. Raising this value increases the simulation speed. If you don't increase

Time Scale, the muscles are sluggish and rubbery. Increase the value to 2.0, as shown in Figure 8.19.

Figure 8.19

The nucleus's Scale Attributes

To check your work so far, you can compare it to `muscleCalibration_v02.ma` on the DVD.

The increased simulation speed requires you to evaluate the simulation using a fraction of a frame due to the fast motion. Caching the simulation using a smaller step produces correct results. If the muscles are calculated per frame, they can pull away from each other, bounce excessively, or cause inaccurate deformations (see Figure 8.20).

To solve a scene, choose nCache → Create nCache and open the tool options. You should use a minimum of 0.5 frames to evaluate the simulation. Figure 8.21 shows the settings.

Figure 8.20

The muscles aren't deforming properly.

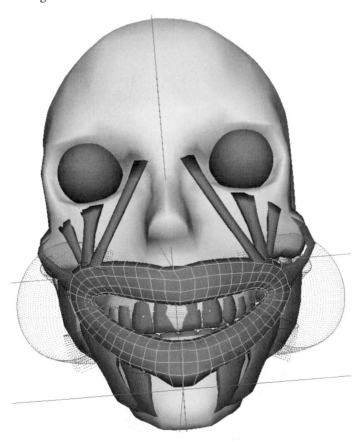

Figure 8.21

Create nCache options

You can also watch the movie `muscleCalibration.mov` from the `chapter8\movies` folder on the DVD. The magnitudes on the zygomaticus majors' fields are too high, causing the muscles to pull excessively (see Figure 8.22). However, when the rest of the muscles are activated, the magnitude will be perfect.

Figure 8.22

The zygomaticus major pulls too much.

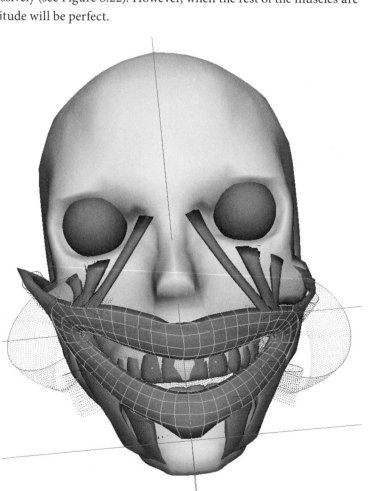

Project: Orbicularis Calibration

The orbicularis oris is connected in the same manner as the other muscles. However, the input data for the outer portion of the muscle is cheated. The intended markers from the performance capture didn't produce sufficient data. You can use data from the zygomaticus major in its place. Here are the steps:

1. Open the orbicularisCalibration_v01.ma scene from the chapter8\scenes folder on the DVD. The scene picks up where the previous project left off.

2. Select the following three nodes:

   L_zygomaticusMajor_MOCAP

   orbicularis_Oris_FIELD_L

   orbicularis_Oris_FIELD_R

3. Choose Window → Hypergraph:Connections.

4. Create a remapValue utility node, and rename it **remapValue_orbicularisOuter**.

5. Through the Connection Editor, connect the translate X of L_zygomaticusMajor_MOCAP to the input value of the remapValue node.

6. Connect the output of the remapValue node to the magnitude of the orbicularis left and right fields. Remember, you can select a new node and click Reload Right to quickly update the Connection Editor.

7. Open the remapValue node's Attribute Editor. Use Figure 8.23 to set its input and output ranges.

8. For the orbicularis oris inner field, you can use L_orbicularisOris_MOCAP. Select both nodes, and open Hypergraph:Connections.

Figure 8.23

Input and output ranges for the orbicularis remapValue node

9. Create a remapValue node. Connect L_orbicularisOris_MOCAP.translateY to the input value of the remap utility node.

10. Use Figure 8.24 to change the values on the remap node's input and output ranges.

11. Use the following numbers to update the nCloth attributes on the orbicularis oris muscle:

Figure 8.24

Input and output ranges for the orbicularis inner remapValue node

Damp	2.0
Stretch Resistance	25.0
Compression Resistance	50.0
Bend Resistance	10.0
Stretch Damp	1.0

To check your work, you can compare it to orbicularisCalibration_v02.ma on the DVD.

You can connect the rest of the muscles to their corresponding motion capture nodes. In Chapter 2, the muscle properties were often changed in order to test the connections between various muscles. You can now lock down the attributes. LevatorNasi, levatorSuperiorus, and zygomaticusMinor use the following values:

Damp	10.0
Stretch Resistance	30.0
Compression Resistance	0.0
Bend Resistance	30.0
Stretch Damp	10.0

Triangularis, depressorLabii, and mentalis use the following values:

Damp	2.0
Stretch Resistance	1.0
Compression Resistance	0.0
Bend Resistance	10.0
Stretch Damp	2.0

Make sure all the muscles match the position of your character's skin. For instance, the eyes were shut on the muscle rig, but they're open on the skinned character. You can move a muscle into position by animating the Output Min on the remap value node. When the muscle is in place, you can save its initial state and delete the animation from the remap node. If the muscle needs to remain in a flexed position, keep Output Min greater than 0.0. Figure 8.25 shows the values used for the superior tarsus's input and output ranges.

Figure 8.25

Input and output ranges for the superior tarsus remapValue node

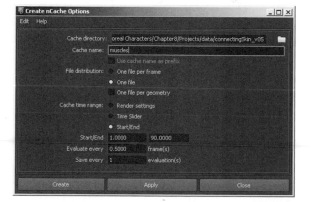

Figure 8.26

Create nCache Options

Muscles must be simulated before the skin. You can make modifications to the muscles after you connect the skin, as long as they're simulated separately. Solving the two at the same time causes a tug-of-war that results in very little motion. You can watch all the muscles in action by playing faceMuscles.mov from the chapter8\movies folder on the DVD. All the muscles were selected and cached with the following settings (see Figure 8.26).

You can also check out the scene file faceMuscles.ma on the DVD.

Skin

The biggest challenge in creating skin is finding the right vertices to connect to the muscles. The skin can do nothing on its own. It needs the muscles to drive it; and without the majority of the muscles connected, it's difficult to judge whether the skin is functioning properly.

The skin needs to be tough. Skin only stretches a little, and it barely compresses. In fact, it's the high resistance to compression that contributes to skin wrinkling. It also has a high bend resistance, enabling it to retain its shape when in motion. These high-resistance values can be difficult to solve. They typically require an increase in the number of substeps used on the solver.

Project: Establishing the Skin

There is no need to simulate all the skin on the head. Neck, skull, and jaw movement are best done using traditional skinning. An Attract To Matching Mesh constraint allows the mixture of traditional skinning and skin simulation. This project takes you through the process and prepares the skin for muscle attachments:

1. Open the establishSkin_v01.ma scene from the chapter8\scenes folder on the DVD. The scene contains all the connected facial muscles. Jack's head geometry has been duplicated from the smooth bound version and converted to an nCloth object.

   The current frame is set to –50.0 to accommodate the cloth. The character is in its bind pose at this frame.

2. Select head_skin and duplicate it. Add it to the JACK_HEAD layer.

3. Rename the duplicate **head_NCLOTH**. Unlock its channels, and delete the extra shape node in the Hypergraph.

4. With head_NCLOTH selected, choose nMesh → Create nCloth. Change the solver to use skin_nucleus (see Figure 8.27). The skin_nucleus node uses the same settings from the previous project.

Figure 8.27

Create nCloth options

5. Shift+select head_skin and head_NCLOTH. Choose nConstraint →Attach to Matching Mesh. Every vertex is attached to the constraint (see Figure 8.28).

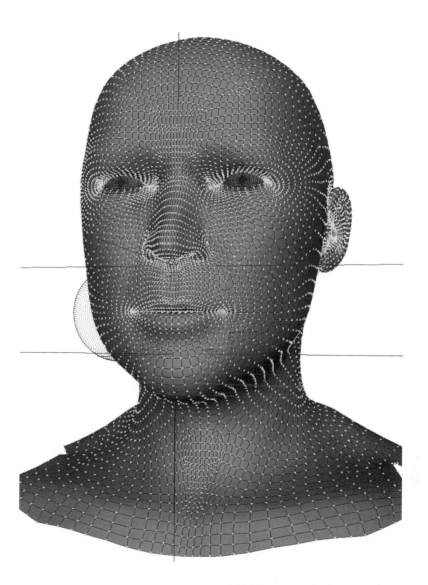

Figure 8.28
The Matching Mesh constraint connects the two geometries.

6. Rename the constraint **skinMesh_CONST**, and turn off its visibility.

7. Open skin_NCLOTH's Attribute Editor. Use Figure 8.29 to set its Collision parameters.

8. Change the resistance values in the Dynamic Properties section to match Figure 8.30.

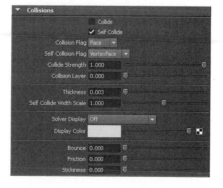

Figure 8.29
Collision parameters

Figure 8.30
Resistance parameters

These values give the nCloth a good stiffness. They allow it to bend and wrinkle, but keep it from sagging.

9. To maintain control over the skin, select Ignore Solver Gravity. Figure 8.31 shows the rest of the parameters.

To check your work, you can compare it to establishSkin_v02.ma on the DVD.

Figure 8.31

Dynamic Properties parameters

Before going any further, it's best to get the character into its first frame of animation. Jack's performance begins at frame 0; but in order to start there, his clothing and skin must be simulated into the proper position. When they're in the proper position, you can set the geometries' initial state.

10. Turn on the visibility for all the layers.

11. Select head_NCLOTH, and open its Attribute Editor.

12. Choose the skin_nucleus tab. In the Time Attributes section, change Start Frame to −50.0 (see Figure 8.32).

Figure 8.32

Time Attributes settings

13. Make sure clothing_nucleus is also starting at frame −50 and enabled.

14. Open the Animation Preferences by clicking the icon in the lower-right corner of the interface (it's displayed as long as you have Range Slider selected under Display → UI Elements). Change the Looping parameter in the Playback section to Once. Figure 8.33 shows all the settings.

Figure 8.33

Playback options

15. Change the playback start and end to −50.0 and 0.0.

16. You can now click Play on the timeline to solve the simulation. This can take an hour or more, depending on the speed of your computer. When it reaches frame 0, it automatically stops.

17. Select all the clothing and muscle geometry.

18. Choose nSolver → Initial State → Set From Current. The current position of the selected geometry is now locked in.

19. Change the playback start and end to 0.0 and 90.0.

20. Change the start frames on both nucleus solvers to 0.0.

To check your work, you can compare it to establishSkin_v03.ma on the DVD.

At this point, the nCloth skin does nothing. It needs to be connected to the muscles. By painting the strength value on the matching mesh constraint, you can remove the weighted head's influence in specific areas. The vertices around the mouth, eyes, cheeks, and forehead need to be controlled by the muscles under the skin. The idea is to remove the influence of the matching mesh constraint from the areas that are connected to muscle and leave the areas where the skin would be connected to the skull or stationary tissue.

Project: Connecting Skin

This project takes you through the process of connecting the skin in order to give it motion. The scene is a continuation of the previous project. The clothing has been turned off. Follow these steps:

1. Open the connectingSkin_v01.ma scene from the chapter8\scenes folder on the DVD.

2. Shift+select skinMesh_CONST and head_NCLOTH. Choose nConstraint → Paint Properties By Vertex → Strength.

3. Set Paint Operation to Replace, and set Value to 0.0.

4. Paint all the areas to be influenced by the muscles black. Make sure you paint the inside of the lips as well.

5. Click Flood about 10 times to soften the painted edges (see Figure 8.34).

6. The main muscle to be connected is the orbicularis oris. Its motion alone represents the majority of the facial muscles. Select vertices along a single edge on the inside and outside of the mouth corner, about 10 total (see Figure 8.35).

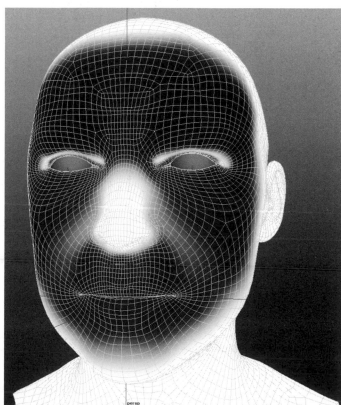

Figure 8.34

The areas that need to be simulated are painted black.

Figure 8.35

Select 10 vertices from the corners of the mouth.

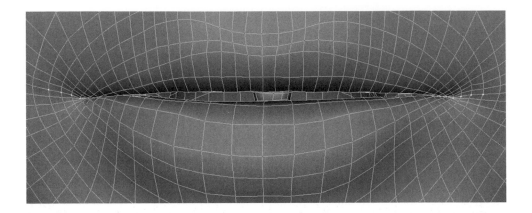

Figure 8.35

Select 10 vertices from the corners of the mouth.

7. Turn off the visibility for the Jack_Head layer. Shift+select a row of vertices from either side of the orbicularis muscle (see Figure 8.36).

Figure 8.36

Shift+select the corners of the orbicularis oris.

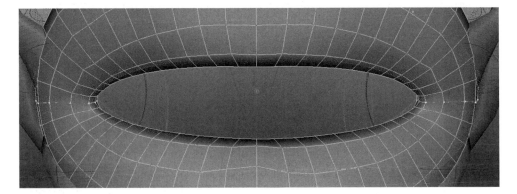

8. Choose nConstraint → Component To Component. The corners of the mouth are now connected to the orbicularis oris muscle.

9. Change the constraint's name to **mouthCorners_CONST**.

10. In the Channel Box, set the Connection Update parameter to Per Frame and Exclude Collisions to On. All of the skin constraints require these settings. Without them, the constraints don't update properly throughout the performance.

To check your work, you can compare it to connectingSkin_v02.ma on the DVD.

11. The lower lip is the next part to connect. Select three rows and four columns of vertices from either side of the bottom lip. Shift+select the orbicularis oris, and choose nConstraint → Point To Surface (see Figure 8.37).

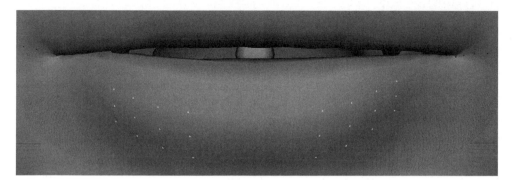

Figure 8.37

Use a point constraint to connect the lower lip.

12. Change the constraint's name to **lowerLip_CONST**, and change the parameters stated in step 10.

13. You can do the upper lip as one constraint or in groups. Use Figure 8.38 to add the point constraints.

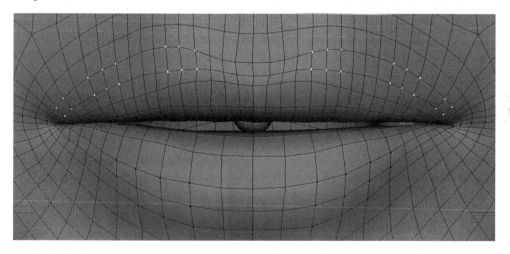

Figure 8.38

Point constraints are used to connect the upper lip.

14. To get the nasolabial folds or laugh lines, add a point constraint from the selected vertices in Figure 8.39 to the levator superioris muscle.

Figure 8.39

Figure 8.39

Add a point constraint for the laugh lines.

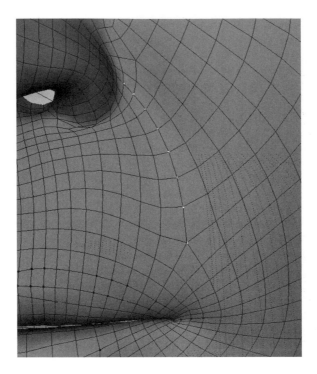

15. The eyebrow area of the skin is connected to the frontalis muscle. The skin sits over the portion of the muscle that is anchored to the skull; therefore it's best to use a component-to-component constraint to connect the two. Figure 8.40 shows the faces used to make the constraint.

Figure 8.40

Connect the eyebrow skin with a component-to-component constraint.

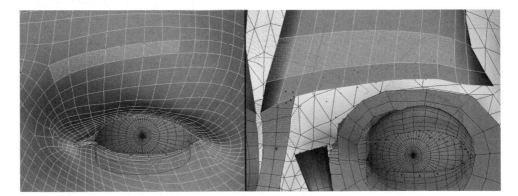

16. Add another component-to-component constraint to connect the skin at the beginning of the eyebrow to the procerus muscle. You can connect the skin vertices to the vertices at the top of the muscle.

17. Add two more component-to-component constraints for the upper and lower eyelids (see Figure 8.41).

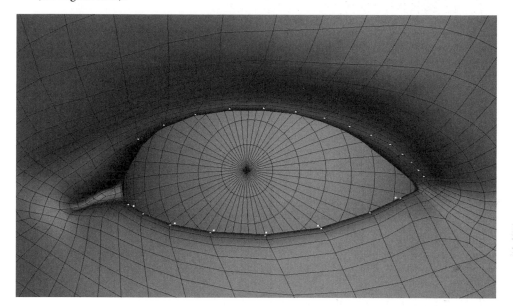

Figure 8.41

Use component-to-component constraints for the upper and lower eyelids.

18. Add a component-to-component constraint for the eyebrow/forehead (see Figure 8.42). Connect it to the last row of faces on the frontalis muscle.

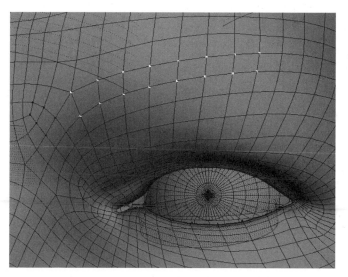

Figure 8.42

Connect the eyebrow/forehead skin with a component-to-component constraint.

19. When the skin is connected, you can simulate it. Figure 8.43 shows the nucleus solver quality settings.

To check your work, you can compare it to connectingSkin_v03.ma on the DVD.

The skin is simulated with the same settings as the muscles. Again, it's important that the muscles play from their cache file. You don't want to re-simulate the muscles at this time, only the skin.

You can compare your scene to connectingSkin_v04.ma on the DVD. The muscles and the skin have been cached in the file and the nucleus turned off. You can also watch the movie skin.mov from the chapter8\movies folder on the DVD.

Shading and Lighting

Getting CG to look real is undoubtedly a combination of every element. However, color and light make the biggest impact. Using them, you can make a simple sphere sitting inside a cube look real. Proper lighting makes things look like they belong.

An enormous asset for photorealistic rendering are *high dynamic range intensity* images. These 64-bit images are used to bounce or cast light into a scene. They're perfect for exterior lighting setups. You can download a free sample from www.doschdesign.com/samples.php.

Project: Lighting

Lighting Jack is a simple process but can be a lengthy one. As you get closer to completing the character, your render times increase significantly. You use a single light source in this project, accompanied by an image that provides indirect lighting. The mental ray preset has been set to Production:Fine Trace and is used for all the renderings. The following steps take you through the process of adding lighting:

1. Open the lighting_v01.ma scene from the chapter8\scenes folder on the DVD. The scene contains Jack with all of his parts, clothing, hair, and so on. The clothing and skin have been cached up to frame 90. To speed up render times, Jack's hair and beard have been turned off.

2. A directional light has already been added to the scene. It has been translated to approximate the sun's position. The light produced is harsh and flat (see Figure 8.44).

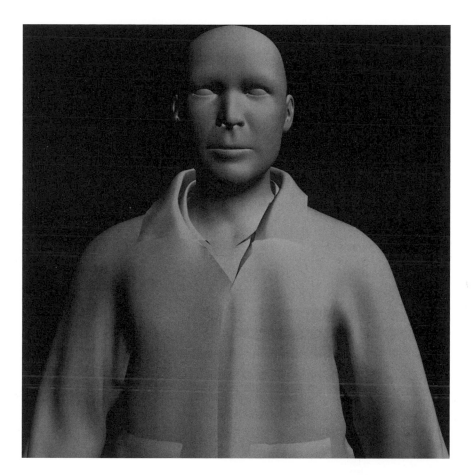

Figure 8.44
Base lighting

Select directionalLight1, and open its Attribute Editor. Open the Custom Shaders section, and click the Create Render Node icon at the end of the Light Shader Attribute field. Select Mental Ray Lights and mia_physicalsun (see Figure 8.45).

3. Change the physical sun shader's attributes using Figure 8.46. Figure 8.47 shows the rendered results.

Figure 8.45
Add a mia_ physicalsun shader to the directional light.

Figure 8.46

Physical Sun Attributes

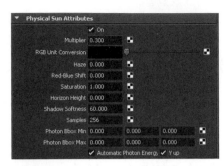

4. The light has a nice falloff with soft shadows; the light's rays hit the character and stop. You can now bring in an image to help bounce light around the scene. Open the Render Settings window, click the Indirect Lighting tab, and choose Create Image Based Lighting.

Figure 8.47

The results of rendering with the physical sun shader

5. The image by itself won't do anything. You also need to turn on Final Gather on the Indirect Lighting tab of the Render Settings. Set Secondary Diffuse Bounces to 2.

6. Open the Attribute Editor for mentalRayIBL1.

7. Add an `.hdr` or `.exr` format image. If you downloaded the sample files from `www.dos-chdesign.com`, load `MOUNT_02LB.hdr`.

8. Change Mapping to Angular.

9. In the Render Stats section, select Adjust Final Gather Color Effects. Using the HSV color scheme, set the value to 3. Figure 8.48 shows the rendered results.

Figure 8.48

The results of rendering with the Final Gather colors intensified

10. The last thing to add is a lens shader to alter the gamma. Open the perspective camera's Attribute Editor. In the Mental Ray section, click the Create Node icon for the Lens Shader attribute.

11. Choose Lenses and mia_exposure_simple.

Figure 8.49 shows the final rendered results.

To check your work, you can compare it to `lighting_v02.ma` on the DVD.

Figure 8.49

The results of rendering with the mia_exposure_ simple node

Subsurface Scattering

The final part of assembling Jack is adding his texture maps. For human skin, subsurface scattering is essential. Perhaps the most important aspect of subsurface scattering are the maps used. It's outside the scope of this book to discuss painting these maps. Beyond the map's detail, you must consider the color information and the correct channels. You can use the following color images as references for creating your own.

GAMMA

The gamma should be adjusted to accommodate your texture maps. If your textures have been individually gamma corrected, i.e., inside a 2D paint package like Photoshop, then it is not necessary to alter them again in Maya. The textures used for Jack have not been gamma corrected. Therefore, the gamma has been set to 1.0 on the mia_exposure_simple node. In addition, in the Render Settings, the Gamma has been set to 0.455 under the Quality → Framebuffer section. Changing these settings alters the gamma for the entire scene. Doing this may or may not produce correct results based on your scene setup.

Figure 8.50

The overall color map

Overall Maps

The overall map is the top layer of the subsurface scattering shader. It's the last layer to be considered by the shader. Use the overall map to provide features that would show up on the last layer of skin, things like freckles or cuts. Anything under the skin, like bruising and veins should be placed on the lower layers. The overall map should have very little color; the actual color of the skin should be determined by the combination of the epidermal and subdermal layers. The map should appear pale and deathly (see Figure 8.50).

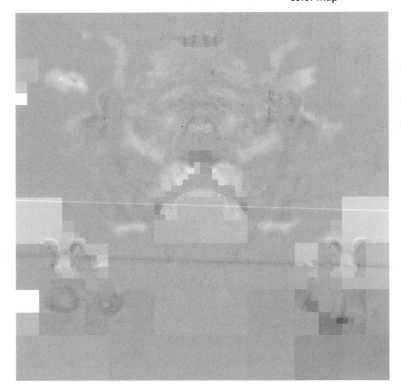

Epidermal and Diffuse Maps

The epidermal map is your prominent color map. It provides most of the features of the character's skin (see Figure 8.51). Adding the epidermal map to the diffuse map channel adds to the color depth of the skin.

Figure 8.51

The epidermal color map

Subdermal Maps

This layer contains blood vessels and fat. Fat is an organ-yellow substance, and the map uses that color (see Figure 8.52).

Figure 8.52

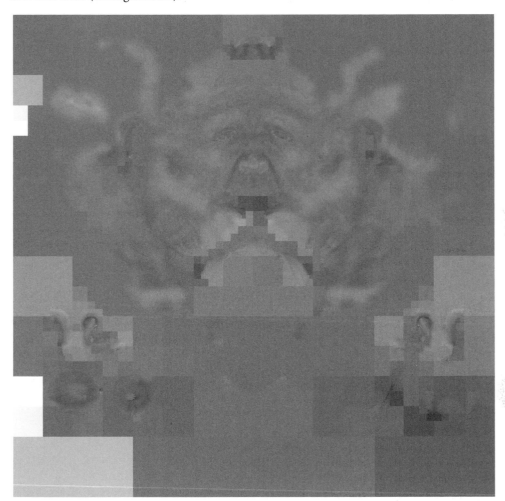

The subdermal color map

Backscatter Maps

Backscatter maps provide the color of the surface when light passes through it from behind. In essences, they're the color of blood (see Figure 8.53).

Figure 8.53

The backscatter color map

Displacement and Bump Maps

Displacement and bump maps are also used on the character. Both of these maps were generated from a high-resolution sculpture created using Autodesk Mudbox. The displacement map is added to the shading group node and not directly connected to the misss_fast_skin_maya shader. The bump map is added to the Bump Shader section of misss_fast_skin_maya shader. Although the map itself is a Mudbox-generated normal map, it's being used as a bump, which provides better results. You can see both of these images in the `chapter8\Projects\sourceimages` folder on the DVD; they're named `head-Disp.tif` and `headNrml.tif`.

When your maps are finished, there are a few extra attributes to set. Subsurface scattering is solved based on millimeters. This means regardless of the scene preferences, each unit is seen by the shader as being a millimeter. To alter this, you change the Scale Conversion attribute, similar to how you modified the nucleus solver's Space Scale. Jack's scene was done in feet; therefore you should set Scale Conversion to 304, converting millimeters to feet.

In addition, you need to tell the shader to include indirect lighting. You do this on the light map node. It's directly connected to the misss_fast_skin_maya1SG Light Map Shader attribute. In its Attribute Editor, select Include Indirect Lighting (see Figure 8.54).

Figure 8.54

Turn on Include Indirect Lighting for the light map node.

Summary

Jack is complete. A significant amount of work was required to bring his static geometry to life. You added hair, clothing, muscles, color, light, and, most important, motion from a human being. Each step is a job unto itself, and each step is equally important in achieving the final look. Photorealistic characters take a tremendous amount of time, skill, and patience.

You can take a look at Jack's final scene file, `final_v01.ma` and movie, `final.mov`, on the DVD. The jacket and head have been shaded and their texture maps connected. The skin has been cached, freeing it from its underlying muscles; they have subsequently been deleted.

As we make our way toward complete digital human reproduction, there will always be something more that can be added to the character. Better geometry, improved texture maps—these things can always be improved upon. As for Jack (see Figure 8.55), his journey is just beginning. Many improvements are already in the works. Soon he will be crossing the galaxy; but for now, you can follow his progress at `www.speffects.com`.

About the Companion DVD

This appendix summarizes the content you'll find on the DVD that accompanies this book. If you need help with copying the items provided on the DVD, refer to the installation instructions in the "Using the DVD" section of this appendix.

- **What you'll find on the DVD**

- **System requirements**

- **Using the DVD**

- **Troubleshooting**

What You'll Find on the DVD

You'll find all the files for completing the tutorials and understanding concepts in this book in the Chapter Files directory on the DVD. You can access the incrementally saved Maya scene files, all the figures shown in the book, and movies from some of the projects.

Each chapter directory is divided into subdirectories so you can easily find the files. Figures from the book are located in the Figures directory, QuickTime movies in the Movies directory, and so on. Note that the content for each chapter varies, so some chapters have more materials than others.

All the Maya scene files are called out in the text of the book. Use these to confirm your settings or test new ideas. The figures are useful to scrutinize detail that doesn't show up in print. Some can also be used for reference to match color and shapes.

Working with files directly from the DVD isn't encouraged because Maya scenes link to external files such as texture maps and dynamic caches. Copy the entire project for each chapter to your local drive, including the empty folders, to ensure that the example scenes function properly.

Please check the book's website at www.sybex.com/go/mspphotoreal, where we'll post updates that supplement this book should the need arise.

System Requirements

This DVD does not include the Maya, MatchMover, and Photoshop software. You'll need to have Maya and MatchMover 2011 or 2012 and Photoshop CS2 (minimum) installed on your computer to complete the exercises in the book.

You'll need to be running Maya and MatchMover 2011 or 2012 to fully use all the files on the DVD (the software isn't included on the DVD). Make sure your computer meets the minimum system requirements shown in the following list:

- A computer running Microsoft Windows 7, Windows XP (SP2 or newer), or Windows Vista or Apple OS X 10.5.2 or newer
- An Internet connection
- A DVD-ROM drive
- Apple QuickTime 7.0 or later (download the latest version from www.quicktime.com)

If your computer doesn't match up to these requirements, you may have problems using the files on the companion DVD. For the latest information, please refer to the ReadMe file located at the root of the DVD.

For the latest information on the system requirements for Maya, go to www.autodesk.com/maya. Although you can find specific hardware recommendations there, here is some general information that will help you determine whether you're already set up to run Maya: you need a fast processor, a minimum 2 GB of RAM, and a workstation graphics card for the best compatibility (rather than a consumer-grade gaming video card).

Using the DVD

For the best results, you'll want to copy the files from your DVD to your computer. To copy the items from the DVD to your hard drive, follow these steps:

1. Insert the DVD into your computer's DVD-ROM drive. The license agreement appears.

> Windows users: The interface won't launch if Autorun is disabled. In that case, choose Start → Run (for Windows Vista, choose Start → All Programs → Accessories → Run). In the dialog box that appears, type **D:\Start.exe**. (Replace D with the proper letter if your DVD drive uses a different letter. If you don't know the letter, see how your DVD drive is listed under My Computer.) Click OK.

2. Read through the license agreement, and then click the Accept button if you want to use the DVD.

The DVD interface appears. The interface allows you to access the content with just one or two clicks. Alternately, you can access the files at the root directory of your hard drive.

> Mac users: The DVD icon will appear on your desktop; double-click the icon to open the DVD, and then navigate to the files you want.

Troubleshooting

Wiley has attempted to provide programs that work on most computers with the minimum system requirements. Alas, your computer may differ, and some programs may not work properly for some reason.

The two likeliest problems are that you don't have enough memory (RAM) for the programs you want to use or that you have other programs running that are affecting the installation or running of a program. If you get an error message such as "Not enough memory" or "Setup cannot continue," try one or more of the following suggestions and then try using the software again:

Turn off any antivirus software running on your computer. Installation programs sometimes mimic virus activity and may make your computer incorrectly believe that it's being infected by a virus.

Close all running programs. The more programs you have running, the less memory is available to other programs. Installation programs typically update files and programs; so if you keep other programs running, installation may not work properly.

Add more RAM to your computer. This is, admittedly, a drastic and somewhat expensive step. However, adding more memory can really help the speed of your computer and allow more programs to run at the same time.

Customer Care

If you have trouble with the book's companion DVD, please call the Wiley Product Technical Support phone number at (800) 762-2974. Outside the United States, call +1 (317) 572-3994. You can also contact Wiley Product Technical Support at `http://sybex.custhelp.com`. John Wiley & Sons will provide technical support only for installation and other general quality control items. For technical support on the applications themselves, consult the program's vendor or author.

To place additional orders or to request information about other Wiley products, please call (877) 762-2974.

Index

D

N

Wiley Publishing, Inc. End-User License Agreement

READ THIS. You should carefully read these terms and conditions before opening the software packet(s) included with this book "Book". This is a license agreement "Agreement" between you and Wiley Publishing, Inc. "WPI". By opening the accompanying software packet(s), you acknowledge that you have read and accept the following terms and conditions. If you do not agree and do not want to be bound by such terms and conditions, promptly return the Book and the unopened software packet(s) to the place you obtained them for a full refund.

1. License Grant. WPI grants to you (either an individual or entity) a nonexclusive license to use one copy of the enclosed software program(s) (collectively, the "Software," solely for your own personal or business purposes on a single computer (whether a standard computer or a workstation component of a multi-user network). The Software is in use on a computer when it is loaded into temporary memory (RAM) or installed into permanent memory (hard disk, CD-ROM, or other storage device). WPI reserves all rights not expressly granted herein.

2. Ownership. WPI is the owner of all right, title, and interest, including copyright, in and to the compilation of the Software recorded on the physical packet included with this Book "Software Media". Copyright to the individual programs recorded on the Software Media is owned by the author or other authorized copyright owner of each program. Ownership of the Software and all proprietary rights relating thereto remain with WPI and its licensers.

3. Restrictions On Use and Transfer.
(a) You may only (i) make one copy of the Software for backup or archival purposes, or (ii) transfer the Software to a single hard disk, provided that you keep the original for backup or archival purposes. You may not (i) rent or lease the Software, (ii) copy or reproduce the Software through a LAN or other network system or through any computer subscriber system or bulletin-board system, or (iii) modify, adapt, or create derivative works based on the Software.
(b) You may not reverse engineer, decompile, or disassemble the Software. You may transfer the Software and user documentation on a permanent basis, provided that the transferee agrees to accept the terms and conditions of this Agreement and you retain no copies. If the Software is an update or has been updated, any transfer must include the most recent update and all prior versions.

4. Restrictions on Use of Individual Programs. You must follow the individual requirements and restrictions detailed for each individual program in the About the CD-ROM appendix of this Book or on the Software Media. These limitations are also contained in the individual license agreements recorded on the Software Media. These limitations may include a requirement that after using the program for a specified period of time, the user must pay a registration fee or discontinue use. By opening the Software packet(s), you will be agreeing to abide by the licenses and restrictions for these individual programs that are detailed in the About the CD-ROM appendix and/or on the Software Media. None of the material on this Software Media or listed in this Book may ever be redistributed, in original or modified form, for commercial purposes.

5. Limited Warranty.
(a)WPI warrants that the Software and Software Media are free from defects in materials and workmanship under normal use for a period of sixty (60) days from the date of purchase of this Book. If WPI receives notification within the warranty period of defects in materials or workmanship, WPI will replace the defective Software Media.
(b) WPI AND THE AUTHOR(S) OF THE BOOK DISCLAIM ALL OTHER WARRANTIES, EXPRESS OR IMPLIED, INCLUDING WITHOUT LIMITATION IMPLIED WARRANTIES OF MERCHANTABILITY AND FITNESS FOR A PARTICULAR PURPOSE, WITH RESPECT TO THE SOFTWARE, THE PROGRAMS, THE SOURCE CODE CONTAINED THEREIN, AND/OR THE TECHNIQUES DESCRIBED IN THIS BOOK. WPI DOES NOT WARRANT THAT THE FUNCTIONS CONTAINED IN THE SOFTWARE WILL MEET YOUR REQUIREMENTS OR THAT THE OPERATION OF THE SOFTWARE WILL BE ERROR FREE.
(c) This limited warranty gives you specific legal rights, and you may have other rights that vary from jurisdiction to jurisdiction.

6. Remedies.
(a) WPI's entire liability and your exclusive remedy for defects in materials and workmanship shall be limited to replacement of the Software Media, which may be returned to WPI with a copy of your receipt at the following address: Software Media Fulfillment Department, Attn.: *Maya Studio Projects: Photorealistic Characters*, Wiley Publishing, Inc., 10475 Crosspoint Blvd., Indianapolis, IN 46256, or call 1-800-762-2974. Please allow four to six weeks for delivery. This Limited Warranty is void if failure of the Software Media has resulted from accident, abuse, or misapplication. Any replacement Software Media will be warranted for the remainder of the original warranty period or thirty (30) days, whichever is longer.
(b) In no event shall WPI or the author be liable for any damages whatsoever (including without limitation damages for loss of business profits, business interruption, loss of business information, or any other pecuniary loss) arising from the use of or inability to use the Book or the Software, even if WPI has been advised of the possibility of such damages.
(c) Because some jurisdictions do not allow the exclusion or limitation of liability for consequential or incidental damages, the above limitation or exclusion may not apply to you.

7. U.S. Government Restricted Rights. Use, duplication, or disclosure of the Software for or on behalf of the United States of America, its agencies and/or instrumentalities "U.S. Government" is subject to restrictions as stated in paragraph (c)(1)(ll) of the Rights in Technical Data and Computer Software clause of DFARS 252.227-7013, or subparagraphs (c) (1) and (2) of the Commercial Computer Software - Restricted Rights clause at FAR 52.227-19, and in similar clauses in the NASA FAR supplement, as applicable.

8. General. This Agreement constitutes the entire understanding of the parties and revokes and supersedes all prior agreements, oral or written, between them and may not be modified or amended except in a writing signed by both parties hereto that specifically refers to this Agreement. This Agreement shall take precedence over any other documents that may be in conflict herewith. If any one or more provisions contained in this Agreement are held by any court or tribunal to be invalid, illegal, or otherwise unenforceable, each and every other provision shall remain in full force and effect.